Hag'em

Memoirs of a Police Dog Handler

A NONFICTION NOVEL

Written By Brad Kuich

Copy Edited by Debbie Roberts

authorHOUSE®

AuthorHouse™
1663 Liberty Drive, Suite 200
Bloomington, IN 47403
www.authorhouse.com
Phone: 1-800-839-8640

This book is a work of non-fiction. Unless otherwise noted, the author and the publisher make no explicit guarantees as to the accuracy of the information contained in this book and in some cases, names of people and places have been altered to protect their privacy.

First published by AuthorHouse 2/6/2009

ISBN: 978-1-4389-0600-3 (e)
ISBN: 978-1-4389-0599-0 (sc)

Library of Congress Control Number: 2008909637

Printed in the United States of America
Bloomington, Indiana

This book is printed on acid-free paper.

Table of Contents

Preface

My story begins with my interest in and love of dogs when I was a young boy. I grew up on a prairie farm situated near the small community of Oyen, in southeast Alberta. We were a small, established family in the area. My paternal grandparents were immigrants from the Dakotas and had homesteaded near Oyen before the outbreak of World War 1. Farm life on the Canadian prairies meant long days of hard work for all family members. During summer break from school, there was little time for holidays. All through my youth, I helped my parents with chores and fieldwork. A successful farmer had to be resourceful, hardworking, and committed.

I have many fond memories of the different farm dogs we had and in particular, one dynamo that we named "Ted." Dad brought Ted home as a birthday gift for me. I remember him saying he looked the litter over and watched for the pup that was the most dominant of its littermates. It was also the first pup that showed a real interest in Dad and approached him without coaching. At any rate, I was elated to receive the six-week-old bundle of fur.

Ted grew quickly and was a constant source of entertainment for the family. The dog did have a mischievous side to him, but was loyal, attentive, and always eager to please. We were unsure of Ted's lineage, but he was of medium size, possibly a cross between a German Shepherd and a Collie. He loved to fetch a ball or just about anything else that we would toss for him. Dad and I got in the habit during early mornings around the farm, to ask Ted where his ball was. It did not matter how long it took, but Ted would search the entire yard until he recovered his ball. He would proudly return with it, demanding some fetch time.

On one spring day, Dad was planting potatoes in our large garden that we always kept. At one point, he turned to check the row that he had been planting and was astounded to see that Ted had dug up all the potatoes he had just laboriously planted. The dog was in the process of haphazardly re-planting the seedlings around the garden. Luckily, Dad always had a soft spot for animals and laughed at Ted's method of gardening.

Ted was fanatical about riding in the old 1951 Chevrolet one ton farm truck. Despite being old, the truck was in good condition and reliable. However, during cold winter days, it did take a little effort to start. The process involved pulling out the choke, turning the ignition key on, priming the accelerator a few times and finally pressing down on the starter, situated on the floorboards beside the accelerator.

During the initial attempt to start the truck, Ted would stand on the bench seat of the vehicle, wagging his tail with anticipation. He intently watched the entire process. If the truck did not start, the driver had to repeat the process. Ted would become anxious and start to bark and paw at the driver until the truck started. The dog would then sit quietly on the seat and wait for a ride around the farm.

During a cold winter evening, Mom and I took a walk along the main roadway south of our farm. Very little traffic was on the road at that time of night. Ted was ahead of us, happily investigating along the roadway, jumping through the snow-filled ditches and fields. The power lines overhead were heavy with frost and hummed in the crisp winter air. The dog yelped in the darkness and ran swiftly back to me. At my feet, he rolled his face on the icy road and pawed at his muzzle. Using a flashlight I quickly realized that Ted had found a porcupine. A number of quills were sticking haphazardly out of his nose. Mom winced at the dog's plight and remarked, "We have to get home right away and get Dad's help. I sure hope he doesn't have any in his mouth."

I recalled a story Mom told of a farm dog before my time that had a run-in with a porcupine. The dog had likely tried to bite the porcupine and received a number of quills inside his mouth. Mom remembered the helplessness that she and Dad felt, since it had been impossible for them to get all the quills out of the dog's mouth. The dog eventually recovered, but went through weeks of pain. With no veterinarians in the area at that time, farmers could only do their best to care for the animals.

We quickly walked back to the farmhouse. Dad detailed me to get pliers from the machine shop at the back of the yard. I held the dog down on the kitchen floor and ever so gently, Dad expertly started to pull the quills out of Ted's tender flesh. The dog fought my efforts to hold him and struggled away from me. Dad had plenty of experience with animals and made a wise decision. Without me trying to hold the dog, Dad called Ted back to him and invited the dog to lie on the floor. Without any constraints and only using verbal praise in soft, soothing tones, Dad started the process again. After pulling two or three quills, the dog would get up and walk away shaking his head. However, after a minute or so, he would return, and allow Dad to continue. After four or five breaks, Dad was confident he removed all the quills. Dad ran his big hands over the dog's face and got a good look inside Ted's mouth. With a slight chuckle he commented, "Can't see any in the mouth. That's good! He must have only had a sniff of that porcupine. I'm sure he won't get close to those things again!" We were all relieved and happy. Ted looked up at Dad and placed a paw on his arm, as if to say "thanks." Ted was obviously overjoyed at the results as well. He spun in circles and barked wildly.

I did not realize it at the time, but upon reflecting, Ted would have likely made an excellent candidate as a police dog. His intelligence, drive, and determination were all good qualities. Later, when I was a dog handler, I would use certain methods of selecting pups for police work from the training and experience I had gained. Coincidently, Dad's method of selection was similar.

My journey to become a police dog handler started a couple years after my graduation from high school. Sadly, my father's health was declining and we reluctantly sold the family farm. Even though I loved farm life, I had no interest in taking over the farm. My older brother already had a career with the Royal Canadian Mounted Police (RCMP) and my older sister, who worked as a nurse, was married to an RCMP member.

After working different jobs in the cities of Calgary and Red Deer, Alberta for two and a half years, I decided to join the RCMP. I needed some financial independence and I really did not want to go back to school. "Trudeaumania" which referred to the spending practices of the federal government under the leadership of Prime Minister Trudeau, was in full swing in Canada at that time. The federal government was spending all kinds of money and all government departments, including the RCMP, were busily expanding. The RCMP was in a hiring frenzy. I was excited about the prospect and elated by the stories my brother and brother-in-law told about their experiences in the force. I desperately needed some challenges in my life.

The RCMP has a colorful history in Canada, especially western Canada. The organization formed up in 1873 - only six years after Canada became a nation. The first leader of the fledgling country, Prime Minister Sir John A. MacDonald, wanted a government presence in the vast northwest expanse of Canada. He intended to establish law and order to ensure Canada's sovereignty. The original force consisted of 300 volunteers, trained and equipped in southern Ontario. It was a long, arduous march to the northwest for this small unit of mounted redcoats. Originally, they were named the North West Mounted Rifles. However, not wanting to alarm the Americans with a military force near their border, MacDonald changed his mind before the group set out and re-named them the North West Mounted Police (NWMP).

In 1904, England's King Edward granted the prefix "Royal" and the force became the Royal North West Mounted Police (RNWMP). In 1920, the name changed once more to the Royal Canadian Mounted Police (RCMP). The force made the famous "March West" and quickly set up outposts throughout the frontier. In 1882, the NWMP set up a marshalling point at Regina, Saskatchewan. Soon after, it became a training center and headquarters. The NWMP called it "Depot Division," but today the official title is the RCMP Training Academy. To this day, many members still refer to it as "Depot".

1980 Innisfail, Alberta. This picture depicts only a small portion of the agility course at the training kennels. The course consisted of various jumps, ramps, swinging bridge, suspended tires and tunnels.

1980 The "tower," part of the extensive agility course at the Training Kennels in Innisfail Alberta. The Tower is approximately 18 feet / 5½ metres high. In the initial stages of training, the dog and handler had to climb the tower together. At the top, the dog and handler had to come down one level at a time. Eventually, the handler could stay on the ground and direct the dog with hand signals to climb and descend the tower.

Chapter 1
Depot and Dogs

After the usual long engagement process, I reported to the RCMP headquarters at Calgary, Alberta on April 29, 1975, at 8:30 AM, three days after my twentieth birthday. I was ushered into the office of a commissioned officer of the force. He was a redheaded man with piercing green eyes and flawlessly dressed in a crisply pressed working uniform. He was clean-shaven except for a handle bar moustache with the ends waxed to a point. He was business-like and aloof during the process. After signing my life away on a five-year contract, he welcomed me on board and wished me every success. I was now a part of the RCMP "family" as he put it. Back in the lobby of the office, a duty constable gave another inductee and me one-way plane tickets to Depot. They also provided cab fare to the Calgary airport.

By 2:00 PM, the same day, my new friend and I were both in green fatigue uniforms, cleaning empty dormitories at Depot. We were to keep working and at 4:30 PM, proceed to the mess hall for dinner. At dinnertime, we were strolling down the street to the mess hall when an NCO met us going the opposite direction. We had desperately tried to fit in to our new, strange environment despite our ill-fitting uniforms. I quickly discovered from this meeting what I could expect over the next 26 weeks of my life. This NCO was a drill instructor. He was all spit and polish with gleaming, high brown boots with spurs. He also wore blue riding pants with the wide yellow stripe down the legs, brown leather gloves, brown serge, and a forage cap. With the shiny peak of his forage cap pulled down low to the eyebrows, he sported the largest handlebar moustache I had ever seen. His dark eyes were riveting as he glared hard at us. His appearance and turnout was immaculate.

He was within three feet of us when he bellowed, "You funny little men!" The comment slightly offended me because I was over six feet tall. It was obvious that our sloppy demeanor had caught his attention. We stood silently, with our mouths gaping open, as he flew into a tirade, hurling articulate expletives at us with his booming voice. He was waving his arms wildly and the arteries in his neck were bulging under a starched collar.

He explained that the likes of us were not supposed to walk and until we learned to properly march, we would run everywhere we went on Depot. He ended the episode by looking at us with a forlorn, dejected face. As he shook his head slowly back and forth, he bemoaned, "Oh Good God, what a sad, sad day for the Mounted Police. Here we have another bloody batch of rabble that just fell off the Old Man's tractor!" With that, he jammed his swagger stick under his left arm and marched off in utter disgust. Ironically, in my case, he was not too far from the truth.

My first week at Depot was what the training staff called "forming up." New recruits for my class were still trickling in from across Canada. I was assigned to Troop 2, which was the second class for the fiscal year of 1975/1976. The troops or classes each consisted of 32 recruits. My troop would have the unwelcome distinction of being junior troop at Depot. There were many other troops ahead of us, probably over 400 recruits.

The senior troop was only a few weeks from graduation and we were in awe of them. They possessed an air of confidence in their immaculate uniforms and highly polished leathers. Soon, they would graduate wearing the legendary red serge or scarlet uniform of the "Mounties."

The red serge included riding breeches, high brown boots with spurs, and a Stetson. Other orders of dress, including the red serge, were still used, but only for recruit training and ceremonial events. The more practical working uniform included a light brown shirt, dark blue patrol jacket, and dark blue pants with a yellow stripe, black ankle boots, and a forage cap. Training at Depot no longer included horses. That practice stopped in 1966. Only members of the world-renowned RCMP Musical Ride rode horses.

For now, we were nothing. As the "new kids on the block," we were relegated to wearing frumpy fatigue uniforms and the other troops and instructors referred to us as "rabble" until the next junior troop arrived.

A 32-bed dormitory on the third floor of "B" Block was the new home of Troop 2. This large, stone block building also housed numerous other troops. During our forming up period there was no training, but to keep us occupied and out of trouble the training staff assigned many tasks for us to complete. Work parties attended to polishing all the brass doorknobs on Depot, washing driver-training cars, polishing the old airplane displayed on a large stand at the south end of the Parade Square, or polishing the cannon balls stacked beside the old field cannons used to help quell the Riel Rebellion of 1885. Needless to say, we continuously grumbled to each other about the mindless tasks.

One day, we received word that a group of RCMP dog handlers and their dogs would be arriving in the next few weeks for a course on crowd control. Kennels and doghouses had just arrived and I was part of a work party detailed to unload and set them up. We reported to the Transport Section and met a tall, lean sergeant dressed in a uniform that none of us had seen before. He was an instructor from the RCMP police dog service-training center, situated at Innisfail, Alberta. His uniform was similar to the brown battle dress worn by Canadian soldiers during World War II. With the legs of his pants neatly tucked into the tops of black Dayton boots, he wore a blue RCMP baseball cap. He had a pleasant disposition, and in total contrast with the treatment we had received from the training staff, was both polite and patient with us.

After we unloaded all the material and put it together, the good-natured sergeant took us away from prying eyes and invited us to sit down with him and talk for a few minutes. "Smoke 'em if you have 'em fellas," he exclaimed. This was a welcome respite, especially for the smokers. Behind the kennels, he explained that a group of handlers from across Canada would be arriving soon with their dogs. After they had completed their training, other groups would rotate in for the one-week crowd control course. He promised that we would get the opportunity to assist in the training of these dog teams and that it would be an exciting, unique experience for all of us. When the smokers

4

were finished, the sergeant thanked us and sent us off. I was eager to see the dogs in action and hoped that their handlers were all easy-going, like the sergeant.

By the end of my first week at Depot, all my new classmates had arrived from the four corners of the country. Nothing could have prepared us for what we would experience over the next six and a half months of our lives. The training staff promised that our time at Depot would be arduous. Depot was a highly regimented atmosphere. Each recruit's turnout had to be impeccable at all times. Male recruits had to get a hair cut every ten days, without exception.

Throughout training, the drill staff regularly inspected our dormitory, including the showers, sinks, and toilets. We were responsible to keep our living quarters spotless. The RCMP blankets and sheets on the narrow single beds had to be flawlessly made and immaculate. The Sam Browne or gun belt of each recruit had to be broken down and set out on the bed. Fur hat, Stetson, and forage cap had a particular order on the pillow. Even all the items in the closets beside the recruits' beds, had a meticulous order. Everything was set out evenly, exacting and in straight lines. Any deviation, even by one recruit could result in the drill staff tearing the entire dorm apart, issuing orders to re-do it until they were satisfied.

A training day started with reveille at 6:00 AM, followed by an inspection at 6:30 AM. After breakfast at the mess hall, classes started at 8:00 AM. At noon we had lunch followed by the time honored, traditional Sergeant Major's Noon Parade on the Parade Square. All troops were required to attend this function. Classes resumed at 1:30 PM until 4:30 PM. The RCMP has many traditions and is proud of its history. The Noon Parade was officiated by the Sergeant Major (SM). The event included a band, made up of various recruits from all the troops.

With all the troops formed up on the Parade Square, the drill staff conducted a close inspection of each recruit. Following several minutes of precise drill movements under the stern direction of the SM, the troops returned to their classes. Noon parade could be a dreadful experience, especially in the relentless, blistering heat of a prairie summer. Standing at attention on hot pavement during the inspection, under a scorching sun was intolerable. The blazing sun turned gleaming boots and leathers dull and everybody had sweat-soaked shirts. Drill staff would scold recruits for a deplorable turnout and hover through the ranks, watching for any movement. I recall having sweat dripping off my nose and at the same time having a trickle of sweat run down my back that made me shudder. If an NCO caught any movement, recruits were often admonished with the usual phrase, "Stand still, you funny little person!" At attention, the recruit could not move and had to look straight ahead. If the corporal caught a recruit looking at him, other customary admonishments were, "Why are you looking at me? Do I look like your mother?" or "Why are you looking at me? Do you like me?" Of course, for the poor recruit, no answer was correct.

During one Noon Parade, a troop mate was in a hurry and forgot to zip up his fly. Flocks of tourists were always on hand to observe the ceremony and lined the perimeter of the Parade Square. It did not take long for a drill instructor to see the open zipper. With the tourists looking on, the corporal placed the end of his swagger stick inside the man's pants and gently stirred the contents. He carefully allowed the stick to hang out of the pants with the other end just inches from the ground. The NCO then told the forgetful recruit that he would return in a few minutes and under no circumstances was the swagger stick to touch the ground. With all of us standing stone still at attention, the tourist's cameras were busily whirring and clicking, documenting the unfortunate event.

Workdays did not end at 4:30 PM. After dinner, there were projects, homework to complete, and extra training for those that required it. Extra training could include driver training, swimming, running, or academics. We were constantly cleaning and polishing our gear, in addition to continually cleaning the dorm and bathrooms. There was no training on the weekends, but we were always preparing for the next week of classes and trying to catch up on some sleep.

The SM was in charge of all disciplinary matters at Depot. If an instructor felt that a recruit was not conforming or committed some infraction (real or not), the recruit was reprimanded, followed with the dreaded phrase, "SM, four-thirty." This meant that after the last class of the day, the victim had to report to the SM's office. Once there, the recruit received yet another chewing out as well as extra duties assigned at the discretion of the SM. In reality these were extra, extra duties, considering all the other work that was already heaped upon us.

Most of the infractions were minor in nature or, in some cases, idiotic. Many of us were so young that we still had peach fuzz on our faces and did not shave regularly. The drill staff seemed to delight in trying to trick somebody with a smooth face. I recall one occasion, during a Friday morning drill class. The corporal put his nose within a few inches of a baby-faced troop mate and asked menacingly, "Did you shave

7

this morning Constable?" The recruit goofed up and honestly replied, "No Corporal, not this morning." The instructor flew into a rant, saying that members of the Mounted Police must shave every day, and concluded with "SM, four-thirty." The reprobate received extra duties and a confinement to barracks (CB'ed) for the entire weekend. I remember he was looking forward to visiting with his girlfriend who had traveled some distance to be with him. Their weekend was ruined and she returned home, without seeing him. It made most of us angry and we tried to consol him the best that we could.

Physical training (PT) classes were difficult, even for those in good condition. Each PT class alternated between weight training and running. We welcomed the running even though the set distance varied from five to ten miles. The weight classes were arduous. In teams of two, we went through an excruciating set of weight exercises, followed by push-ups, jumping jacks, sit-ups and the lethal squat-thrust-stands. At the end of the class, we had to break the weights down and place them back in the storage room. The PT instructors would threaten a visit to the SM for anybody that dropped a weight on the gym floor. I recall being so exhausted, I could barely hold a twenty-pound weight, let alone carry it.

Injuries in the self-defense classes were common. Self-defense involved a combination of wrestling and judo, holds and the use of pressure points to subdue and arrest violent people. To learn all of this, we of course had to practice on each other. Sometimes the competitive nature would surface, especially in such a group of young men. During a sparring session, one man was accidentally kicked full force in the groin. An ambulance took him to the hospital in Regina, with a bad case of swollen testicles. Some of the ghoulish members of Troop 2 thought that our comrade was lucky since he got time away from the training schedule. When he returned to us a few days later, we kept pestering him to show us his testicles. He repeatedly declined our requests, but judging from the way he walked, they must have been swollen. The ghouls started asking him if he got lucky with any of the nurses while in hospital. He only looked back at them with an incredulous expression on his face.

Another unfortunate recruit had a tooth punched out of his mouth. Two more had cracked ribs. Others had black eyes and everybody experienced bruises. We practiced carotid arteries chokeholds, which were a favored method of subduing suspects. We called it, "doing the chicken." This term was appropriate since a well-placed chokehold often made the semi-conscious victim's body shake or twitch involuntarily like a freshly butchered chicken.

Even swimming classes were strenuous and the instructors remorseless. During the first class, the draconian method of identifying non-swimmers in the troop was having everybody simultaneously jump into the deep end of the Olympic size pool. I remember the three non-swimmers crawling and clamoring over the swimmers. Their pleas for help, while rising well above the loud admonishments of the instructors, went unanswered. Surprisingly enough, by the end of training, we all could swim continuously for one mile.

Not surprisingly, firearms' training was intensive. The firearms instructors spent hours drilling us with firearms safety and combat style shooting on the large indoor ranges. Many of my troop mates had never fired a handgun, rifle, or shotgun in their lives. If anyone was caught not paying attention at all times, the instructors would descend on them with their wrath, and the reprobate usually got the "SM, four-thirty" routine. As training progressed, firearms training became more enjoyable for the entire troop thus developing a competitive spirit to see who the best shot was.

Driver training was demanding. Each driving instructor was assigned four recruits. The five would go out into the city of Regina or to the country on numerous three-hour drives in a driver-training car. The instructor explained and demonstrated what he wanted at the start of each class and then sat in the front passenger seat. He would observe and coach the recruits, who each took turns to drive. Initially my instructor, Constable Ring, was critical of my driving. He would yell profanities and at times strike me with his metal clipboard. I must admit that I was not the only one that got the same treatment, but I felt that he had singled me out and was going to ensure that I received his full attention. He put me on remedial driving. After regular classes, I had to seek out a recruit from senior troop that would take me out driving. I would have to do extra driving until Ring deemed that I had sufficiently improved. I started to hate that instructor, with his whiny voice and gaudy comments.

When Ring was transferred to Depot as an instructor, he had not yet received his promotion to corporal. A few other new instructors were also waiting for their promotions. All instructors at Depot were mostly corporals along with some sergeants. At times, the stiff regimentation at Depot was briefly relaxed with the tradition of allowing recruits to throw newly promoted instructors into the swimming pool. Of course, the recruits had to catch the instructors and win the inevitable battle to get them in the pool.

On the day that the promotions came through, we got the green light and I was actively looking for Ring. I was getting frustrated since I could not find him. Numerous recruits had gathered at the pool with some of the other newly promoted instructors. During the pandemonium of trying to throw the instructors in the pool, I saw Ring was already in the water. I felt cheated by not getting to him first, but was pleased just the same to see him choking on a mouthful of water. Ring had his back to me as he treaded water. I got down on my knees at the pool's edge, grabbed his shoulder, forcefully pushed him under the water, and held him there. Suddenly, a fully clothed drill instructor flew through the air, yelling obscenities. As he hit the water with a resounding splash, I let go of Ring, who was struggling and sputtering in the pool. He did not see who had shoved him under, but it felt good to get some revenge.

My driving improved and Ring took me off the extra driving list. It must have really improved, since he did not yell as much and the clipboard episodes ceased. In fact, near the end of training, in front of my troop mates, he congratulated me on my new driving skills and wished me every success. This was high praise indeed from an instructor and I felt a stab of guilt for pushing him under water.

Academic classes at Depot involved a large number of topics, including criminal law, federal and provincial statutes, the RCMP Act and Regulations, narcotics, note-taking, crime scene work, basic investigative techniques, forensics, domestic violence and officer safety. Some of the classes could be stale and uninteresting. After the strenuous physical classes, coupled with the constant sleep deprivation, recruits were liable to fall asleep. This was a big problem for the students, since the academic instructors did not tolerate anybody falling asleep during their lessons.

To combat this, if someone felt sleepy, it was their responsibility to get up from their desk and stand at the back of the room. During some of the more dreary lectures, I recall most of the troop standing at the back of the classroom and some still fell asleep standing. If a recruit was caught sleeping in class, they were never punished. The two neighboring recruits on each side of the offender got the "SM, four-thirty" routine. On one occasion, I fell asleep during a lecture from a guest speaker from the university. His presentation was dry and I found myself fighting to stay awake. It felt like somebody had placed sand bags on my eyelids. I was sitting at the front of the class and the next thing I remember is waking up to the lecturer looking directly at me. My neighbors did not realize that I was sleeping. In fact, they were standing at the back with half the troop. The guest teacher was just wrapping up his presentation, when our instructor walked back into the room. I felt the bottom of my world fall out. I was waiting for the man to report me to our instructor, but he did not say a word. For reasons unknown, he did not turn me in and I got off scot-free with a forty-five minute afternoon nap.

One of the many duties at Depot was guard duty from 10:30 PM until 6:00 AM. Most of us had the distinction of this duty at least three or four times during training. Once on night guard, my patrol partner and I were on our assigned route when we decided to take a short rest at the Infirmary. There were no patients at the sick bay and the beds seemed to invite us to lie down and stretch out. We compensated by sitting in chairs at the entrance, facing each other. The next thing I know, I received a thump on my forehead. I looked across at my friend with bleary red eyes and asked him what happened. He was also holding his forehead and looking at me accusingly.

We quickly figured out that we had both fallen asleep at the same time and during our slumber, our unconscious bodies had slumped forward at the same time, causing a head-on collision. To our horror, the sun was peaking over the flat, prairie horizon. We had slept for over an hour. On rubbery legs, we beat it back to the guard's post, all the while trying to come up with a plausible story for our absence. As we burst into the guardroom, we startled the guard commander, who was sleeping in a chair, with his feet on the desk. The guard commander was always a member of a more senior troop and he had the authority to report us to the SM. Nevertheless, under the circumstances, we had one up on him. Using discretion, he dismissed us early, if we promised not to say anything.

The regimentation and discipline at Depot was unceasing. Troops did not receive "marching orders" from the drill instructors until about six weeks into training. Until that time, a troop would have to form up and run (in step) to all their classes. Even on off duty time, members of troops without "marching orders" had to run everywhere they went on Depot. When the troops received their marching orders, they had to work hard to maintain that privilege. Drill instructors were quick to cancel the order if they felt the troop was not maintaining a high degree of proficiency in foot drill.

Depending on the daily training syllabus, a troop may have to move to four or five different places on Depot for instruction. This required that the troop had to form up on the street and march to each class. If it was a physical class, everybody had to change prior and after the class, shower and change back into uniform. I recall finishing a self-defense class, rushing to shower and change back into uniform within 10 minutes and form up on the street, in front of the self-defense gym. We marched half a block to the PT gym and raced inside to change into our PT gear. We formed up again in the gym, for an inspection by the PT instructors, prior to the class commencing. After that class, there was another 10-minute shower and then we would rush out to form up for the march to the next class. Being late for any classes was inexcusable and not tolerated. When moving about as individuals or small groups, troop members had to march, on and off duty.

During foot drill at the Drill Hall, the instructors demanded perfection and inspected us closely to ensure our uniform and dress was always impeccable. A piece of lint on a necktie or an undone button could result in push-ups. The usual expression was, "Give me twenty-five of your best!" which of course meant 25 push-ups. I know from personal experience that it is difficult to do push-ups on a highly polished hardwood floor wearing high brown boots with riding pants, brown serge, and Stetson, leather gloves and a gun belt.

At first, we all detested foot drill, but as the weeks wore on we became more proficient. We grew accustomed to the lambasting of the drill instructors. In fact, we started to joke about it in the dorm. A couple of troop mates could imitate particular drill instructors and would play skits that involved other troop members. This often had the entire dorm roaring with laughter.

During our busy schedule, we caught glimpses of dog handlers around Depot. We were told that since we had been at Depot for a number of weeks, it was now our turn to assist with the training of these teams. There had been a couple rotations of handlers through Depot and we would work with the latest group. I was excited at the prospect and finally one day, the training staff announced that we had to quickly change into mufti (civilian clothes) and report to the old riding stables.

We arrived filled with trepidation, but were happy to have a break from the grueling training schedule. As we entered the arena of the stables, I immediately recognized the dog handler sergeant that I had met during my first week of Depot. He strolled over to meet us and introduced himself as Jim. Since we had become accustomed to a structured life style, it was shocking for a senior NCO to be so informal. He invited all of us to gather around him so that he could brief us "without havin' to yell my damn head off!" After ensuring that we could all hear him, he explained that we had an important role to play in the training of the police dogs.

What Jim wanted to accomplish was to simulate a situation for the dogs to break up an unruly crowd and disburse them. We would be the crowd, acting in a riotous manner. We would advance on the dogs, yelling and screaming, acting aggressively and throwing objects at the dogs and their handlers. Jim told us that the handlers would then use their dogs to disburse us. So far, we were accepting of the idea. He warned us that once things got under way, everything would speed up and it was imperative that we keep our heads up. Jim distributed empty tin cans and rolled up paper to us. These objects were chosen to provide some realism for the dogs, while not causing any injuries Jim said that he would be coaching us from the sidelines during the exercise.

With some anxiety, we stood together looking to the other end of the arena. We started to comment amongst ourselves whether this was going to be much fun. One troop mate mentioned that he talked to a couple members of a more senior troop the week before. They had been through this and related that they had the hell scared out of them.

The doors opened and a single line of six handlers and their German Shepherd dogs emerged. Two more dog handler sergeants followed in behind them. Each dog wore a harness with a long line attached. The dogs were anticipating some action. They strained in their harnesses as the handlers held the long lines and maintained control of the dogs. All the dogs were barking, whining, and glaring at us. To those dogs, we must have looked like a bunch of rabbits. It was unnerving to have these dogs sizing us up. One of my troop mates started to break out in a sweat and kept repeating, "Oh, shit, oh shit" under his breath. I took my eyes off the dogs and glanced around at my fellow rioters. Everybody had eyes as big as saucers.

One dog stood out more that the rest. He was an intimidating big brute, with coal-black fur and gleaming red eyes. He acted most aggressively by pacing back and forth in front of his handler, barking continuously, and flashing rows of sharp, white teeth. Globs of his saliva flew through the air as he barked. To say the least, it was frightening to watch this canine preparing to take us on.

The dogs and handlers were now in a row in front of us. Jim signaled us and we apprehensively started to move forward. Immediately all the dogs went into frenzy, straining hard against their harnesses and digging into the earth floor of the arena. All the handlers were having a difficult time remaining stationary and in line, while controlling the dogs. Jim yelled at us to start acting more like rioters than a "bunch of old women." He encouraged us to move faster, yell, scream, and throw the items at the dogs. Heartened by Jim's support, we flew into our role with enthusiasm. Nevertheless, that was short lived.

None of the dogs backed down from our advances. The dogs and handlers started to slowly press forward, but we desperately held our ground with Jim constantly egging us on. Suddenly, without warning, the dogs were charging us at full speed. The handlers would let the dogs have more line as they moved ahead. They would reel the dogs back in just to let them charge ahead again. We started to loose our nerve. The charging canines were suddenly moving at lightening speeds, narrowly missing biting some of us, while the handlers swept their charges back and forth.

By now, the situation turned into chaos. We were faltering and disorientated. Some troop mates were visibly terrified. The handlers expertly broken us into smaller groups and forced the groups tightly together. Men were standing on others that had fallen to the ground during the bedlam. The troop mate that had been repeatedly talking to himself, prior to the exercise, had totally broken down. Tears were rolling down his face and he shook uncontrollably. He would later confide to us that a large dog had attacked him when he was a small child. This experience had certainly not changed his attitude about dogs.

Mercifully, Jim finally stopped the exercise and had the handlers stop their advance. He asked them to exit the building and the dogs reluctantly went with their handlers. Obviously, they were not finished with us, especially the big, black dog. He kept twisting in his harness, trying to break free to come back at us again. He wanted more of the action. It was relatively quiet and we tried to gather ourselves. Some tried to act macho and laugh off the dreadful experience, but to me it just sounded like nervous laughter. All of us stood wide-eyed, shaking with fear. We kept looking to see if the dogs were coming back for more. Jim smiled as he congratulated us. We did not share his keenness. We tried to gather ourselves and get some dignity back in our lives. It was a shocking, dreadful incident for all of us.

Jim invited us to gather around him once again. We thought it was all over, but the sergeant informed us that we had one more obligation. We all groaned in unison and started to mutter amongst ourselves. Jim quickly took back charge of the situation, held up his hands to quiet us down, and told us to listen. We were to remain in one group but spread out. We were all to stay calm and not move. The handlers would escort their dogs back into the arena and move through the group. Jim further explained that despite the fact the dogs had been in a rage, they now had to realize that the exercise was over and had to be composed. The walk through the former rioters would calm the animals. Justifiably, we were not eager to be willing participants. The sergeant reassured us that as long as we did not move, nothing would happen.

We nervously stood quietly as the canines returned. The animals were still keyed up, but the handlers reassured the dogs by talking to them in low, soothing tones, and petting them. The canines started to calm down. I felt anxious as the dogs moved behind me. The urge to turn and watch the dogs was overpowering. Jim kept encouraging us to stand still and not look at the dogs. He informed us not to look directly into the eyes of a passing dog. Locking eyes with a dog would only make a dog feel threatened and it would respond aggressively. We all stared straight ahead and did not move. After a minute or so, Jim ordered the handlers to take the dogs away. The handler of the black beast was sadistic. As he made a last pass behind one recruit, he reached out and grabbed the man's lower leg. Just for a second, the startled trainee was certain that the dog had latched onto him. He later told us that he nearly passed out.

We gladly went back to our regular training, but on two or three more occasions, we returned for more riot control work. I was amazed at the psychological effect the dogs had on us. Six men with dogs could easily disperse 32 people. I was captivated and hoped that I could find more information about the police dog service. I knew at that time I definitely wanted to be a dog handler.

The basic training at Depot went by quickly. We now realized that to be successful and get through Depot, we had to rely on each other and work together as a team. We learned to depend on each other. The training staff had thrust us together and hurled many difficult tasks at us. In return, they demanded perfection. Since most of us were only 19 or 20 years old, it made their job easier. We were too young to know any better. The oldest member of my troop was 32, which earned him the nickname "Gramps."

We came from diverse backgrounds across the country, but we all had one thing in common. We wanted to become members of the RCMP. The training had brought all of us close together. We had developed the "Esprit de Corps" or "Team Spirit." Most of us received transfers to detachments across Canada and assigned to general duty, which is everyday uniformed police work. A few went to other duties including one member that received a stint at the federal Parliament Buildings in Ottawa, Ontario, "guarding the tulips."

A week before our graduation, representatives from several specialized units within the RCMP attended to give presentations about what they could do for the general duty investigator. These guest speakers included members from drug squad, bomb disposal, serious crime and homicide, fraud, surveillance, police divers and a dog handler. They related some of their own experiences as members of the Force.

For me, the handler's detailed presentation was captivating. He appeared to be an intelligent man with a quiet disposition. He was of medium height with a slim build. Standing behind the lectern, with his RCMP ball cap perched on the back of his head; he related some of his own experiences as a dog handler and gave a detailed description of his duties. We learned that RCMP dogs not only broken up riots, but could also help investigators solve crimes. He was amiable and answered numerous questions.

I asked what the process was to become a dog handler. He responded that firstly, it was our responsibility to contact the dog handlers at our new detachments. Taking the opportunity to express an interest in working with the handlers and assisting with the ongoing training of the dogs was the first step. I could hardly wait to arrive at my new detachment and meet the handlers.

One thing that intrigued me was my first impression of the handlers I had met and observed at Depot. They all seemed to be patient, amiable, and respectful, with quiet, calm dispositions. I later discovered that for the most part, that was true. Nevertheless, despite the easy-going exterior, most handlers I worked with over the years were fiercely competitive, hardworking individuals, dedicated to their canine charges and police work.

Chapter 2
Introduction to Police Work at Burnaby Detachment

After the graduation ceremony of Troop 2 at the end of October 1975, my first posting was the municipality of Burnaby, a bedroom community of 120,000 people next to the city of Vancouver, British Columbia. As I had expected, my assignment was general duty in a "zone" in south Burnaby. A zone was like a detachment within a detachment. I was part of a team of about 18 members, appointed to the everyday policing of that zone. The detachment had a total complement of over 200 members at that time. Management assigned a member of my zone to be my trainer for six months. He had several years of service and was responsible for my on-the-job training.

Over the next four and a half years, I would work general duty in south Burnaby. During that time, I responded to countless complaints including noisy parties, break-ins, drunks, disturbances, armed robberies, assaults, sudden deaths, homicides, domestics, and assistance to the public. We conducted investigations, submitted charges and attended court. We patrolled the streets and neighborhoods, dealt with traffic offences, arrested drunk drivers and did foot patrols.

I recall many incidents and experiences working in Burnaby. On one occasion, my trainer and I were returning to the detachment at 6:00 AM, after completing a long night shift. As we made our way through the quiet streets, the urgent voice of the dispatcher requested a car attend a shooting. As she announced the location of the incident, we realized that we were driving passed the address. We advised that we were on scene and the complainant came out to meet us at the request of the dispatcher.

A young man in the basement had shot himself with a rifle. As I descended the stairs, I discovered that the man was still alive. He was lying on his back with the rifle beside him. The paramedics were on the way and I held him in my arms. I covered the bullet hole in his chest with a washcloth. Frothy blood had been coming out of the wound each time he exhaled. I kept encouraging him to hold on, but just as medical help arrived, he died in my arms. I watched life leave the terror and regret filled eyes that stayed glued to mine during the entire ordeal. I will always remember the rattling noise in his throat as he expired. It turned out he was the same age as me and we were born the same month.

A homicide occurred at a house in north Burnaby, while I was working an evening shift in south Burnaby. Other cars attended, took custody of the suspect, and secured the scene. The detachment Watch Commander later called upon me to attend the scene and assist with the investigation. By the time I arrived, all other uniformed members had departed. The plainclothes investigators and forensics team were still gathering physical evidence. My shift had just ended, but being a junior member, I was anxious to help. I had seen dead bodies before, but the scene I witnessed shocked me.

Earlier that evening, the owner of the house and two other men were drinking heavily. One houseguest made explicit comments about the owner's young daughter. The drunken father flew into a rage, went to his bedroom, and emerged with a shotgun. Without warning, he shot one man in the face at pointblank range. The force of the blast threw the victim backwards and he landed in the sofa, in a seated position. The corpse slumped to the right, with the upper body hanging over the side of the sofa. The assailant then turned his attention on the second houseguest, who in a state of terror and shock, was running to the front door. As the man was scrambling out the door, the suspect fired a second blast. The buckshot entered the back of the man's left elbow, continued down the length of the forearm: shredding it. He continued out the door, ran out into the street, and flagged down a police car that happened to be driving through the neighborhood. Re-enforcements promptly arrived and the suspect surrendered. An ambulance took the second casualty immediately to hospital. He survived, but the wound left his arm disfigured and crippled.

As I entered the house, I immediately saw the corpse. Half the face and head were missing and a mass of gray matter and blood had formed on the floor. It was a sickening sight, but added to that was the strong odor of liquor, sweat and blood. As I was taking in the sight, an orange house cat emerged from the shadows. Being inquisitive, it slinked up to the mess on the floor, sniffed it and took an exploratory lick. I felt myself getting sick, but made every effort to conceal it from the old salts from the forensics team, who seemed to enjoy watching my plight. I am sure that I was as pallor as the dead man. An investigator scooped the feline away from the scene as the body removal service arrived.

Another investigator briefed me about my involvement in the case. The corpse was on its way to the morgue at the hospital, where it would remain until a scheduled autopsy early the next morning. It was my job to escort the body to the morgue and maintain continuity of it. At the morgue, I would lock the body away and retain the key. I could then go home and return the next morning, witness the autopsy, gather blood and tissue samples and take them to the RCMP laboratory for analysis.

From my experience, witnessing an autopsy is intriguing, provided you remain objective. For me this was difficult to do. A small, high-speed circular saw opened up the remaining portions of the skull. The massive cutting of tissue and the removal of organs was upsetting. The combined smell of blood, human waste, and large quantities of un-digested beer was overpowering and something I will always remember. At the time, I felt honored that the investigators chose me, a junior member, to look after the most important exhibit. Later that afternoon my bubble quickly burst when I discovered that since I was still a trainee, they did not have to pay overtime for escorting the body after my regular shift or for attending the autopsy on my day off.

On another occasion, while on patrol on a Sunday evening, I received a call of a shooting at a high-rise apartment block on Kingsway Avenue. Kingsway is a major thoroughfare across south Burnaby and continues into the city of Vancouver. The victim had been sitting at her kitchen table, wearing her bathrobe after a shower. She heard a muffled bang in the apartment beside her and a mille-second later, a bullet came through the wall. The missile whizzed passed her face, traveled down a hallway, and imbedded itself in a closet door. The woman flew out of her apartment in a state of panic and ran to the manager's suite for help. The manager called the police.

I attended with two other members and found the victim hysterical. The manager provided the name of the lone male occupant living next door to the woman. The three of us drew our service revolvers and knocked on the door of the suspect suite. There was no answer and we opened the door with the key that the manager provided. The apartment was dark except for a light on in the bathroom. My breathing was labored and my heart pounded as if I had just sprinted up hill for a mile.

We burst in with one of my counterparts doing a grand entry. He had his weapon in both hands, with his arms fully extended. In true "Rambo" fashion, he went into a combat crouching position.

His uniform pants must have been too tight, because they split wide open with a resounding rip. As this happened, a middle-aged man emerged from the darkness, with hands high, yelling, "Oh, shit boys, don't shoot! For God's sake, don't shoot!" I handcuffed the man and searched him for the weapon, but he did not have it on him. I did a cursory search of the apartment and by chance, found it hidden in a laundry basket in the bedroom.

It turned out that the suspect, Reg, along with a friend, had been at a bar earlier that evening. They engaged in conversation with a stranger, who ended up selling Reg a handgun. The suspect and friend returned to the apartment and started playing with the revolver. Reg sat at the living room table with the gun. Without checking to see if it was loaded, he aimed it at the wall and pulled the trigger. Without hesitation, the friend ran out the door leaving Reg sitting in a state of shock. Reg's ears were ringing from the blast, but he could still hear his neighbor screaming as she ran down the hallway. He did not know what to do, so he hid the gun and turned out the lights, sat in the dark and hoped everything and everybody would just leave him alone.

Later, I checked the serial number of the gun to determine if it was a registered firearm, and/or stolen in Canada. My enquiries were negative, but I did a further computer search in the United States. Six years previously, authorities in the State of Alabama, reported a stolen revolver matching the make, caliber and serial number of the gun I seized. I could only wonder how many hands that weapon had passed through over the years and what its history included. After the court case, I returned it to Alabama.

On a cold, rainy midnight shift, a fellow member, Ray, and I responded to a complaint. A man on the 16th floor of a high-rise apartment building had called the Crisis Line, contemplating suicide. We arrived at the address to find a despondent man named Stan. He was a tall, slender man in his 40's. We purposefully engaged in a lengthy conversation with him. His predicament involved a job going nowhere and a failed relationship. After about 15 minutes, he seemed to relax and we convinced him to go to the hospital for examination.

Stan was already dressed, but asked if he could pack a few personal items in case he had to stay at the hospital. Ray agreed to stay with him while I used the telephone to call our dispatcher to request an ambulance. Some kind of electrical interference in the building was affecting our portable radios and we could not transmit.

Ray was in Stan's bedroom while I talked to the dispatcher in the living room. Suddenly, I heard a thumping noise in the bedroom. I called out to Ray, but he did not reply. I dropped the phone and ran into the bedroom. Ray was against the wall beside the head of the bed. The bedroom window above the bed was wide open. Ray's face was white and his forage cap bobbed up and down on his head, because the back of the cap was pressed hard against the wall. His eyes were wide with astonishment as he hung on tightly to Stan's legs. The top half of Stan's body was hanging out the window. I jumped onto the bed, leaned out the window, and grabbed the jumper by the belt around his waist. I remember looking at the street far below us with the cold rain slashing across my face. With one great heave, we pulled Stan back to safety. He struggled with us until we handcuffed his hands behind his back. He then laid on the bed sobbing.

After the paramedics attended and took Stan for treatment, I asked Ray what happened and why he did not respond when I called out to him. Ray was standing by the bed while Stan packed. Suddenly, Stan took a flying leap onto the bed and bounced head first out the open window. Ray re-acted by wrapping his arms around Stan's legs on the way out. He said that he was in such a state of shock that he could not speak and despite the fact we had worked together for almost a year, Ray could not remember my name. A week later, the commissioned officer in charge of the detachment presented both of us with a written commendation for our quick action in saving Stan's life.

My duties were many and varied while I was a general duty member at Burnaby detachment, some of which were terrifying, emotional experiences. Any incidents that involved children, I found the most disturbing. I recall responding to a domestic disturbance involving a couple that were known drug users and reprobates. This troubled household also consisted of a boy about three years old. I and other members had attended on previous occasions and all had concerns about the welfare of the toddler. Social services were constantly involved, but only with mixed results. I sadly remember trying to referee the combative man and woman as the child sat on the dirty kitchen counter, staring into oblivion, repeatedly muttering four-letter words.

During an evening shift, I attended a complaint about people causing a disturbance and fighting in the parking lot of a popular drinking establishment in south Burnaby. Upon attending, I saw a few people in the parking lot, but nobody was fighting. A staff member pointed out a young man about my age that was near the others in the lot. The staff physically removed the man from the bar because he was threatening people and trying to pick fights. They just wanted the man to stay away from the premises.

I drove up to the man, got out of my patrol car, and called him over to me. He was about the same size as me. He did not appear to be intoxicated, but was definitely upset and angry. His torn shirt was possibly from the altercation with the staff members. He came over to me, but was not cooperative and would not answer my questions. He became belligerent and started to walk away from me. I placed my hand on his arm to stop him, when with cat-like speed; he turned and pushed me violently against the side of my car.

I re-acted by grabbing him and we both slammed against the front of the car. We started to grapple and wrestle with each other. Entwined, we ended up rolling across the hood of the police car and falling in a withering lump onto the pavement.

I had ended up on the bottom and winded from the fall. He pinned me and started punching me wildly about the face. Anger and fear together brought out the adrenalin that now surged through my body. I pushed him away and jumped onto him. I tried to apply a chokehold, but he was fighting like a demon. I did not have backup and it was impossible to get to my police radio. The bar staff had gone back inside and were not aware of the altercation.

I was conscious that a crowd was starting to gather around and from the comments made; none of the spectators were rooting for me. I was also afraid that some of the people might join the fray and start pummeling me. My opponent suddenly smashed the side of my face with his elbow. He coughed up a giant wad of phlegm and spat directly in my face.

Perhaps it was the training. At Depot, it was always a 110 percent effort and never give up when the chips were down. On the other hand, maybe it was just because I was no longer scared, but angry as hell. The next thing I knew, I had my foe's head jammed under the front tire of the police car. With spittle dripping off my nose, I pushed his face hard into the tire tread and got a hold of his neck. As I squeezed, he went limp. I handcuffed him and pulled his semi-conscious body into the back of the car. The crowd did a complete turn-around and started to cheer for me. Some even commented that it was bad form for the man to spit on me.

One hot summer's day, I discovered a naked man in a back alley. He was laying full length in the dirt, desperately trying to do swimming strokes. Of course, for me the most upsetting part of the scene was the man's ten-year-old son standing over his prostrate father. With tears streaming down his face, the boy pleaded with his father to get up and come back inside the house. The man had suffered a mental collapse.

Another night, a fellow member, and I responded to a single vehicle accident. Witnesses observed a small, foreign made convertible roll into a deep ditch. There were no streetlights in the area and the ditch was narrow. The car was upright, tangled in the undergrowth and the driver was still behind the wheel. We struggled over twisted metal and brush to the male driver, who was unresponsive. My partner opened the driver's door and the man fell into our arms. As we caught him, grey matter and blood fell into our laps. He had not utilized his seatbelt and the collision had crushed his head.

On another occasion, I attended a disturbance on the third floor of an apartment building during a busy midnight shift. The suspect in the disturbance had a history with the police. He was unpredictable, dangerous and had threatened members that had dealt with him in the past. He also owned firearms. As I opened the stairwell door to the third floor hallway, I could hear the man around the corner, talking in a loud voice. From the tone of the voice, he sounded angry and intoxicated. He was yelling profanities, repeating, "I'm ready for those bastards this time! They aren't goin' to take me away! I've got something for them this time!"

I drew my sidearm and cautiously peeked around the corner. He was standing in the dim light of the hallway with his back to me. He was swaying back and forth and swinging his arms. I caught sight of something in his right hand. As I called out to him, he swung around and pointed the object in his hand directly at me, as if he were holding a firearm. It all happened so fast. As he spun around, I was aiming at his chest and squeezing the trigger of my revolver. My weapon was within a fraction of firing, when I suddenly realized that he was pointing an empty beer glass at me. My heart was pounding in my throat and I suddenly felt exhausted.

My work life was extremely busy, but I always went out of my way to be around any of the four dog handlers posted at Burnaby. They often attended crime scenes to assist in looking for evidence or tracking suspects that had fled on foot. They usually showed up at alarms and searched buildings found insecure or broken into. They often attended complaints involving violence or potential for violence, as back up for the general duty members. With the exception of the sergeant in charge, I found these men friendly and approachable,

The sergeant was an older, gruff character named Willam that some of the younger members found to be abrasive and intimidating. Actually, I am sure that some of the more senior members and NCO's thought the same way. He was short and squat, with a beefy face and thick neck. Willam seemed to be a loner, but according to the handlers that worked for him, he was always a fair and respected boss. He had that "old school" appearance. He constantly wore a forage cap, rather than the more comfortable and practical ball cap preferred by the other handlers. Willam even wore the cap when he drove his police vehicle. At the time, dog handlers wore brown denim pants, rather than the long blue trousers with the yellow stripe. Instead of the blue patrol jacket, they wore green rain jackets. Willam opted for the patrol jacket, complete with a uniform shirt and necktie.

During my first year at Burnaby, I volunteered some of my off-duty time, to ride with the other three handlers as an observer. It was difficult to do, since I was still a trainee and had to devote other off-duty time to my job. I found the police dogs and the relationship they had with their handlers intriguing. The more I was around the handlers, the more convinced I became that I wanted to join the police dog service. To this end, I knew that I had to approach Willam and ask more about the process to become a handler.

On a quiet afternoon shift, I overheard Willam on the police radio. He advised the dispatcher that he would be at his office in the detachment. I was in the detachment at that time and had just completed a stack of paperwork. I walked down to the ground floor, where the "dog office" was located. This was our first one to one meeting. The office door was open and Willam was sitting behind his desk, with his forage cap on as usual, focused on some paperwork of his own. He did not look up when I approached the open door.

Apprehensively, I tapped on the doorframe with my knuckles and he looked up at me. He had a dark, round, cynical face with a Fu Manchu moustache. With a big phony smile he asked, "So, you think you wanna be a dog man?" The question astounded me and I did not know what to say. Feeling quite intimidated, I fidgeted with a paper I had in my hand. Finally, I bleated, "Well, I would sure like to try." The smile disappeared from Willam's face as he shot me a glare that made my hands instantly sweat.

He pointed at the chair in front of his desk and replied, "Sit-down! You know, all you wet-behind-the-ears kids wanna be dog handlers! What's so special about you?"

This was the start of our first real conversation and the beginning of an interesting working relationship between Willam and me over the next three years. He told me that the other handlers had been talking to him about me. I had told them about my interest in police dogs and they had relayed that to Willam. As we talked, Willam became more amiable. My initial gut feelings told me that deep down Willam was not the old grouch that everybody labeled him. In some ways, he was odd or even unusual, but as I would later discover, when it came to knowledge of police dogs, he commanded a lot of respect.

I heard many stories from other handlers about Willam's abilities and perseverance. However, there was one account that I heard directly from an eyewitness. During a dayshift, I met Willam for coffee and a man riding with him that day, turned out to be a senior NCO with the RCMP stationed in Manitoba. He was on holidays and visiting family in Vancouver and stopped to reminisce with Willam for the day. Years before, Willam and the NCO had worked together at the same detachment in southern Manitoba.

In a pensive manner, the visitor related to me the case of a murder suspect on foot in a remote area during an extremely cold, winter night. Willam and his police dog tracked the suspect all night, with the NCO as his backup. The man said that the cold was severe and they both became exhausted from the long, intense pursuit. The NCO wanted to stop and rest. They did not have radio communication and nobody knew of their position. The fatigued Willam coaxed and persuaded his back up to keep moving despite the harsh elements. At daybreak, they finally captured the suspect and search aircraft discovered them shortly after. The old NCO credited Willam for saving his life. Willam responded to the story by only shrugging his shoulders dismissively.

Willam said that what I needed to know about police dogs was not all found in books. It took a special appreciation of the animal and a commitment to work with them. Willam went on to describe the prerequisites required to become a handler. Firstly, I needed the investigative experience that would take some time to acquire and good progress reports from my supervisors. I had to commit my energy and time, usually on my regular time off, to work with all the dog handlers, mostly assisting with the ongoing training of the police dogs. The handlers would also continually assess my aptitude around the dogs.

Potential handlers also had to participate in the RCMP puppy program. This involved raising a potential police dog from pup to adult training age, under the close supervision and tutorage of a handler. The job consisted of forming a one-on-one bond with the pup. The potential handler exposed the pup to as many different environments as possible, including busy streets and crowds, rides in vehicles, buildings, stairways, shiny floors, escalators, and elevators. As the pup got older and bigger, there were walks in parks and rural areas. Playing fetch was highly encouraged. Contrary to common belief, the pup learned basic obedience slowly and never forcefully. Maintenance of the pup included a proper diet, as well as regular grooming and check-ups at the veterinarian. There was never a guarantee that the potential dog would actually become a police dog. Statistically, only one out of ten dogs selected ever became a working dog. It depended on temperament and the health of the potential dogs. The tough part of this job was giving the dog up when it reached adulthood.

The other requirement for a potential handler was to attend annual dog handler refresher courses as a quarry. On the two-week course, the quarry had to assist with scenarios set up by the trainers for the dog handlers. Both the trainers and dog handlers assessed the quarries during the course. Quarries had to demonstrate an ability to work under pressure, use good common sense, and be self-motivated. The trainers would also be watching for the patience and skills needed to be a handler.

Just to be considered for dog handler duties was a big order to fill, and would require a lot of work. Willam and I concluded our meeting, with him stating that it was a long, competitive process and that I should give careful consideration before committing. It was sound advice, and I promised to let him know of my decision.

After a few weeks, I bumped into Willam at the detachment. I told him that I wanted to start the process, no matter the time and effort required. I had set my sights at becoming a dog handler. I took every opportunity to work with the Burnaby handlers, mostly on my off duty time. In return, the handlers good-naturedly gave me the title, "Wanna Be."

One of the most important tasks that police dogs perform is tracking people. I found this to be truly amazing. A harness with a line attached that is about 20 feet long, secures the dog. The handler holds the line and by "reading" the indications of the dog, follows the track. From the early stages of training, the dogs are encouraged to ignore other animal scents and tracks.

Watching a well-trained dog follow the scent of a human is extraordinary. Scent in tracking consists of three factors. First is the particular scent that each person has. Each living person sheds thousands of microscopic particles every day and these particles make up an exclusive smell. The dog's powerful nose can discriminate between individual scents. I have observed countless times during training scenarios, where dogs will ignore cross tracks from other quarries while tracking. Once a well-trained dog is "locked on" to a particular scent, he will follow it disregarding other human scents.

The second feature that makes up a track or scent is what other smells a person may have on their body. This would include deodorants, after-shave, lotions, perfume, or creams. If the person is say a mechanic, there may be grease, oil, or gasoline on the body or clothes. The particular odor of the clothes is also important, such as bleach, cleaner, and fabric softeners.

The third part to make up a track is the vegetation through which the quarry moves. Heavy vegetation like thick bush and high grass will hold and trap human odor for many hours. In addition, crushed or disturbed vegetation has a different smell than if it is not disturbed. (In dog handler training, we got down on our hands and knees and smelled a patch of grass. Next, we lightly scuffed our boot on the grass and smelled it again. Even the human nose could discern that the scuffed area smelled more intense.) In contrast, sparse or minute vegetation will not hold scent long, nor change much when the quarry moves through it.

The handlers would have me quarry for them and lay out tracks at their direction. These exercises would help keep both the dog and handler keen in this skill. The length of the tracks varied from a few blocks to several miles. Occasionally, if there were more than one quarry, I had the opportunity to accompany a handler and dog on a training track.

One aspect of tracking that astounded me was that the dog always knew which way to go. In other words, the dog's nose was so discerning that he could tell the freshness of the next footprint from the last one. During some training tracks, we would "cut" a quarry's track, meaning that the dog was directed across the track at a right angle. After the dog indicated the track, nine times out of ten, the dog went the right direction. If the dog did go the wrong way, it was only for a few feet. He quickly sorted it out, turned, and went the direction the quarry was walking.

Sometimes in actual investigations, it was necessary to work a back track, or in other words, have the dog work a track from where the suspect(s) came from. Experienced dogs had no difficulty doing this. As an example in 1983, I assisted the provincial Conservation Officer (CO) Service, near Salmon Arm, BC. The CO discovered a man in a field near a road that he suspected had shot a deer out of season. The suspect was unarmed, but had blood on his hands and clothing. I had my police dog Trapper work the man's track backwards for nearly a mile, through thick brush. Halfway through the track the dog indicated a high-powered rifle hidden behind a tree. At the end of the track was a recently shot, gutted deer carcass. The CO confronted the suspect with all the evidence Trapper had uncovered and the man admitted to the offence.

Training a dog to search for articles is another interesting exercise where the quarry places out a variety of items for the dog to locate. Large articles included things such as a jacket, shirt, hat, boots, tools, and firearms. Small articles were spent shell casings, coins, buttons, or bits of cloth and leather. For a large article search, the quarry would vary the number of articles each time.

The area searched could be a field, alleyway, or a bush area. For small articles, the numbers also varied and areas searched would be considerably smaller. During large article searches, the dog was usually off line and the handler directed the dog with voice commands and hand signals. The handler moved the dog into the wind, in a back-and-forth pattern, through the search area. The handler watched for "indications" when the dog found an article. During small article searches, the format was the same, except the dog worked much closer to the handler, in a more confined search area. What the dog was indicating was the human scent on the article, the particular scent of the article and the fact the combined smells were foreign to the area searched.

With narcotic searching, the first smells introduced to the dogs were the "soft" drugs, namely marihuana and hashish. Areas searched included buildings and vehicles. The dogs were on leash, with the handler directing the dog in a search pattern to cover the entire search area. As the dog indicated the hidden drug, it would sit and the handler then rewarded the dog with a ball or a leather tug. The "hard" drugs, cocaine, and heroin (with their derivatives) were then introduced. The dog never touches any of the drugs, since contact can be hazardous, especially in their purest form. To ensure consistency, the federal department of Health and Welfare provided all training drugs. Handlers and quarries wore protective gloves any time they worked with these drugs, to avoid health complications.

Protection or aggression work is another important profile for police dogs. An adult German Shepherd dog can exert over six hundred pounds per square inch of pressure with their mouths. Even with protective padding, this can still be a painful, yet exhilarating experience for the recipient. Sometimes the aggression training was held in conjunction with building searches. This involved having access to a warehouse after hours to train dogs to find hidden or barricaded persons. The quarry hid with the protective gear on.

As a quarry, I remember numerous occasions of finding a suitable area to conceal myself in a dimly lit warehouse. I would nestle down and always wait with great trepidation. It was quiet and customary to wait several minutes for the scent to expand and settle after having moved around the building. This of course gave me time to reflect and sometimes wonder why I was sitting, waiting for a super-charged canine to find me.

After the wait, the handler and dog entered the building with the dog usually whining or barking in anticipation of the hunt. The handler called out that it was the police and for any persons hiding, to surrender or he would release the dog. Keeping with the training exercise, I remained quiet and hidden. After a few moments, the handler released the dog with a "search" command. They then started a search pattern through the building to locate me. With the dog now in search mode, I could hear him panting and the toe nails clicking on the flooring as he quickly patrolled. There were no other sounds except for the odd verbal encouragement from the handler. No matter how many times I did this, it was always unnerving to know that inevitably, the dog would find me.

Depending on the size of the search area and the amount of air movement, it did not take long for the dog to catch the scent and charge into the source of it. The dog always hit the padding with a furious bite and the "fight" was on. It was the responsibility of the quarry to ensure that the dog was not injured during the struggle. After a short battle, I inevitably surrendered. After searching me to ensure I did not have any weapons, the handler and dog escorted their "prisoner" out of the building.

As Willam emphasized, it was important for me to raise a pup for the RCMP. A considerable amount of my off duty time was now devoted to working with the handlers and caring for a canine candidate. For me it was a rewarding experience to raise a potential police dog from a fury puppy to a young adult, but it was also extremely heartbreaking just as Willam had explained. For the pups that made it through the program in good health and passed all the temperament tests, they went to the Training Kennels at Innisfail, Alberta. The dog was then partnered with a handler for training.

Willam could see my distress and offered advice and consolation in his own way. He reminded me that other potential handlers across the country were going through the same thing. I was not alone. It was important to do the best job possible, because the competition was close. If I really wanted a chance to become a handler, then I had to keep my priorities in order and keep my emotions in check. Willam also said that I was giving the potential dogs a tremendous advantage. Raising the dogs with compassion, support, and proper training would help them to become good police dogs. For the right dogs, it would mean an exciting life for them.

Willam continuously offered his support to me. He would tell me, if I did become a handler, how important it was not to abuse the use of a police dog. I always remember him saying, "Sending a dog on a person, you better make damn sure that you are justified! That is the same thing as drawing your gun! Like drawing your gun, you only draw it if you intend to use it. Therefore, you had better remember that you have to be justified in lettin' that dog go! At the end of the day, they'll be lookin' at you." Willam strongly believed that the dog was only as good as his trainer. It was important to have integrity and be responsible for your actions.

In puppy rearing, one of the big health concerns was hip displaysia in the German Shepherd breed. This terrible disease was partially the result of generations of indiscriminate breeding practices. Displaysia can only be properly diagnosed with radiographs and not until the dog is about six months old. One of my puppies named "Gar" was progressing well. He did not show any problems, but the veterinarian recommended an X-ray during one of Gar's check-ups. The dog had displaysia so bad that the doctor put Gar down the same day. I was in a state of shock and disbelief. The pup had never shown any signs of pain or discomfort before. When I got home on that grief-stricken day, I went into the backyard to Gar's kennel. I wrapped his favorite old blanket in my arms and had a good cry. Again, Willam and the other handlers were supportive and some told me of their own experiences of losing dogs. It was not too long before I took on another pup and tried again. Two dogs that I raised went on to be working dogs. Despite Willam's talks, I still found it heartbreaking to see them go on to another handler. After the dogs left, I usually consoled myself with that customary trip to the back yard.

Chapter 3
The Training Kennels

In the early fall of 1979, I was selected by the RCMP Training Kennels to attend a two-week annual refresher course for the police dog service. I was excited at the prospect of attending. It was also satisfying to have some recognition of all my hard work and patience over the past three years. All the dog handlers' stationed at large detachments near Vancouver, including Burnaby, Coquitlam, North Vancouver, Surrey, and Richmond were scheduled to attend. Other dog handlers posted at smaller detachments east of Vancouver in the Fraser Valley were attending also. Half would attend the first week and the second half during the last week of the course. All the quarries, including myself, would stay for the entire two weeks at the Canadian Forces base, situated at Chilliwack, BC.

Instructors from the Training Kennels would officiate the training. The purpose was to assess each dog team, to ensure that dogs and handlers were still meeting all the qualifications. To do this, the instructors would use the quarries to set out numerous and varied scenarios. This, in turn, would give the instructors and handlers the opportunity to assess each quarry for suitability as future dog handlers. For the quarries, this was the chance of a lifetime. An unfavorable evaluation meant exclusion from further consideration. I recall there were about 14 quarries on this course and the competition throughout was close. About 25 dog handlers in total, attended along with four instructors.

Right from the start, I noticed that for the handlers, this was more like "old home week" than an assessment. During the initial meeting on the evening before the course, all the handlers and instructors had a chance to meet each other. Most knew each other from various training courses and operational situations. Some had been stationed together at other detachments over the years. We, as quarries, stood in the sidelines watching and listening. It was a time for these handlers to re-kindle old friendships and probably make some new ones. Inevitably, the meeting turned from amiable small talk to a "bitch and stitch" session directed at the training staff, usually regarding higher echelon decisions about training or operational concerns. After that, it was time for war stories, where each handler had an experience about a particular case or cases they worked. These stories always included how well and how hard their particular dogs worked under extraordinary circumstances. With this, I could see the keen competitiveness coming out. Each handler had a good story to tell and for the most part, the stories were incredible and action-packed. Most handlers injected a little humor in their stories, which made them that much more interesting.

The training staff reminded all of us that we were guests on a military establishment during the course and we were to conduct ourselves accordingly. They would not tolerate any tomfoolery on or off duty, and threatened disciplinary action for any incidents. For the quarries, this would also include a one-way ticket off the course. The days were long and the course demanding. Many hours of our workdays were off the base, outdoors in the rain and cold. I tried to concentrate and put my best foot forward. I had gained a lot of experience working with the handlers in Burnaby and made good use of that knowledge. Besides assisting with building searches, large and small article searches, drug searches and aggression training, all quarries were detailed to lay long bush tracks in the mountains surrounding the city of Chilliwack. The tracks were four to six miles long.

On one exercise, I had to hike through thick brush in a steady, drizzling rain, for about five miles. The rain gear that I had was inadequate for the circumstances. The wet gear stuck to my sweat-soaked undergarments. By the time I reached the area where the training staff told me to stop, I was a wet, tired, cold mess. I took refuge under a large cedar tree beside an old logging trail, while the rain intensified. I knew that I would have to wait for at least two hours while the track had time to age before the handler worked it.

I found some relatively dry tinder and branches under the surrounding trees and prepared to start a small fire to warm up and perhaps dry my clothes. I could not find the matches that I was sure I had packed. Getting increasingly frustrated at not being able to find the matches, I started to shed all of my wet gear. Before long, I was standing in the bush, wearing only my underwear and hiking boots. As I was making one last attempt to find the matches, Wesley, the senior instructor of the course, drove around the bend on the road. I stood stone still, hoping that the old staff sergeant would not see me. Wesley was an astute man and observant. He slowly drove passed me with a look of total amazement on his face. He stopped, reversed his vehicle, and stopped in front of me.

Wesley did not say anything to me as a wide grin spread across his face. He went to the back of his warm, cozy truck and pulled out a pair of coveralls. He tossed the dry clothing to me along with a book of matches. Silently puffing on his pipe, he got back in the vehicle and drove off. I am a size extra large, tall, but I was beyond caring and squeezed into the medium coveralls. I got a small fire going, which warmed me and I did my best to dry my gear. The handler and dog tracked me down a couple hours later. I did not say anything about my strange attire and I did not bother to mention my chance meeting with Wesley.

Billeted in eight person rooms within one large barrack, the training staff mixed handlers with quarries. The idea being that everyone would have the opportunity to know each other and for the handlers to better assess the quarries. In our room, we all seemed to get along well, perhaps too well. One early morning, after a night of partying, conversations had deteriorated to discussions about the smoke detectors on the ceiling of our room. Some wondered if the devices really worked. To resolve the concern, one roommate lit a cigar and standing on a chair proceeded to blow smoke on a detector. Of course, we all encouraged him. Repeated attempts by the smoker had no effect and we all became disillusioned with the effectiveness of the alarms. Suddenly the entire barrack was filled with the incessant ringing of loud bells. We threw open all the windows and the smoker tossed the cigar, all in a vain attempt to silence the alarms. In the distance, we saw the fire trucks leaving the base fire hall, with lights blazing and sirens screaming. The unceasing noise had everybody in the building awake. All the unsuspecting members of the course, including the instructors, were milling about in the hallways. Everybody was in a state of confusion. Amid shouts and swearing, partially dressed and half-asleep people made their way out the front entrance.

We were standing outside the barracks in the pouring rain, when the military firefighters promptly arrived on the scene. Suited up in their firefighting gear, they barged into the building to investigate the alarm. I glanced over at Wesley, who was standing across from me. His glasses were foggy and the rain was pounding off his head and shoulders. I felt guilty and could not look into his face. All I could think of was him discovering that we were the people responsible and being kicked off the course. Soon the firefighters emerged empty handed and somebody asked if they knew what had set off the detectors. One disgruntled firefighter replied that the alarms had gone off before and believed they were too sensitive. Another just grumbled, "A loud fart would probably set those damn things off!"

To my indescribable relief, the instructors accepted the analogy and everybody went back to bed. Nothing further was said, except by one of the older seasoned handlers. He was a sound sleeper and in the commotion, nobody thought to wake him. He was not aware of the incident until early the next morning. He went into a fuming tirade and exclaimed to everybody within earshot, "What the hell is wrong with you people? If that had been a real fire, I would have probably burned to death! What a nice bunch of assholes I gotta work with!" None of us could blame him for his concern.

The two weeks flew by and I became even more captivated by the training of the dogs and the characters that handled them. Besides the competitive nature of the handlers, I was amazed at the devotion each handler had towards his dog. Dog and handler were definitely a team. Nobody got between the two. At no time, did another handler or even a trainer attempt to handle, touch, or even talk to another handler's dog. I had observed the same with the Burnaby handlers and respected the unwritten code of conduct. As quarries, we knew that petting or addressing a dog meant a one-way ticket off the course.

Wesley was a wealth of knowledge concerning police dogs. He encouraged the handlers to spend more than just the required time training and maintaining their charges. To demonstrate this, he asked a handler to place his ball cap on the ground. Wesley then instructed four or five others to place their caps in a line with the first ball cap. The handler then brought his dog out and under Wesley's coaching, had the handler walk his dog down the line of caps. When the dog got to his handler's cap, the dog was encouraged and praised. The dog now knew what was expected and the process repeated a few times, with different caps. The dog would quickly indicate his handler's cap each time. It was just a simple exercise in scent discrimination. It proved how discerning a dog's nose was.

Wesley told us that years before, when he was a handler, he had trained one of his dogs to salute. It was still during a time when constables and NCO's were required to salute commissioned officers of the RCMP in a show of respect.

Wesley always enjoyed telling others how well trained his dogs were. To teach the dog to salute, he simply blew lightly in the dog's right ear. The dog responded by lifting his right paw to his ear, in an effort brush off the wind in his ear. Each time the exercise was done and as soon as the dog started to lift his right paw, Wesley said, "Salute." Soon the dog understood that when his handler said "Salute," he would lift his right paw to his ear. According to Wesley, many commissioned officers were delighted and surprised, when even the police dog saluted them.

On the last day of the course, the trainers evaluated the handlers and dogs. In turn, the trainers and handlers began to assess each quarry. We were all anxiously waiting for the decisions, when Wesley and one of the handlers emerged from the barracks. I remembered that the handler had been pestering Wesley all week about a concern over his dog. Wesley had his hands full running the course and now it appeared that he was going to address the situation. The handler and Wesley walked across the parking lot to the handler's car. We watched both men approach the car and I noticed that the handler's dog was spinning happily in the back of the vehicle. The dog had a week of exhilarating training and upon seeing his handler with Wesley; he now assumed there would be more. Wesley got in the front passenger seat and the handler was behind the wheel.

Sometimes dogs react to a build up of tension and excitement. In this case, it could not have happened at a more in-opportune time. As the dog was spinning, he had a huge diarrheic outburst that splattered the inside of the vehicle and both occupants. The vile, wet stream covered the backs and heads of the men inside. It all occurred within seconds and most of us witnessed the unfortunate event.

As both car doors flew open, we all turned in unison and walked off. Wesley, with shoulders hunched over, raced for the barracks. The handler, standing by his vehicle, let out a long, loud string of colorful language mostly directed at his canine. The dog stared back out at him through brown stained windows, happily wagging his tail. The handler tore off his soiled uniform shirt and threw it to the ground as we all scampered around a high hedge. Safely out of earshot and sight, we broke into uncontrollable laughter.

Near the end of the day, the trainers called the quarries inside, one at a time for an interview. By the time my turn rolled around, I was filled with trepidation. Wesley quickly put me at ease saying that I had successfully met the standards and they would recommend me and two or three of the other quarries on my course for dog handler training. I was so elated that I did not really hear what he said next.

He tried to make it clear that this was the first refresher course for the year. He and the trainers had to attend three other courses across the country, to accommodate all the handlers stationed in Canada. Of course, there would be more quarries to assess and when that was completed, they would place my name on a national list. My position on the list would depend on seniority and operational demands.

I returned to my regular duties at Burnaby detachment on cloud nine. All my years of hard work and sacrifice had paid off. To me, it was a great sense of accomplishment. Wesley advised me that I would receive a copy of the training staff's recommendations and a copy of the national list, but it would take about two months. The papers had to ride the RCMP red tape highway. I buried myself in my work and tried to remain patient.

At about two months, as Wesley promised, I received the list. I tore open the envelope with shaking hands and saw, to my utter disappointment, that my name was number 17 on the list. This equated to at least a one-year wait and I felt deflated. I decided that I had to keep my nose to the grindstone and try not to be disillusioned. I continued to volunteer my time with the local handlers and participate with the puppy-rearing program. Throughout the winter, I heard rumors that the list had changed. A few candidates went into training, but a couple others dropped off the list for various reasons. The news made me feel more optimistic, but the local handlers told me not to get too excited. No schedules existed for dog handler courses in the near future, due to the lack of available funding and no operational requirements were identified for the following year. I was now number nine on the list.

By mid-April 1980, I had resigned myself to the possibility that I would not be taking the dog handler course for that year. While enjoying a quiet morning at home, the telephone rang. It was the Chief Superintendent of the Burnaby detachment. He was the man in charge and I knew that the "Old Man" was not in the habit of phoning young constables at home and I was shocked. He was a polite, articulate man with an infectious smile, but everybody knew that he was not to be taken lightly. He was always fair, but did not have any patience for those that ended up on his wrong side. Staying on the straight and narrow was the easiest way to get along with him.

Firstly, he apologized for phoning me at home on my day off. He had received a memorandum from the police dog services, channeled through the RCMP's staffing and personnel section. The police dog service wanted to know if the Old Man would release me from my duties at Burnaby to attend the Training Kennels. My training would commence in one week. I was flabbergasted because the Kennels had gone over several names on the list to pick me.

The only thing that stood in my way now, was that the Old Man had to decide whether he could let me go at that time. I knew that the detachment had staffing issues and a twinge of fear rose in me. The Old Man could elect to keep me because of the labor shortage. The boss must have sensed my panic when I blurted out that working with police dogs was my goal. He cut me short with his calming voice, "No, no, Brad, I am aware that you have worked hard to get this far. I will not stand in the way of your career path. You are going! I just wanted to know if one week is enough time for you to prepare. That is damn short notice. I can ask for an extension on your behalf." I nearly dropped the phone. I was elated. I told the Old Man that one week was enough time for me and thanked him for his concern. He chuckled, congratulated me, and wished me every success. I thanked him profusely for his consideration.

I reflected on all that I had learned working with other handlers and their dogs. Numerous times the dogs had proven how their noses were such a discerning and powerful tool, well suited for police work. It fascinated me at how the dogs all enjoyed working. They were one-person dogs, committed to working with their handlers. I was such a regular around the Burnaby dogs and they were very familiar with me. When it came to hard work, courage, intelligence, temperament and stamina, these dogs were all the same, but of course, each had its own personality. One particular dog would always welcome me with a wagging tail and play bows, but I knew that he was setting me up. He would bite anybody that tried to touch him. Another dog totally ignored my presence, until it involved some type of exercise, at which time I received his undivided attention.

Niki, my second working dog, had a nasty habit. During training exercises when a group of other handlers and quarries were standing, talking, and socializing, Niki would saunter up to them in a friendly manner. As he got within range, the dog would intentionally flick his head up, bumping them in the crotch with his nose. It was usually only enough to cause a little discomfort. Niki quite often looked back at me, with a mischievous look on his face. I never bothered to correct the dog, since those that were familiar with Niki's antics, just covered their respective crotches whenever the dog walked passed I actually found it somewhat humorous to watch grown men standing around, instinctively covering themselves anytime Niki walked by searching for a potential victim.

Some people believe that police dogs are primarily mean and unpredictable. In reality, having such an animal is detrimental and dangerous for everyone, including the handler. The handler needs an animal that can be trusted and in turn, the dog must be able to trust its handler. The domestic dog has been with people for centuries and has adapted well to living around humans. We have learned a lot about dogs by studying the habits of their distant cousins, the wolves. Like the dog, a wolf's eyes are at the front of the head. The sharp eyes pick up movement and are an important tool for this hunter. The eyes of prey animals such as rabbits and squirrels are located on the sides of their heads. They have an excellent field of vision to keep them safe. If they see danger, they can quickly flee or hide.

Wolves live in groups or packs. Within each group, there is a hierarchy with a leader and subordinates. Each pack member has a particular function to ensure the group remains a cohesive, efficient unit of hunters. Some members of the pack do not have a strong instinct for hunting. They are the "hanger-ons," relegated to other duties, such as baby-sitters for the pups. When feasting on a kill, these members usually eat only after the more dominant ones have finished their share. The leader keeps order in the pack and ensures that it remains efficient in the never-ending quest for food.

The ideal police dog has to be similar to the leader of the wolf pack. He or she must possess all the drive and determination of a hunter. The dog must want to do the job and thrive on seeking. The dog must be tenacious and have courage. A certain amount of independence is also required, but the dog must also want to please. The police dog works only because he or she enjoys the work and wants to please the handler. The RCMP had and still do have some female police dogs.

It is always important to see things from the dog's perspective. The police dog, like the wolf, considers the handler and itself to be a pack. It is the job of the handler to ensure that the dog understands and accepts the fact that the handler is the undisputed leader of the pack. To achieve this, the handler has to use good common sense, be patient, and always use good judgment. Besides that, the handler must make certain that the dog is always healthy, properly fed, safe, maintained and exercised. The handler must take full responsibility for the dog's actions.

Through consistent handling, training and positive reinforcement, the dog will understand and accept the handler as the leader of their pack. If the human does not remain consistent, the dog may become unsure or uncomfortable in its role within the pack. The dog may assume that the handler is not as strong as it first thought is, and take advantage of the situation to its benefit. The handler must also keep in mind that the dog is by nature an opportunist.

A well-trained dog, given proper direction and care by the handler, will strive in every way possible to please the human. The dog and handler will form a strong bond and therefore become a cohesive team. During my time as a dog handler, I had to depend on my canine partner many times. On at least one occasion, I had to depend on my dog for my life!

I arrived at the RCMP Police Dog Service Training Kennels, situated near Innisfail, Alberta on the last week of April 1980. Innisfail is a prairie town situated in central Alberta along Highway 2. The area around the town is all farm and ranch land and the Kennels are on 17 acres, about a mile south of Innisfail. The facility consists of numerous indoor and outside kennels, administration buildings, storage sheds, exercise yards, and a large agility field. Kennel personnel maintain the Kennels and care for any dogs that may be on the premise. There was an inspector in charge, or in RCMP terms an "Officer in Charge" (OIC), and five trainers on the site. No operational police work was conducted, only the training of police dogs. The trainers had all been active dog handlers for many years and now, with their expertise, trained new handlers. In 1980, there were approximately 14,000 RCMP members across Canada and only about 85 dog handlers. Having the opportunity to join this small group of specialists was certainly an honor.

Accompanying me was a young male German Shepherd named "Tark." I had raised the dog through the puppy program and he was now of trainable age. I had some misgivings about Tark's potential, since he behaved young for his age. The only problem at the time was no other trainable dogs were available and I had to do my best with this young dog. Another candidate named John, arrived the same day and we would train together. He had a young dog as well, but John was more optimistic about his dog. Four other trainees were at the Kennels as well, but they were almost half way through the course. Usually, there are four trainees and dogs assigned to work with one trainer. In our case, just John and I would be working with a trainer.

Our instructor, a gregarious sergeant named Gus, welcomed both of us to the Kennels and quickly assessed our dogs. He was a big-boned man with a large frame. He did not say too much about our canines, but only wanted to set a positive working environment for all of us.

We learned that training started at 8:30 AM sharp, Monday through Friday. Our accommodation was at the military base near the farming community of Penhold. The base was about 14 miles north of the Kennels and we had use of a marked

RCMP kennel truck to commute. It was our responsibility to be at the Kennels before 8:00 AM, take our dogs for a quick morning run, feed them breakfast, and clean their kennels. We had to ensure that all our gear and the kennel truck was ready for the day. At 8:30 AM, Gus joined us from the administration building to start our day of training. The ranchers, farmers, and communities were all familiar with the kennel trucks filled with dogs and handlers, traveling the secondary roads, highways, and streets in the area. It was normal to see police officers and dogs running through fields, along ditches, down alleyways and jumping fences. I recall an occasion later in the training, after our group had grown to five trainees. Gus was driving the van along a country road when a passing farmer flagged us down. He had lost his wallet in the barnyard the day before and asked if our dogs could help locate it. We happily agreed to assist. After an hour of fruitless searching around his outbuildings and barn, the farmer's wife emerged from the house with the lost wallet. She had located it in the clothes hamper. The red-faced farmer offered coffee for our troubles and we crowded into a warm kitchen and happily devoured a large plate of freshly baked muffins and drank a pot of hot coffee.

The RCMP dog handler course was 16 weeks long and broken down into three levels. John and I were at the beginning of Level 1 and I remember Gus asking us, "Can you say day one?" The unexplained question surprised both of us. The entire course was physically demanding for both dog and handler. Level 1 tracking started immediately. Gus drove us out in the country to a grass field where there were few distractions for the dogs.

The first task in tracking is the "master track." Under Gus's instruction, I put a tracking harness on Tark while Gus held the attached line. In an animated fashion, I then walked away in a straight line, out of sight of the dog. While walking, I encouraged the dog to come to me, but the trainer held the dog back. Once out of sight of the dog, I kept quiet, walked a few hundred yards, and hid in some undergrowth. The dog became excited and distressed at my disappearance. After a few minutes, with Gus holding the line, Tark followed my scent using his nose. He quickly located me and I praised the dog profusely for a job well done.

The next step involved John acting as quarry for me. This time, with John using lots of enthusiasm to attract Tark's interest, he walked away, while I held Tark and encouraged him. We waited a few minutes for the scent to settle. Then, using the command word "Soo," (pronounced, "Sue") with me holding the line, the dog and I followed the quarry's scent. Gus ran with me, offering advice and encouragement. Upon finding John, I praised the dog. In turn, John did his "master track" with Gus' assistance and then I quarried for John. At first, both dogs were bewildered, but quickly clued in and grew excited by the lively exercise. Gus had an easy-going demeanor and was a patient instructor. He would encourage both of us and offer constructive criticism and advice when warranted.

"Master tracks" were no longer needed and under Gus' instruction, we gradually started to lay longer tracks for each other. We let the tracks sit for greater lengths of time before we worked them. Under Gus' close tutorage, we also started to lay tracks with a few ninety-degree corners. While tracking, the dogs make "indications" that the handler must learn to "read." Strong or obvious indications made by a dog while tracking include, pulling hard in the harness, and keeping the head and nose close to the ground. Slighter indications consist of how the dog holds his tail or ears while tracking. The more subtle indications vary between dogs. All our tracking was in rural settings. We had to traverse through fields, pastures, and bush, going over fence lines, crossing creeks, streams, and roadways.

When the dog comes to a corner in the track, he indicates a track loss by bringing the head up, slowing down, and allowing slack in the harness line. The first thing the handler has to do is stop. The next step, especially for a new dog, is to tighten the line and then using the line as a guide, sweep the dog in a circle, until it re-locates the track. Once the dog indicates the track's new direction, timing is paramount. With verbal praise and encouragement from the handler at the time of re-location, the dog's head will go down again and the line again becomes taut. After repeating the process a few times, dogs and handlers start to catch on to the art of tracking. In fact, in most cases, the dog catches on faster. An experienced dog will automatically start to circle at a track loss or a corner. Of course, it is up to the handler to read circling as a change in track direction. Gus came with us on all our tracks, offering his expertise.

Tracking is done at a jog, but depending on air movement, weather conditions, age of the track and the terrain, the speed could fluctuate from a fast walk to an all out run. With more experience and training, I could estimate the age of tracks, depending on all the factors including terrain and weather. I could also tell when I was catching up to a suspect. As the scent was getting "fresher," the dog would become more intense and want to break into a lope.

As the Level 1 tracks became longer and older, Gus had both of us place large articles, such as clothing, along the track. The quarry tucked the articles under grass or foliage on the track, so that the dog suddenly got a large whiff of scent and stopped to investigate. After the dog uncovered the article, the handler praised the dog. Sometimes there may be a quick tug-of-war, but the dog was quickly encouraged to continue tracking. Another part of tracking was the introduction of "dead-ends." While laying a track, the quarry stopped, turned, and walked back on the track for 20-30 yards, and then either turned right or left and continued walking. When working the track, the handler learned to identify the dead-end, work the dog back in circles, until the track was re-located.

Gus always gave explicit instructions for those laying a training track. He determined the direction and length of each track. He expected each of us to follow his instructions to the letter. On one occasion, I saw him take another potential handler aside. The handler had goofed-up on directions twice in two days. In front of everybody, Gus took a black marker and drew a large "L" on the back of the man's left hand. He then drew a large "R" on the right hand. Everybody laughed including the errant, red-faced handler, but directions were never a problem for anybody after that episode.

Gus determined the number of articles on a track and dictated where he wanted the articles dropped. He decided on the number of corners and where they were on the track, along with any dead-ends. To train the dog and the handler, it was very important to know everything about the track. While working the track, Gus could say to the handler, "OK, there is a corner coming up. Stop when the dog's head comes up. Be ready to circle him and praise him when he re-locates." Alternatively, "There should be an article on this leg of the track. Watch for the indication." As the dogs and handlers became more proficient, we were working rural tracks three or four miles long and aging them over an hour. Gus was making fewer comments and corrections, since both John and I were reading our dogs well.

It was critical, especially for the dogs that each training exercise ended on a positive note. Each dog had its limitations and it was important not to go beyond the dogs capabilities. However, there were standards the dogs and handlers had to meet. Both our dogs progressed, but at times, I noticed that my dog's tenacity was flagging. Gus had noted this as well, but felt there was still time on the schedule for improvement and we should remain optimistic.

During Level 1, the emphasis is on tracking, but other profiles included protection work, individual and group obedience and agility. For protection work, John and I switched roles. Firstly, he put on a large padded arm. While holding Tark on line, I remained stationary while John worked the dog up with lots of animation. I enthusiastically encouraged the dog to bite the padded arm. When the dog did bite, I praised him with added energy. Gus was always on hand observing and offering advice to both of us in our roles. Then John and I changed jobs and I helped train his dog. Both dogs had to display courage while being threatened and ignore loud noises such as gunfire. The dogs were never physically harmed in any way. It was also important that the dogs show an even temperament. The dogs had to be able to "turn off" once the protection exercise was concluded.

Individual and group obedience was ongoing throughout the training day and added to that was a trip or two over the obstacle course each day. All obedience was on leash. Again, it was imperative for the morale of the dog that the handler was never overbearing. Obedience had to remain fun and upbeat for the canine.

As the six-week mark approached, both John and I had concerns about our dogs. Their interest was waning, despite Gus' suggestions. I believe that Gus did his best to keep both of us optimistic and hopefully not to telegraph our misgivings to the dogs. Dogs are very intuitive. They easily notice the moods and feelings of their handlers.

The Training Kennels did not have replacement dogs available for us at that time. Two dogs had just arrived, but their physical examinations were still not complete. In addition, the dogs were not part of the puppy-rearing program and purchased after only short assessments.

The process to obtain trainable dogs is sometimes uncertain and depends on a long list of variables. For police work, we needed hunters, or dogs with the strong instinct to seek and find. We needed dogs that were intelligent, courageous, tenacious and of even temperament. There were many other requirements including familiarity with people, loud noises, and shiny floors. The dogs had to be comfortable around a multitude of distractions, including other animals. Lastly, but just as important, the dogs had to be in excellent health and free of any joint problems. The optimum training age is between one and two years of age. A dog any older than two had to have exceptional qualities.

Gus threw all caution to the wind and decided to arrange for another trainer at the Kennels to assess John and me along with our dogs. We would all have to pass a stringent Level 1 test. The other trainer was a well-known perfectionist and demanded the best from both dog and handler.

A good part of the test was a two-mile long rural track, with numerous corners, articles on the track, a dead-end and at least two road crossings. The trainee would not know any details of the test track. Gus and the other trainer accompanied the trainee and his dog, but did not offer any assistance other than to show the trainee where the track began. John and I worked our test tracks, but we could immediately tell that the assessor was not pleased at what he saw. We both failed. The perfectionist was critical of both our efforts, but we stood our ground. With Gus' backing, we convinced him that both dogs were ultimately not suited for police work. They both displayed drive, but not enough. To our relief, he finally accepted our explanation and the trainers decided to remove our dogs from the program and we would start again with new dogs. I was both distressed and frustrated over the event. We had worked hard to bring the dogs along and had done our best. John and I later learned that there had been a previous disagreement between Gus and the other trainer. They eventually settled their quarrel and I was somewhat consoled to know that perhaps the judgmental attitude of the trainer was unwarranted. This meant that John and I had to start the course over again. In a futile effort to make us feel better Gus exclaimed, "Hey guys! Can you say 'day one'?" We were not in the mood for jocularity and John offered to punch him in the head.

Chapter 4
"Trapper"

About two weeks prior to our failed assessment, we returned to the Kennels from a long day of tracking in the country. It was close to quitting time, when an old car pulled into the visitor's parking lot. The trunk lid was up with a plastic dog kennel tied in with old binder twine. The driver informed us that a trainer from the Kennels had been to his house in Calgary a few days previously. The trainer had assessed his dog and agreed to purchase it, providing the owner brought the dog to the Kennels. The man seemed anxious and said he just wanted to return home, a distance of over 100 miles.

We were annoyed that the man had crammed his German Shepherd into the small kennel and made the dog endure the long drive in the trunk. Gus encouraged the owner to open the kennel immediately and get the dog out. When he opened the crate, a long, lean, dark tan colored dog unfolded himself and emerged from the confined space. He deftly landed on the ground and gazed around. The trainer that purchased the dog was finally located and he came out to speak with the man. After a short conversation, the trainer led the dog to a waiting kennel. The owner did not seem interested in saying goodbye to the dog and nervously waited for the trainer to provide him with the necessary paperwork. I overheard the man say that the dog's name was "Trapper."

About the same time that Trapper arrived, another potential police dog named "Max," appeared at the Kennels. During the next two weeks, further assessments and medicals were required for both dogs. Word got around through kennel staff and trainers that both dogs showed excellent potential, however Trapper's behavior was causing some concern. He growled at some of the staff members and some thought he might be unpredictable. One trainer said the dog snapped at him during an assessment.

The day after our botched Level 1 test, John and I reported for our new "Day One." We both felt out of place without canines at our sides. The Kennels gave Tark and John's dog away to good homes, as was the normal practice. Gus nonchalantly approached us in the parking lot. He seemed deep in thought and just stood looking at us for a few moments. Finally, he shook his head, reached deep into his pants pocket, and withdrew a quarter. While rolling the coin skillfully through his sausage-sized fingers, he explained his dilemma. "Look, I've been trying to come up with a diplomatic way of doing this. I have two dogs and you two gloomy looking characters." His face suddenly beamed with a big toothy grin and went on. "We'll flip to see who gets what dog. Whoever calls it gets to put a leash on that Trapper. Guess he snapped at another staff member yesterday. However, we gotta work with what we got! OK, who's gonna call it?" I volunteered and with a dry mouth nervously croaked, "Tails." Of course, John had "heads." With trepidation, we watched Gus toss the coin high into the air. He caught it in a big, meaty hand and flipped it over onto the top of his other hand. He looked under his hand with mock suspense and smirked when he saw the result. Gus looked up at me and slowly moved his hand so that I could see the coin. Gus whispered, "Tails! John, you got Max. Brad will be happy to get the alligator." John let out a sigh of relief. I unsnapped the choke chain and leash from my belt as I started walking to the kennel like a condemned man. My mouth got dryer and my gut started to churn at the prospect of meeting the "alligator." I glanced back to see Gus and John, both with beaming grins on their faces.

During my walk, I wondered how I was going to work out my predicament. What could I do if this animal tried to bite me? Trapper was in an enclosed kennel run and I walked up to the back entrance. He was at the back of the kennel and immediately saw me at the door. A low guttural growl came out of him and he curled his lips to flash some large, white teeth. He lowered his body slightly, moved close to a wall and glared at me with gleaming, dark eyes.

My hand shook as I gently unlatched the door and slowly opened it. As I carefully entered the kennel and closed the door, Trapper let out another growl. I still had the sense not to lock the door in case I had to get out fast. Keeping my back to the wall, I moved to a corner and slid down into a crouched position. I spoke in a low, soothing tone in an attempt to calm the animal. I was careful not to look him in the eyes, since he might feel further threatened. With no other thought of what to do, I remained in my position and stared at the floor in front of me, but kept the dog in my peripheral vision. I tried my calming voice again, by repeating, "Good dog, good dog, its OK, I'm not going to hurt you", but had to stop since the back of my throat was so dry that it made me cough. Trapper continued to stare angrily at me, but at least he was no longer growling. I felt encouraged and extended my hand towards the dog's nose. He stood stone still and just glared back. As the seconds ticked by, my arm started to ache, but I suddenly felt a warm puff of air on my hand and the cold touch of his nose. I withdrew my tired arm for a few moments and then reached for his nose again.

I swallowed hard and turned to glance at the dog's face. The menacing glare was gone and he now seemed curious with his new kennel mate. My arm filled with pins and needles and I put it down again. I inched a little closer and put my arm back out for the dog. A cold nose touched my shaking hand as I spoke to him again. I was able to scratch the top of his nose and he did not withdraw. Soon, I was gently petting his head and face. Trapper seemed more at ease as I cautiously took the choke chain and slipped it over his head. He did not object and I attached the leash to the choker. He finally sat and his big tail swished slowly back and forth like a big broom. My knees were aching so I stood up for relief. I looked at the dog and asked in a low questioning tone, "Hey pal, do you wanna go play?" He stood up, cocked his head to one side, and looked at me expectantly. I took that as a "yes" and with a gentle tug on the leash, we emerged from the kennel.

Gus saw us and waved me over to the agility field where he was with John. John had Max on leash and they were getting to know each other. Gus instructed us to give our new dogs some light exercise on a few low hurtles and play with them. Trapper reacted eagerly to the obstacles and was keen to please. He responded enthusiastically to my praise and my initial gut feeling towards this dog was very positive. We were on the way to cementing a strong friendship. Trapper never growled at me again. I was on top of the world. Gus could see that everybody was happy and yelled at me across the field, "Can you say 'day one'?"

Before our small group could re-start training, three more trainees and dogs arrived at the Kennels. The training staff assigned them to our group. Gus now had the responsibility of five handlers and dogs. He took the job on with enthusiasm and continued to provide us with his expertise throughout the course. Our group got along well and friendships quickly developed. The training was demanding, but we always found time for some fun and Gus had a great sense of humor.

Every Friday afternoon, training ceased and a general clean up was conducted of all the kennel vehicles and equipment. We used pressurized water hoses to wash the inside and outside of the vans. We removed all items, cleaned, sorted, and placed them back in the vehicles. One warm afternoon, clean up turned into a water fight within our group. It escalated to include the other group in training. At one point, we took a large plastic garbage can onto the roof of a kennel building, filled it with water, and poured it on an unsuspecting soul that walked out of the door. The force of the water drove him to his knees. Eventually both groups joined forces for an assault on the training staff. We started hauling hoses and water buckets to the administration building. The OIC and some staff members had barricaded themselves, but the Old Man finally put a stop to the water war. He threatened disciplinary action and we all reluctantly retreated.

One day our group used two marked vehicles. We left the Kennels in the morning, traveling north on Highway 2. Three of us, including me, were in one van with Gus driving. The other two members in the second vehicle, pulled up along side of us in the fast lane. I looked over to see the passenger standing on the back seat, with his bare posterior pressed against the window. I brought this awful sight to Gus' attention. He quickly looked around to make sure none of the motoring public was nearby and ordered all of us to return the favor.

Driving to work early one morning, we picked up a few beer bottles that were at the side of the road. Gus always emerged from the administration building in the mornings with a large mug of coffee and when he got in the truck, he always placed the coffee in the cup holder on the dash. As usual, on this particular morning, Gus came out to meet us with his coffee. He opened the truck door and a beer bottle fell onto the pavement. It did not break, but hit the ground with a loud clink and un-ceremoniously rolled along the length of the vehicle. His eyes narrowed and there was not the usual grin. His face really darkened when he looked inside and saw another beer bottle, sitting upright in his favorite cup holder. The Old Man was a strict autocrat and did not tolerate any breach of the rules and regulations, especially when it came to liquor. Even a few empty beer bottles could cause a lot of grief in Gus' life. He snarled at us, "You dumb sons-of-bitches! Get these bottles out of this truck, now! I've had enough of your crap for one week. Load the dogs up! Today we work never-ending tracks!"

During training tracks, the quarry always finished the track by hiding, either behind something or even under some brush. The idea was that the dog had to track right up and find the quarry by only using his nose. By this point in our training, all the dogs in our group were becoming ardent trackers. I found Trapper to be very keen and enthusiastic and a pleasure to work with. All the rural tracks were getting longer, perhaps four or five miles. Never-ending tracks are different. The quarry had a thirty-minute head start, and kept moving until the handler, and dog caught up. This meant that our tracks that day were six to eight miles long. Since the tracks were so fresh, the pace was a fast jog over rough terrain. As soon as one quarry was caught, another handler laid a track for him to work. Each one of us walked and ran 14 to 18 miles that day. Gus spent a leisurely day in the truck, sipping his coffee and eating lunch. The dogs loved the challenge and it helped build their stamina. We returned to the Kennels, but Gus had not yet forgiven us and made us go through the agility course. Not only did the dogs have to jump and climb the obstacles, but Gus ensured that we did so as well. We did not complain out of fear that he would make us go through it again. We decided not to pull any more stunts, at least not for a while.

A well-respected member of the other group in training was a fun-loving character. He was a hard worker that enjoyed his time off as much as dog handler duties. He had to return to his home detachment for a court case and would be away for a few days. It also gave him the opportunity to spend time with his wife and three children. He drove a police vehicle to the Calgary airport and flew home. On the return trip from Calgary, he was driving northbound on Highway 2 when a southbound vehicle clipped another southbound vehicle. The second vehicle lost control, crossed the median and crashed head-on into the member's vehicle. At highway speeds, there was no time to avoid the accident and all the occupants of both cars died in the crash. The offending vehicle fled the scene, but police stopped it later that day. The driver was intoxicated.

We did not know about the accident until the next morning when we reported for work. The Old Man announced it to us in the front parking lot and provided all the details. He was visibly shaken and by his appearance, it was evident that he had a sleepless night. We were all in a state of shock. Some walked away to be alone and sort out the news. None of us could work that day. The remaining members of the other group packed all the victim's possessions and shipped it back to his family. We took the time to grieve the loss of a good friend and co-worker, but quickly returned to our training routine. Gus was confident of our progress and announced a Level 1 test for our group. We happily anticipated the challenge.

Trapper and I aced the Level 1 test. The rural track went off without a hitch. Trapper easily worked the corners, dead-end, road crossings and located all the hidden articles along the track. We had a different assessor than my first Level 1 test. He was pleased with our progress and commented that I was reading my dog well. The bite work and aggression went well, including the obedience. We could now start Level 2 training.

The distances in Level 2 tracking were shorter. Most tracks would now be about two or three miles in length, but would be in more semi-urban environments. The dog and handler had to deal with more distractions including people, vehicles, and animals. A typical Level 2 track usually started in field or bush on the outskirts of a town and worked into an industrial area. The tracks still had large articles with a hidden quarry at the end.

The training staff introduced large article searching, now that the dogs were well grounded in tracking. This consisted of using a number of large articles such as old jackets, hats, boots, tools, and firearms. The articles had to have lots of human scent on them. The quarry, again under the watchful eye of Gus, placed three or four large articles out in a field about 200 yards square, in an area with limited distractions. It was important to tuck the items under grass or brush so the dog could not see them. The dog had to locate them only by scent. We usually waited at least one hour, or sometimes a half-day, to let the scent settle around the articles.

Under Gus' tutorage, the handler started the dog down wind to the field. Using the command "search," the handler then walked with the dog in a back and forth pattern, into the wind. When the dog picked up the scent of an article, the handler learned to read the dog's indication, encourage the dog to follow-up on the scent and go to the object. Once the dog got the article, the handler praised the dog and there would usually be a tug-of-war contest with the article. The handler had to remain upbeat and animated throughout the exercise to keep the dog excited and interested. Different areas were used as the dogs progressed. A search area could include ditches, bush, pastures, or farm fields. It was the responsibility of the handler to ensure that the dog covered the entire search area and always be cognizant of any change in wind direction. This training prepared dog and handler for operational work, searching for stolen or missing property and evidence at crime scenes.

Drug searching started with introducing the dogs to the scent of marihuana. Gus took clean cloths and placed them in an airtight container with a quantity of the drug. After the cloths were in the container for a few days, they absorbed the strong odor. He then distributed the cloths to the handlers. The reason for the cloths was for the protection of the dogs. During this introduction phase, it was likely that the dogs would come into direct contact with the contraband. Under Gus' supervision, the handlers introduced the cloths to the dogs with plenty of animation and praise. The dogs became excited and more intense with little games of finding the cloths in easy to find hiding places, while handlers encouraged the dogs with the key command word of "pot." The dogs quickly realized what the handlers expected of them when the handlers said the word "pot."

After the dogs knew what to look for, the next part was the introduction of the "sit confirmation." Training in the drug profile was usually in buildings such as shops and garages. The military at the Penhold base, often allowed us to use vacant barracks or airplane hangars. Using the real drug, Gus hid small amounts in easy to find locations, while the handler looked on. The handler then brought the dog on leash, into the search area. Using lots of enthusiasm, the handler gave the command, "search pot," and directed the dog over the hidden drugs, one at a time. As soon as the dog indicated the drug, the handler encouraged the dog to pursue the scent to the source (drug). Again, timing was paramount. With the dog was almost touching the drug, the handler made the dog sit. As soon as the dog's posterior touched the floor, the handler would place the dog's favorite toy in his mouth. For most police dogs, especially with such high prey drive, the ball is a favorite. The handler then praised the dog with lots of excitement. At first the dogs were puzzled, but quickly realized that as soon as they found a drug, they sat, therefore confirming the find to the handler. For the dog, the reward was their favorite toy along with a little playtime. It was an enjoyable exercise for everybody, even for our teacher Gus.

As the dogs and handlers became more skillful with this profile, we placed out even smaller amounts of pot. We varied the number of "hides" from four to eight, depending on the size of the search area. Like any other searching profile, it was important that the handler covered the entire search area. We became more innovative by hiding drugs in and under furniture, under tables, in other containers, under mattresses and inside walls. We used vehicles and quickly became proficient in search patterns to locate drugs in and outside the vehicles. Gus was always busy offering advice and observing the handlers and dogs.

Protection work intensified. We placed greater emphasis on the control of the dog during bite work. Gus introduced running attacks. A quarry, with protective gear, ran from the dog. The handler then sent his dog with encouragement. The quarry only stopped when the dog bit the protective arm and held on to it. The handler then joined the dog and made the "arrest." All the dogs in our group took to this work with gusto and courage.

Obedience training also intensified, with some off line work and voice commands given at a distance from the dog. Group obedience was now more challenging and fun with five dogs and handlers. Great care was taken to never "brow-beat" the dogs. All the obedience exercises were upbeat and exciting. We still used the agility course on a daily basis, but with a portion of it off leash, emphasizing control only with voice commands.

We worked each profile daily, as we had done in Level 1. It was a fast-paced training schedule and I now realized that Tark would have been over-whelmed. However, Trapper enjoyed the challenges and loved to please. I too, found the work to be exciting and was amazed at how quickly all the dogs adapted to the training. A whole, new world opened up for them and they took pleasure in training to become four-legged policemen. For the handlers, the competition to have the best dog was becoming more evident. Six weeks after our last exam, Gus felt that we were ready for our Level 2 test.

Our assessor was pleased with our progress. The Level 2 track was about two miles in length. This included several road crossings, articles on the track, corners, a dead-end, and distractions such as people and vehicles. The handlers did not know any details of the track and had to rely on the actions of the dog. For the large article and drug searching profiles, the handlers only knew the boundaries of the search areas. The number of articles and drug "hides" were also unknown to the handlers. The assessor closely watched the aggression and obedience work, looking mostly for control. Having control of the dogs during the agility course was also important. We all passed and were ready for Level 3.

If successful with Level 3 training, we could easily complete the entire course within the sixteen weeks. We were all anxious to get to our new postings and put all we had learned into "real dog work." While we were in training, we were encouraged not to become involved with operational police work, unless absolutely required. One particular day, while traveling through the town of Innisfail, we overheard on the police radio that a prisoner from the nearby penitentiary, had escaped from his guard while attending a dental appointment in town. The detachment members were frantically trying to locate the operational dog handler stationed in the city of Red Deer. At that time Red Deer was a small city of approximately 65,000 people, about 15 miles north of Innisfail. The handler stationed there was responsible for Innisfail and numerous other towns in the area. The prisoner had violently assaulted the guard and escaped on foot. The members were anxious to re-capture this man since he was serving time for manslaughter and considered dangerous. The guard was now with the police and able to show the members where he last saw the culprit run. Attempts to locate the Red Deer handler were negative, despite repeated efforts.

We were closely monitoring the events. Gus was sitting on the edge of his seat. His lips pursed as he intently listened to the radio. We were frantic and tried to convince Gus to ignore protocol and help the detachment members. At first, we pleaded and then became frustrated. One of the more outspoken members of the group angrily commented, "Come on Gus, forget the rules! Let's help these guys out. The bastard assaulted a guard!" Two others started punching and shoving at Gus as he drove along the street. Truthfully, he was anxious to be involved. Gus had been a handler for a number of years and we knew that he missed the action. Compared to operational work, being a trainer was rather routine. Gus suddenly exclaimed, "Alright, that's it! Hang on!" He punched the accelerator as a resounding cheer let loose in the van. Training vehicles did not have emergency equipment, but Gus expertly maneuvered the truck to the scene.

Within minutes, we careened around a corner and slid to a screeching stop in front of two detachment members standing at a street corner. They knew we were from the Training Kennels and were visibly relieved to see us. All six of us piled out of the van as Gus approached the investigators. One member commented, "Boy, are we glad to see you guys! Are you able to give us a hand?" Gus quickly replied, "I sure hope so, but I've gotta know some more details." The injured guard popped out of a police car. His face was bloody from a large cut on his forehead. He also looked very angry. I wondered why only one guard was with the prisoner. The member related that the guard last saw the prisoner running west from the intersection where we were gathered, about twenty minutes ago. The man was dressed in brown institutional clothing and a green jacket. He did not have handcuffs on and the guard gave a physical description of the escapee.

Gus turned to see all of us clamoring over each other, at the back of the van. The doors flung open and we all tried to be first to get our dogs out. The dogs knew something was going on and all barked with excitement. As we jostled around trying to pull dogs out of their individual pens and put harnesses on, the detachment members stood by with perplexed looks. In an exasperated tone, Gus yelled at us, "Come on for Chris sakes, you guys! Somebody get a dog harnessed up and get the hell over here!" Gus turned to the silent members and threw his big hands up in disgust.

Trapper was in harness and I moved him away from the others onto the boulevard. I watched the dog put his nose down on the short grass. He slowly wagged his tail and started to move west. It did not register with me immediately, but the dog and I were standing on the escapee's scent. I looked up at Gus and sputtered, "I, I think he's tracking." With a look of distain on his face, Gus shot back, "No shit, Sherlock. Praise him and go with him!" I weakly praised the dog and the line snapped tight as Trapper got his head down and leaned hard into the harness. He picked up speed and I suddenly felt exhilarated. I looked over at Gus and he now had a big grin on his meaty face. This was what a "real" track felt like. The feeling was short-lived. We only went about 200 yards, when the dog stopped dead, turned his head sharply to the left and darted over to a large pile of brush at the side of the road. I could not see anything and was slightly baffled at the dog's actions. In a split second, Gus pushed passed me, jumped up, and came down with both knees on the chest of a man hiding in the center of the pile. I heard the painful whoosh of air from the prone man as Gus' 250-pound frame came crashing down.

I pulled Trapper out of the way, as the guard suddenly appeared and started kicking the half-conscious prisoner. The detachment members started to restrain the guard, when Gus quickly grabbed him by the collar with both hands. He pulled the man close and hissed, "Stop it, right now! It's all over. Settle down or I'll throw you in a police car." The guard realized he was way out of line and quickly regained his composure. I could not really blame him for being angry, but he was obviously badly injured and needed medical attention.

Without fully comprehending the situation at the time, I had been in a very vulnerable situation. Being that close to a desperate escapee was sobering. It could have been disastrous for my dog or me if the man had a weapon. It was obviously dangerous work, but having the ability to use a dog to track down a human was thrilling.

Level 3 was more intense. Tracks were now about a mile in length, but all in urban environments. We tracked through alleyways, parks, and residential neighborhoods. This was very challenging since we had to work around numerous distractions. Articles were on the tracks, with a multitude of corners and road-crossings. Handlers had to slow the dogs down to pick up the quarry's smell in "low scent areas," such as short grass, dirt, and pavement. The handlers had to refine their line work when tracking through these environments. It proved to be exacting work. As usual, Gus was huffing and puffing along side each of us, offering support. We were all reading our dogs well and Gus preferred to let us work "unknown tracks." We learned to rely on our dogs to find the quarries.

Large article searching was still part of training, but now Gus introduced small article searching. Small articles included buttons, shell casing, bits of leather, cloth, plastic, coins, and pieces of shoelaces. A number of the these objects were tucked away in much smaller areas than the large article searches, perhaps 20 to 30 feet square. The search area could be in a park, industrial or residential area and sometimes an alleyway. Again, using wind direction, the handler worked the dog in a tight pattern through the search area. Upon finding an article, the dog was encouraged to go into a "down" position. The handler quickly praised the dog and presented the dog with his ball. This would prepare dog and handler to search crime scenes involving small pieces of evidence.

Drug searching now included the hard drugs: cocaine, heroin, and all their derivatives. These drugs were of high quality and therefore probably fatal if a dog ingested even minute amounts. The sit confirmation curbed the dog's natural inclination to grab anything they found and made the training safer and easier for everybody concerned. Now drug searching included the soft and hard drugs. We tried innovative situations, such as burying drugs in the ground, or placing them in suitcases and on quarries.

Gus was responsible for the large quantities of training drugs that we carried. One day, at the Penhold military base, we all helped Gus with re-packaging some heroin and cocaine for a search. After concluding our drug searching exercise, Gus was accounting for the drugs and to his horror found that 30 grams of high-grade cocaine were missing. The color drained from his face, as we all frantically started looking for the lost drug. Our searches did not locate the package. Gus was becoming anxious and we all tried to re-trace our steps, in hopes of discovering how we could lose the drug. John decided to check the garbage can once more. It had already been searched two or three times. Earlier, we had tossed some of the old packaging in the can. John dug through some disgusting garbage, but his efforts proved successful. He held the package up in his hand with a look of triumph. Gus was close to crying with relief as he walked on his knees to John. In front of several military staff, Gus turned John around and started to repeatedly kiss John's rear-end. John stood red-faced, with a look of embarrassment, as Gus continued.

Protection or aggression work reached a new level, with more emphasis placed on off-leash work. The handler now had to show control of the dog with voice commands only. A few evenings of building searches were added in conjunction with aggression work. Obedience progressed to giving the dogs commands at a distance, using hand signals only. The agility course was now all off line with the handlers maintaining control of their dogs with only a few voice commands and more hand signals. As in the other levels, each working profile was worked daily. One handler and his dog, from another group, were identified as an explosives team. They were not trained in the narcotic profile, but were introduced to explosive material such as, black powder, C-4, and detonation cords for dynamite. The team validated in all the same profiles as the other teams, and the RCMP stationed them at one of the international airports in Canada.

We all expected transfers from our old postings upon completing the course. During our Level 3 training, the Old Man interviewed each of us separately. If I successfully completed the course, I was going to Prince George, BC. Originally, John was supposed to accompany me to Prince George, but at the last minute, the OIC changed his posting to Vernon, BC. We later learned the reasoning behind the change. The Old Man was an ardent supporter of hockey teams within the police community of British Columbia. Another member of my group had a reputation as a strong hockey player and the Old Man decided that the Prince George team needed another valued player. It seemed that the higher echelon did not always have the best interests of the members at heart, when it came to transfers. Nothing against the hockey player, but I did not think it was the best use of judgment to change the career path of two members for the sake of a good hockey team.

Level 3 testing was scheduled for the second week of October, just before the onslaught of the cold prairie winter. The testing was successful for all members and dogs in our group and the OIC ordered us to make immediate arrangements to return to our old detachments and await the transfer process to start. All our transfers were within British Columbia. Since the dog handler community within the RCMP was so small, we would all cross paths with each other on refresher courses, re-training new dogs at the Kennels and operational requirements over the coming years. I returned to Burnaby with Trapper for a month and anxiously waited for all the paperwork involved in my transfer. I had to return to my general detachment duties, but with every opportunity, Trapper and I continued our training with the Burnaby handlers.

1982 Prince George. Trapper was approximately 3 ½ years old. I am dressed in the working RCMP dog handler uniform of the time.

1982 Trapper and me in front of police transport at the time in Prince George. Call sign was 13Echo1

Chapter 5
Prince George

Trapper and I arrived in Prince George in mid-November 1980. Coming from the balmy coastal weather of the Vancouver area to the bone chilling winter of Prince George, was certainly a big change. At that time, Prince George was a community of about 75,000 people. Everybody referred to it as the "Gateway to the North" for the province of British Columbia. It is the last big community before going into the far reaches of the north. Although it is about 600 miles northeast of Vancouver, it is still in the geographical center of the province. High mountain ranges cover most of British Columbia. Prince George, nestled in the confluence of the mighty Fraser and Netchako Rivers, relied heavily on the lumber industry, with numerous large mills producing paper and building materials.

The detachment was one of the busiest in the province, with over 150 members. Trapper and I were one of four dog teams for the city. Besides the city, we also provided support for the small satellite detachments of Vanderhoof, Fort St. James, Fraser Lake, Burns Lake, Quesnel, McBride, and Mackenzie. Another handler was posted at Fort St. John, a community 300 miles northeast of Prince George. Nevertheless, if he was away or needed further assistance, we were required to work his area, which included Fort St. John, Chetwynd, Tumbler Ridge, Dawson Creek, and Ft. Nelson. His area extended north to the border of the North West Territories.

All the handlers took turns on call during their off-duty time and had to be available to work on short notice. Upper management assigned police vehicles to each handler and because of the distances involved in getting to calls out of town, the vehicles had a stockpile of equipment. Winter gear included parkas, wind pants, gloves, mitts, facemask, thermal underwear, rations for dog and handler, backpacks, boots, sleeping bag, compass, first-aid kit, candles, matches, shotgun, shells, mukluks, and snowshoes. We were always prepared to leave town at a moment's notice.

Added to the day-to-day operational police work, dogs and handlers had to continue training in all the working profiles. During work shifts, when time permitted, I would conduct different exercises to keep Trapper and I motivated. To further hone our skills, all the handlers met once a week for an entire day of training.

It was definitely an exciting job. One day, I could be working downtown Prince George and the next, anywhere in northern BC. The duties always varied and I usually did not know what challenges we would face from day to day.

A few days after arriving in Prince George, I worked a night shift. This particular night was extremely cold with temperatures dipping below minus 40 degrees Celsius. Despite the extreme cold, I could not believe how busy the detachment members were. People did not seem to notice or care about the inclement weather. We all spent the night responding to calls of impaired drivers, public disturbances, fights, break-ins, prowlers, and domestic disputes. Just after midnight, the dispatcher broadcast a report of a large fight in the streets of the downtown area. Several cars responded, but I was the last to arrive. In front of me, 40 to 50 men and women were drinking, swearing, and fighting in the street. Most were in their shirtsleeves and all seemed equally oblivious to the cold. Several members lined up on the sidewalk, with buttoned up storm coats, mitts, and fur hats pulled over their ears. They all moved around in a vain attempt to ward off the cold.

I walked over, stood in line with the rest, and asked one member what we planned to do. He nonchalantly replied, "They'll get tired soon and start to realize they're freezing. When they start goin' back into the bars, we'll just encourage them go inside. After that we'll latch onto a couple of stragglers and a few smart-mouths." Just as he finished with the explanation, a few combatants comprehended that their bare skin was freezing and started to go back inside.

I saw one shirtless man wind up and deliver a haymaker at another man. It was a well-aimed blow but the distance to the target was way off. Without making contact with anything but the bitterly cold night air, the momentum made the man do a complete pirouette and crash to the icy road. He made a few hopeless attempts to get up, but his dress shoes kept slipping and he resigned himself to sitting on the street, muttering to himself. The members moved amongst the revelers, encouraging them inside. I assisted taking custody of a few die-hards and rescued the shirtless ballet dancer. We then departed to attend more incoming calls.

During my first year at Prince George, some coldly disturbing events took place involving reclusive people. One Sunday morning, while I was working a dayshift, a call came into dispatch reporting a shooting. It occurred at the hamlet of Summit Lake, about 25 miles north of Prince George along Highway 97. It was a bitterly cold day and there had been fresh snowfall early that morning. The caller reported he was the shooter and wanted to turn himself in to police. It was a most unusual request and three cars started heading north, including myself. A member of the Prince George Rural detachment was on duty and patrolling near Summit Lake. He waited outside the hamlet until we arrived to assist. By the time we converged on the sleepy village, the dispatcher still had the caller on the line. He was at the pay phone in front of the post office. As we approached, we could see he was a pensioner, but stood erect in his tall, chiseled frame. He had a wild white beard and a fur hat pulled over his ears. Despite his age, he looked lean and fit. His movements were fluid and he looked tough and hard-bitten. Luckily, he was passive and surrendered without incident. I had Trapper beside me and was prepared to use the dog, if needed.

The suspect lived in a dilapidated cabin on the outskirts of Summit Lake with another grizzled pensioner. During the cold winter, they agreed to switch off each night with the duty of ensuring the fire did not go out. Last night was his companion's turn. The pensioner woke in the middle of the night to find the fire had gone out and the cabin was ice cold. In a fit of rage, the murderer got out of his bed, grabbed the shotgun, walked over to the sleeping victim and shot him point-blank in the head.

He re-started the fire, went back to bed and had a fitful sleep. Early in the morning, feeling well rested, he got up, put his clothes on, and walked down to the pay phone. He felt it was his civic duty to report the incident. The scene was a terrible mess. The dog and I were not required, since all the evidence had been located.

For some time afterwards, we kidded each other with statements like, "Is the fire still going?" or "Don't let the fire go out!"

In May of 1981, the dispatchers had a call of a deranged man in a cabin on the outskirts of Prince George. Trapper and I attended as backup with three members of the rural detachment. The cabin turned out to be a partial log structure recessed into a small rock bluff. It was more like a hole in the ground. The doorway was so low, that a person would have to double-up to enter the edifice. The rightful owner of the establishment was present and stood nearby. He told us that a stranger, who seemed to appear from nowhere, walked into his cabin and kicked the owner out. The suspect was still inside and the members kept calling to him to come out to talk. He replied un-intelligibly, hooting and yelling. The owner also mentioned that his five high-powered rifles were loaded and inside with the unknown squatter. This sudden piece of news made us all pretty nervous and apprehensive.

After more negotiations, the man emerged from the opening, on his hands and knees. I was shocked at his appearance. Dirt and grime covered his long, thin face. Soot covered his filthy gray-brown hair and scraggily beard. The clothes were threadbare and soiled. He grinned eccentrically bearing yellow, decayed teeth. He had a crazed, wild look and talked gibberish. As the wild-man stood up, and walked towards us, he tripped and fell to the ground. We quickly gathered him up and took him away for assessment at the hospital.

It took some time to discover that the man lived even farther in the bush than where we had found him. So many reclusive years had slowly deranged him. During my time in Prince George, I dealt with many people that chose to live cloistered lives in the secluded areas of the province. Many were interesting and colorful characters, but for some, the remote, lonely lifestyle compromised their physical and emotional health.

Trapper and I were quickly getting our "street smarts" with the continuous onslaught of police work. One night, there were four break-ins, all in quick succession, at businesses in the downtown area. The thief or thieves stole large amounts of jewelry and other expensive items. While patrolling the area, I noticed a man running down the street with two suitcases. I jumped out of the police car and yelled at the man to stop. He kept running, but when he heard Trapper barking, he stopped abruptly, dropped the suitcases, and threw his hands up high.

The suitcases contained all the stolen goods and the suspect admitted to the break-ins.

During a dayshift in June 1981, Trapper and I attended a residence in the city, regarding a break-in. A witness saw one male suspect run from the scene. Trapper picked up the track, going through back yards, over fences, down alleys and under a highway bridge. I knew from the actions of the dog that we were closing the distance. He was more intense and tried to lope. Finally, we came into a back yard and the dog circled wildly. The track had ended in the yard, but we could not locate the suspect.

The front door of the house opened and a large brusque looking man stepped out. Holding the door open, he looked back inside and with a loud, commanding voice, shouted, "Out! Oooouutt! Oooouutt!" A younger male voice responded from inside the house, in a pleading tone, "Please, no! No, please don't make me go out there!" The big man was relentless and made the same demand again. A haggard, tired, sweaty individual slowly emerged from the house. The big man held the door open with his right hand and with the left arm extended, pointed the way out of the house. The little man slowly walked down the steps and fell to his knees in front of Trapper and me. With a beseeching look, he pleaded, "Oh, please Mister, don't let that dog bite me! Oh shit no, please!" I ordered the suspect to remain on the ground and not move or the dog could have him. I called for another car to pick up my prisoner.

The house owner told me later that the little man pounded on his door a few moments before the dog and I arrived. The suspect obviously knew we were chasing him and hoped the big man would let him in the house under the pretext of using the phone. The owner allowed the man inside to use the phone. When the big man saw the dog in his yard, he put it all together and ordered his visitor out of the house.

On a summer night in 1981, Trapper and I were tracking a suspect in an attempted murder. The culprit ran from the scene, armed with a rifle. With another member as my backup, we chased the man for nearly two hours, through residential areas and bush. At one point, it was evident that the fugitive swam a pond in the city, referred to as the Fort George Slough. Near the end of the hair-rising pursuit, the dispatcher called me on my portable radio. She advised that a man fitting the description of our culprit was running through yards of houses that were a block ahead of our direction of travel. I knew we were closing in since Trapper had renewed energy and was surging in his harness. As we bailed over one last fence, a male voice in the dark exclaimed, "OK, I give up! I give up!" It was too dark to see the person, but he certainly saw us. We threw ourselves to the ground and Trapper, oblivious to the danger, was fixated at getting to the suspect. It took all my strength to hold the dog down, until we could order the man to come out. He was unarmed and told us he threw the rifle in the slough before swimming across it. Trapper and I searched the track, but were unable to locate the firearm.

On another summer's night, I had just returned home from a busy night shift and was about to go to bed when the phone rang. The dispatcher told me that an armed robbery just occurred and Trapper and I were required. It was 4:00 AM when I attended the downtown nightclub where the robbery occurred. The owner and staff were huddled in front of the bar. A distraught, attractive young server was seated on a stool, crying hysterically. One of the bouncers that I recognized was nearby. He was a big muscular man. He stood silently, with his head hanging down and hands stuffed in his pockets.

The investigators told me that the club was just locking up, when the bar staff heard loud pounding on the metal door that led to the alley. The crying server, who was the girlfriend of the bouncer, opened the door and was confronted by two men, wearing ski masks. One man was armed with a shotgun and the other with a long knife. The knife-wielding suspect grabbed the woman and held the knife to her throat. His shotgun-toting partner demanded all the money from the bar. The bouncer boyfriend responded by slamming the door shut, leaving his terrified girlfriend to the mercy of two armed robbery suspects.

The culprits lost their nerve, released the woman, and fled the scene on foot. The woman pounded on the door, screaming and pleading until the owner finally opened the door to rescue the victim.

I harnessed Trapper and he quickly located the suspects scent traveling eastbound in the alley. I had my shotgun slung over my shoulder as we worked along. The dog indicated two ski masks stuffed under a wooden step in the alley. The track continued east for a block, then northeast across an open lot, to a wooden fence with several slats missing at the bottom. As Trapper and I got to the fence, he indicated into the tall grass near the fence opening. I clicked on the flashlight and caught a slight reflection in the grass. My heart was banging like a sledgehammer in my ears, when on closer inspection, I discovered it was a double-barreled shotgun. By the look of the flattened grass, it was evident the suspects lay waiting to see if anybody followed them. I was relieved they abandoned their position.

I continued the track for a short distance, but lost it on pavement and could not re-locate it. Trapper searched the area for any other evidence, but found nothing. I returned to the bar in time to watch the young server as she gave her statement to an investigator. She was more composed, but continually shot her now ex-boyfriend with withering, glaring looks.

It was my day off at about 1:30 PM on a cloudy Sunday afternoon in early July, 1981. I was taking Trapper to a bush area near my house for some exercise when I overheard frantic transmissions on the police radio. A high-speed pursuit was in progress about 60 miles east of Prince George, along Highway 16, near an area called Hungary Creek. Constable Benton, an RCMP highway patrol member, had tried to stop a suspected drunk driver, but it turned into a chase. A computer check of the license plate by the dispatcher revealed the man was Jim

Jones. I had dealt with this man directly about three weeks previously. He was violent, unpredictable and had access to high-powered rifles. At that time, I had tracked him down and investigators charged him with attempted murder. He was now out on bail, awaiting trial.

During the chase, Benton's police car experienced mechanical problems. As the big car lost power, Jones sped away out of Benton's sight. Benton was no doubt upset at losing Jones. Highway patrol members generally ensure that their high performance cars are always in good condition. Benton was standing outside his useless car, when Jones suddenly drove passed him, now traveling westbound. Benton reacted by firing two rounds into the trunk of Jones' car just before it disappeared over a hill. As Benton fired his weapon, an elderly couple approached Benton's position, also traveling westbound. Benton flagged the folks down and commandeered their car. The confused couple was left stranded in a remote area, beside the broken down police car. Benton resumed his pursuit of Jones in their older model sedan.

Dane, my boss at Prince George, was on duty that day. He was several miles away, on the opposite side of the city. Even though I was not on duty, I called Dane on the radio and informed him that I was driving eastbound to assist with the chase. Since I was much closer, he agreed that I should assist Benton. Dane had many years as a handler. He was a big, strong, hard-bitten character that was surprisingly fast and agile for his size. He did not put up with any nonsense, but was always fair and I enjoyed working for him. He was a patient man and understood that new handlers needed the experience to become competent.

Benton called to say that he had not re-located Jones, so I started to check some of the side roads off the highway. I found Jones' car about 200 yards south of the highway on an abandoned gravel road. The suspect had obviously fled from the vehicle and I saw the two fresh bullet holes in the trunk. I did not see any blood on the seats or on the ground. I radioed the dispatcher of my location and soon after Benton drove up with his commandeered brown sedan. Since I had tracked Jones before, I knew he was quite clever; nevertheless, Trapper and I had caught him. Other units were attending to assist with the search for Jones. One member offered to pick up the stranded couple that had given up their vehicle. They were about 15 miles east of our location, still waiting for Benton to return.

I quickly started to harness Trapper, who was anxious to work. With the harness only partially on, he was already trying to locate a track. Anytime he even saw the harness, he became excited. He knew what was going to happen. Impatiently, Benton asked to accompany me as my backup. He had already borrowed a shotgun from another member. I did not know Benton well. I had reservations about him, especially after shooting at Jones and taking the old couple's car. The only weapon I had was a snub-nose revolver and I was not in uniform. Considering whom we were chasing, I felt better having added firepower. Benton was nervously handling the shotgun and I noticed that it did not have an attached sling. It would be difficult to carry, especially running over rough terrain. This area was mostly cedar trees with thick undergrowth, ridges, hills, fast moving creeks, and rock. Carrying a shotgun while running through rough terrain would be demanding.

Despite my gut feelings, I accepted Benton's offer. Trapper was restless and immediately located a track away from the vehicle and we blasted through the thick bush. True to form, Jones was back to his old tricks. The track continued through heavy foliage, going in circles and making dead-ends. After about 300 yards, we entered an open area filled with deadfall. The track was now proceeding east, parallel to the highway. After about a mile, the track made a wide circle and started westbound. We climbed a steep ridge, came back down, and went up again. On a third trip up the ridge, I reached out to what I thought was a branch, to pull me up the hill. I did not have gloves on and latched on to a Devil's Club. This plant is covered with thousands of tiny, sharp needles that pierced the inside of my hand. I yelped in pain as I let go of the plant. Trapper crashed through a large patch of clubs. I braced for the worst and I felt hundreds of needles hit my bare arms.

We came to an abandoned gravel pit, overgrown with brush and crossed an old service road. We came to a creek and lost the scent at that point. It was obvious that Jones had walked down the middle of the creek. We hiked along the creek side, knowing that Jones would have to of come out. The fast-moving, cold water and slippery rocks would not only slow Jones down, it would also make for a very uncomfortable walk. Dane was monitoring my progress, as I gave updates on my portable radio whenever possible. He was trying to cut the track ahead of me, to take over and allow Trapper and me time to rest. I just wanted to catch Jones. After about 200 yards, we cut the track coming out from the water. We continued through bush for about half a mile before entering a clearing.

Before crossing the clearing, I stopped Trapper. I kneeled down and motioned Benton to do the same. I took a minute or so, just to check the clearing for any movement and catch my breath. Benton remained behind me and we did not talk. Trapper wanted to move ahead and as we started, a thunderous shot made me dive to the ground. My ears were ringing like bells, as I pulled Trapper down beside me. I looked back at Benton who was still standing upright, shotgun in his hands, with the barrel pointed at the ground. His eyes were wide with his mouth agape. I could not understand why he was still standing. At that moment, I was certain Jones had shot at us, until I noticed smoke waffling out the barrel of Benton's shotgun. Looking down at the ground, there was a hole about the size of a dinner plate behind my right foot. Benton tried to talk, but he was in shock. His face was ashen and his voice was gone.

Thoughts of Jones shooting at us dissolved, as I realized that Benton's shotgun had nearly blown off one of my feet. Benton had not made the weapon safe and he had been running with me for over two hours, with an unsafe shotgun. In a weak voice, he finally said, "I didn't think there was one up the spout." My shock gave way to anger and I retorted in a quivering voice, "If you shoot me with a shotgun, make sure you do me in!" I had seen too many hideous shotgun wounds and added, "Just go to the highway. Forget it, I'll go on alone." Benton did not reply. He simply turned and made his way to the road. I continued the track, wondering if Jones heard the gunshot. If so, he probably believed the police had shot at him again. The track meandered for another hour through the bush and finally ended on a gravel logging road near Highway 16. I could not re-locate the track and guessed that an unsuspecting motorist may have picked up Jones.

Trapper and I were sore, tired, and thirsty. I let the big dog flop down into a shallow pool of water in the ditch. He was only trying to cool himself down from all the exertion. I went to him, scratched him behind the ears and spoke to him soothingly, just to let him know I appreciated his efforts. My hand and arms were painful from the cuts and scrapes of the Devil's Club. To say the least, I was a sweaty, sorry mess and emotionally, I was still upset with the errant gunshot. I was also disappointed that Jones had escaped.

I informed dispatch of the track loss and Dane quickly cut in to say he would meet me at my location. Within a few minutes, he drove up and climbed out of his truck to talk. He commented on how beat up we looked and asked, "What the hell happened with Benton?" When I sent Benton away after the gunshot, he found his way back to the highway and Dane approached him to find out why he had returned. Dane had not heard the shotgun blast, but could see Benton was badly shaken. Dane was perplexed that Benton would not discuss why he had come out to the road.

I told Dane what happened and the cigar he was chomping on nearly fell out of his mouth. He exclaimed in his gravely voice, "Yer kidding? Holy Mother of God! The dumb son-of-a-bitch!" Dane gave Trapper and me a much-appreciated lift to my vehicle. During the drive, Dane's surprise rapidly changed to anger. The cigar moved vigorously from one side of his mouth to the other and the knuckles on his big hands were white as he gripped the steering wheel, while talking incessantly.

At my vehicle, Trapper had a long, well-deserved drink from his water pail as Dane and I discussed the situation. At first, since Dane was an NCO, he considered initiating disciplinary action against Benton. However, after more discussion, we figured that Benton would have enough to explain with shooting at Jones. He was not likely justified since he was not in grave danger when he fired the shots. Leaving an elderly couple stranded on a lonely highway also was not good common sense and besides their vehicle was not suitable for high-speed pursuits.

I chalked the experience up as a lesson – a hard lesson. In future, I would be very careful who came with me as backup, and would ensure that all firearms were safe. I also made certain that I always had thick gloves and long sleeve shirts available.

At the east end of the city, off Highway 16, was the old Prince George Regional Correctional Center. Periodically, inmates escaped on foot from the institution and the police always attended to investigate. The investigators usually called a dog hander to assist in the search for the escapees. One afternoon just after my first Christmas at Prince George, an inmate walked away from a work gang. He was possibly in possession of a hatchet. Trapper and I arrived about 40 minutes after the escape and the dog quickly picked up a track in the surrounding bush. The weather was unseasonably warm and the ground was bare except for some patches of snow. The track was very fresh and we moved swiftly along. From time to time, I saw fresh footprints in the wet snow patches.

The terrain was rough and the bush thick. As the dog ran ahead, the line slipped through my wet gloves. The dog was so intent on the fresh track, that he ignored my repeated calls for him to stop. Trapper moved too fast for me to keep up to him and I lost sight of him. I desperately tried to catch up and luckily, I could see dog prints along with the escapee's tracks. The track was eastbound, but now shifted northeast towards the highway. I worried for Trapper's safety if he caught up to the suspect, especially if the man had a hatchet. My other concern was the track going to the highway. The dog would be so intent on following the scent, that he would not take notice of the traffic on the busy road. To make matters worse, I suddenly realized that my portable radio had slipped off my gun belt.

After about a mile, I came down a hill to the highway and to my indescribable relief saw Trapper standing in the ditch. He looked back at me expectantly and I yelled at him to stay. As I joined him and picked up the line with shaking hands, Trapper quickly turned and pulled the line so tight that my arm nearly came out of its socket. We raced westbound along the ditch. The dog's head came up and he turned right, wanting to cross the highway. As we crossed the road, I noticed a police car parked in a pull out with two occupants. I motioned to them, trying to make them understand that I did not have a radio. The passenger, who happened to be a guard from the jail, ran to me and slapped a revolver into my outstretched hand as I dove into the ditch. Before I could say anything, he ran back to the car. I jammed the weapon into my back pocket and continued.

Another half mile later, the track crossed the highway again and proceeded straight up a steep embankment for about 200 yards. As we crested the top, the escapee was standing about

50 yards ahead of us. He did not see or hear us. He was staring straight ahead at the prison. The inmate just realized that he had made a complete circle and ended where he had started.

Keeping in mind that he might have a weapon, I waited a few moments, trying desperately to catch my wind. Trapper was beside me, intent on the prisoner. Gathering all my strength, we made a dash for the man who suddenly turned to face us. I yelled at him to raise his hands but he did not comply and I crashed into him at a full run, knocking him to the ground. Trapper bit the lower leg of the man who responded with a scream of terror and pain. It was over. He was in custody again. The prisoner was not armed, and after turning him over to the prison, I searched the track. Trapper found my portable radio but did not recover a hatchet.

Trapper and I were also attending calls outside of Prince George on a frequent basis. In March 1981, we attended a rural residence on Bearhead Road, near the town of Vanderhoof. This town is on Highway 16, about a ninety-minute drive west of Prince George. An exhausted 28-year-old woman had walked to the house. She was badly battered, covered with her own blood and suffering from exposure. She was unable to provide any information because of her weakened condition and nobody knew who she was.

The investigator did not know where the assault took place and asked if I could follow her footprints in the snow. We hoped to find out where she came from and, in turn, gathering more evidence. It was starting to get dark and the temperature had been just below freezing. With the fast encroaching nightfall, I felt the temperature dropping as the breeze from the north intensified.

We followed the track for nearly two miles, through open pastures, fields, and bush. My snowshoes kept me from sinking in the snow and made the hike tolerable. I found impressions in the snow where the victim had fallen or stopped to rest. Trapper found the woman's wallet and some other personal papers. The dog also indicated numerous drops of blood in the snow. Eventually, we came to a fence line near a roadway, where it was obvious that the beating had taken place. The impressions and scuffmarks in the snow told a story of a brutal confrontation. Blood spatters in the snow were likely the result of violent blows from a blunt weapon. We searched the area, but did not find any weapon. The tracks in the snow showed that the woman had been able to get away from her attacker and run across the open field. The culprit had possibly let her escape. Despite the pain and massive blood loss, she had kept going. Identifying the crime scene was an important part of the investigation.

It had become fully dark and the coyotes howled in the distance. The breeze had turned into a wind, which swirled through the treetops. I remember shivering even though I wore a large RCMP issue storm coat and mukluks. A bright half moon poked out between fast moving clouds. The moonlight gave the macabre scene an even more eerie feel. The temperature dropped further. I radioed the investigators and gave them my location. They soon joined me, with a forensics specialist who processed the scene. The culprit turned out to be her estranged husband and investigators arrested him. My heart went out to the woman that suffered such a despicable assault.

In July 1981, Constable Hawkins, an investigator with the Quesnel detachment planned to arrest a native that had several outstanding warrants in relation to numerous offences. The suspect was a resident of the remote Klus Kas Reserve, about a one-hour flight west of Quesnel. Hawkins requested a dog handler to assist with the arrest and I was detailed to accompany him. The suspect was also known to carry a sawed off .22 caliber rifle.

The detachment hired a civilian helicopter service to fly Hawkins, my dog and me to the Reserve. Pockets of fog hung in the trees surrounding the Quesnel airport, as we lifted off before daybreak. It was just light enough to fly and the civilian pilot was very excited about having us on board his helicopter. Apparently, he had never assisted the police before.

Before taking off, we briefed the pilot on what we hoped to accomplish. He advised us that he had made several trips to the community in the past and was very familiar with the layout of the Reserve. From the information we had, we knew the suspect resided in a large tent situated at Klus Kas. The pilot confirmed that by saying he had seen the tent during one of his trips in.

As we got closer, we noticed the pilot becoming too eager as he talked excessively over the headsets. He commented that he wished he could announce our presence and belt out music over the loudspeakers as we arrived at the Reserve. Hawkins glanced back at me and rolled his eyes. He shared my mounting concern over our wound up pilot.

He did, however make one sensible suggestion. We could fly in a semi-circle behind a number of hills on the west side of the Reserve, to muffle our approach. The pilot concluded by saying, "I can bring us in low, and land her right in front of the tent. You guys can run in and have him before we wakes up!" It sounded feasible and we agreed to the maneuver.

As the sun broke free of the eastern horizon, we came in low behind the hills as planned and popped out at roof top height over Klus Kas. With the nose up, the pilot expertly landed his machine within 100 yards of the only tent on the Reserve. I unbuckled my seatbelt and already had Trapper in his tracking harness. As the skids touched down, I bailed out with the dog at my side. Hawkins joined me at the front of the helicopter. The wind gusts from the rotors beat on our backs as we raced for the tent entrance.

I threw back the front flap and we entered the tent. A sleepy suspect raised his head and started to reach under his pillow. Trapper jumped on the bed and I jammed my service revolver in the man's surprised face and ordered him not to move. Trapper growled and flashed some teeth a few inches from the face of the now wide-awake suspect. Hawkins quickly handcuffed the man and checked under the pillow, to discover a loaded, sawed-off rifle.

We all emerged from the tent to a pilot that was beyond containing himself. He had shut the helicopter down and was exuberantly pacing back and forth in front of the machine. We bundled the captive in the back seat. Trapper and I would have to share the space with him on the trip back to town.

I noticed people on the Reserve who were just starting their day. Women and skimpily clad children were slowly making their way to the creek to gather water. The wide-eyed children seemed fascinated by our presence, but I could also detect fear on their small, innocent faces. It was saddening to see these people living in such conditions. Hawkins told me that the Reserve did not have running water, electricity, or communication with the outside world. Most of the wooden cabins and houses did not have glass in the windows, or doors in the doorways to protect the occupants from the elements. It seemed as if time had forgotten about the place.

Hawkins asked the pilot to fly a few minutes further west of the Reserve to a cabin situated on a small river. He had to talk with the resident about another unrelated file. As we came in close, the trees were too thick to allow a safe place to land. The pilot decided the dock on the river was adequate and touched down. Pine trees swayed wildly from the rotors and seemed too close for comfort. From the expression on our prisoner's face, he shared our concerns. He leaned in to me, motioned towards the pilot with his chin and yelled over the noise, "Hey, where the hell did you find this guy?"

In August 1981, Trapper and I assisted the Burns Lake detachment with an old file concerning a missing person. Burns Lake is about a four-hour drive west of Prince George. The summer before, a common-law couple set up a camp at Powderhouse Creek, a few miles west of the town. The man and woman had a reputation of fighting with each other and the man had a history of violence. After a few weeks, others in the community were becoming concerned, since the woman Arlene, had not been seen for some time.

In the interim, the man, named Henry, had moved the camp back into Burns Lake. Notified of Arlene's disappearance, the police talked to Henry. He said that Arlene had moved away from Powderhouse Creek three weeks before. He admitted that they had a disagreement, but stated she left on her own accord. From Henry's answers, or rather, lack of answers, the woman's disappearance was suspicious. Henry had not mentioned or reported Arlene's absence to anybody.

A search was conducted at Powderhouse Creek over a period of several days involving provincial search and rescue, community members and the police. The searchers did not find the woman or any of her belongings. The local detachment conducted a lengthy investigation, including re-interviewing Henry, but his story did not change.

After a year, investigators still pursued the case. At the time Arlene vanished, the water was shallow in Powderhouse Creek. Water from this creek flows into nearby Burns Lake. The members thought the culprit might have buried her in the creek, despite the water. Now that it was dry, they asked if my dog could search the creek bed. To me it was a long shot, but I agreed to try. It was only about 300 yards long, from Highway 16 to the lake.

It was a warm Saturday afternoon when we started. I had Trapper work closely to me, searching a tight pattern in hopes of locating some scent seeping out of the dry earth. If the victim were there, it would have been a shallow grave, allowing scent to drift upwards. It was slow, methodical work and the surrounding area was covered with thick brush, marsh, and stinging nettle. Despite the heat, Trapper continued working very well. He loved water and always enjoyed a long swim. When he did go swimming, I always had to keep calling him back to me. From experience, I knew if he got too far out, he would ignore my calls and remain in the water until he was ready to come out. Although Trapper was a purebred German Shepherd, he acted like a Retriever around water.

As the afternoon wore on, I could see Trapper eyeing up the lake. I allowed him to have a twenty-minute break and enjoy the cool water.

After the dog had his swim, the staff sergeant in Prince George called on the radio, enquiring when I planned to return to Prince George. I was required for the night shift in the city. The staff sergeant, not unlike most other senior RCMP members at that time, had little patience for young members like me and did not like to wait for answers. I was diplomatic and convincing enough when I said that I had a lot of searching to do and I would keep him advised. Remembering the expression on the face of Jerad, the Burns Lake corporal, I knew that he was obsessed with solving this case. I did not want to let him down.

Late in the afternoon, Jerad showed up and we spoke for a few minutes. I told him about the old staff sergeant's enquiries and that I wanted to continue searching for as long as possible. I suggested expanding the search, to include the areas searched the year before. Perhaps something was missed or overlooked. To do this, I would have to stay overnight and search the next day. Jerad's face lit up with the idea and promised to deal with the old NCO on my behalf. This was probably a homicide investigation and anxious friends and family needed answers.

At dusk, Trapper and I stopped searching and went to Burns Lake. No members were at the detachment except for an elderly civilian night guard. He was friendly and in the mood to talk. It turned out he was a local history buff and had lived in the area most of his life. I asked if he knew how Powderhouse Creek got its name. He explained that years ago, barges hauled equipment and supplies up and down the lake. Dynamite was stored in a powderhouse at the creek. Consequently, the name Powderhouse Creek stuck.

After the visit, I fed Trapper and settled him down in the police truck. I got a room at a local motel and fell into a deep sleep. Before 5:00 AM, I was up and dressed. No restaurants were open yet, so I decided to search a few hours and then return for breakfast. It was a quiet, peaceful Sunday morning. At the creek, the birds sang uninhibitedly as the sun rose and the bright rays stabbed through the trees at almost a 90-degree angle.

Despite the beautiful setting nature provided, I knew why I was there and I felt uneasy. I directed the dog into a wooded area that we had not yet searched. Why I chose that area, I cannot recall. Trapper was about 30 yards ahead of me, enjoying the early morning run. Suddenly he slowed and his tail flicked to one side. He stopped and his head went down to the ground. I saw him sniff a large lump on the ground. To me it seemed that the singing birds ceased their morning oration. I gazed down at the lump the dog indicated. It looked like something covered in moss, but I had never seen red moss. I touched it lightly with the toe of my hiking boot. It was soft, but I could feel something hard in the middle.

Carefully, I used my foot to turn the lump. It moved easily. With the bright sunshine piercing through the trees, I continued to turn it. I held my breath as the object revealed itself as an intact human skull. The red moss turned out to be hair, which had turned color with decomposition and exposure to the elements. I suddenly felt detached and unaware of everything around me, even Trapper, who remained at my side.

The training brought me back to reality. It was important not to disturb the scene and I needed help immediately. Leaving the skull, Trapper and I walked out the same way we came in. I broke out into a run and quickly covered the distance back to the police vehicle. My lungs took in the fresh morning air and the sunshine warmed my face, neither of which offered any comfort. None of the members in Burns Lake was on duty yet, so I had to call Prince George dispatch to relay a message to the member on call. I composed myself before hitting the radio repeater. After a few moments, the dispatcher cut in, "Car calling Prince George?" Holding the mike with a shaking hand, I replied, "Prince, thirteen echo one here. Would you please phone the member on call at Burns Lake and have him meet me at Powderhouse Creek immediately. Also, could you call Jerad and have him attend?" Alyss, the dispatcher knew something was happening, but she was smart and knew enough not to ask too many questions. She acknowledged my request and told me to stand by.

I made some hasty notes of what I had found. I knew I had to write a report later and might have to attend court. It was important to have good notes. After a minute or so, the radio crackled, "Thirteen echo one, Prince. I've contacted the members and they are on the way. Is there anything else I can do for you?" For the time being, all I could do was wait and replied, "No, not right now. Thanks, Prince." Alyss signed off by saying, "Good luck Brad. Prince George clear." The radio went silent and I continued with my notes. It was difficult to remain seated. I wanted to go and continue searching.

There was no traffic on the highway. Breaking the silence in the clear, morning air, I heard a vehicle driving west at high speeds towards my position. It turned out to be a police car, driven by one of the junior members from the detachment, with Jerad as the passenger. It careened off the highway and bounced over the dirt trail towards me. It slid to a stop beside my vehicle, with a great cloud of dust enveloping all of us. Jerad popped out and yelled over to me, "What the hell have you got?" He was wearing a uniform shirt, blue jeans, and had a bad case of "bed head." I pointed towards the bush and replied, "Dog found a skull." Jerad's eyes went big. He was beyond containing himself and blurted out, "Where? Show me!"

I led them to the skull, but despite the grisly find, the corporal was giddy with excitement. "It's Arlene! I know damn well its Arlene! This is the finest damn dog work I have ever seen in all my years! I'm gonna buy that dog of yours a big steak!" I was proud of my dog, and in my mind's eye, I hungrily and enviously watched Trapper eating that big steak.

The young constable was carefully walking around the immediate area when he exclaimed, "Oh my God guys! Have a look at this!" We walked over to his position, about 30 yards from the skull. He pointed to a tangle of brush and we could barely make out a fully clothed, headless, human skeleton. The foliage partially concealed the corpse. It had taken a sharp eye to see it.

Predatory animals will often chew the head off a carcass and carry it away, sometimes for miles. With human remains, it is no different, but this case seemed to be an exception to that theory. The corporal was sure we had found Arlene. The clothing on the corpse matched what she usually wore. In those days, we did not have DNA testing. I do not recall if there were any dental records, but investigators were sure it was the right victim.

I left the scene for the rest of the morning, while the investigators started the painstaking task of crime scene work. The coroner attended and an RCMP forensic specialist arrived to photograph the scene and take details for a planned drawing. Jerad telephoned my staff sergeant in Prince George and got the man out of bed. He was so pleased with the progress that he told Jerad I could stay in Burns Lake for as long as they needed me. The old NCO also offered his assistance in the way of more resources for the Burns Lake members. In other words, he could pull strings if needed.

I stayed for another day and searched the scene again, after the investigators completed their work. We did not locate any further evidence. I was present when the investigators re-interviewed Henry. I remember, even at a distance that he looked rather vulnerable and shaken. Despite the investigators best efforts, he stuck to his original story. A post-mortem of the remains was unable to determine the cause of Arlene's death. Because of the lengthy exposure to the elements and predators, they could not find any signs of trauma. It was a very frustrating case for me and to this day, I still think about it. I hoped the recovery of the remains brought some closure to the family, but it was probably of little consolation. Of the two people at Powderhouse Creek during the summer of 1980, one could not talk and the other would not talk.

I was working a Sunday afternoon in Prince George in the fall of 1981, when I overheard radio traffic between members concerning the discovery of a human body, about 30 miles east of the city. The nude body of a woman was lying in a shallow ditch beside a dirt road in a logged area, about one mile south of Highway 16. The victim's clothing was draped over her body and face. One member carefully pulled the clothing back, to reveal bullet holes in her chest. Casings from .22 caliber shells lay on the ground near the corpse. I attended without being called and quickly harnessed the dog. I circled the dog around the ghastly scene in an effort to locate any human tracks, but that met with negative results. Next, we started to search the area, hoping to find more evidence. About ten yards from the body, Trapper found the woman's shoes. We searched until nightfall, without finding anything further.

While driving back to the scene the next morning, I decided to check around the bridge where Highway 16 crossed the Willow River. The bridge was about eight miles from the murder scene. It was a long shot, but I thought it was a likely place to discard evidence. The embankments were long, steep, and covered with dense brush. Near the river, Trapper located a woman's black purse in the undergrowth. Inside, it contained picture identification of the murdered woman. Up until that time, investigators did not know the victim's identity. They surmised that the suspect had thrown the purse over the bridge, while driving towards the city. Police divers searched the river, but did not locate any further evidence.

Over the next four days, Trapper and I, plus two other dog teams re-searched the logged off area. We searched the ditches of Highway 16, 30 miles in both directions from the scene, as well as all side roads, pullouts and rest stops, but did not find any other evidence. Investigators did eventually find the suspect and he was convicted of first-degree murder.

I attended several homicides during the first couple of years as a dog handler. One of the most disturbing murders has remained vivid for me over the years. Perhaps it had to do with the innocence and vulnerability of the young victim. This was a prime example of the callous disregard for human life and the barbaric actions of persons that I hardly consider human beings. It has left me with a jaded and bitter attitude.

Hikers in a bush area west of the Hart Highway (Highway 97) truck weigh scales discovered the body of a missing 13-year-old girl. It was in the north part of the city. Investigators swooped into the area and a considerable amount of time went into the processing. The sight was hideous. It was November and the lifeless body lay on the cold ground. She had been sexually assaulted and strangled. In a brutal way, the suspect used a filet knife to mutilate and disfigure her body. Near the corpse were unique car tire impressions embedded in the sandy soil.

Investigators later matched the marks to the car owned by a suspect they identified.

After all the evidence was gathered and the body removed, Trapper and I, along with two other teams combed the area for further clues. Near the end of our fruitless search, with nightfall approaching, I was overwhelmed with hate, sadness, helplessness, and disgust. The courts convicted the suspect, but to this day, it bothers me when I see a filet knife.

Not all my experiences were so repulsive. One summer's day, I was exercising Trapper in a bush area in the north part of the city. Three boys, all about 10 or 12 years old, were playing with a small dirt bike about 200 yards from me. The machine bounced through the ditch and the young driver lost control. The bike flipped as the youngster flew off and crashed to the ground on his hands and knees. I noticed him get up just as his two companions ran to him. All three stood for a few moments. The bike rider was holding his right arm. They seemed engrossed in conversation but suddenly ran to me.

The boy presented his arm to me and with a worried look, asked, "Do you think they can fix this?" A distinctive "U" shape replaced where the boy's wrist should have been. Trying to hide my shock and remain collected so as not to further alarm the boy, I nonchalantly replied, "Oh sure, they fix stuff like that all the time." I ushered the boy into the front seat of my police truck and gently buckled his seatbelt. I told him to hold his injured arm to his chest and not move it. I turned to the remaining boys and told them to immediately go home and have a parent return for the dirt bike.

As they ran off, Trapper bounded into the vehicle and quickly came up to check on our young passenger. The boy received a sniff on his left ear and a large kiss on the cheek. On the way to the hospital, the dispatcher attempted to contact the boy's grandparents, whom he lived with. Nobody was home but the dispatcher kept trying.

At the emergency, the nurses asked me to stay with my new young friend until the grandparents could attend. I happily agreed and stayed by his bedside, holding his uninjured hand. I offered moral support while the doctor examined him and held his hand extra tight when painkillers were administered with a rather large needle. A distraught grandmother finally arrived and I reluctantly gave up my post. The next evening, I dropped by the boy's residence and was astounded that he had a cast from his hand to his shoulder. The grandparents were gracious and grateful folks. I wished the boy a speedy recovery and gave him my RCMP ball cap as a keepsake of our meeting.

During the summer of 1982, a prospector was reported overdue and missing from his camp about 30 miles south-west of the town of Mackenzie. The camp was situated in a remote bush area, accessible only by walking in or flying to it. The area was dotted with marshes, small lakes, and ponds. Only aircraft with pontoons could land on the lakes in the area. The prospector was an older man, familiar with living alone in the bush over extended periods. Varieties of precious metals supposedly permeated this area and the man was obsessed with finding the "mother lode." The prospector had hired a private airplane to fly supplies to his camp at pre-arranged times. On the last trip in, the camp was still there but the man was missing. It was very unusual for the prospector not to show up for the plane. The pilot made a return trip the next morning, but again did not locate his client. He reported the incident to the Mackenzie detachment and the investigator initiated a missing person investigation.

A big part of the investigation would involve resources such as the provincial Search and Rescue volunteers (SAR), aircraft and dog handlers. Trapper and I would assist Mel, another dog handler from Prince George, who was already in the area searching. When I arrived at the Mackenzie detachment late in the evening, Mel just returned from the bush after a full day of searching with SAR. He briefed me about the latest developments on the situation.

The first concern he had was that certain ore deposits in the region affected the compasses that we relied on. From his experiences, the compass needle could vary up to 180 degrees at certain locations. In other words, we could not totally rely on these instruments for direction. Mel said that the SAR volunteers depended on the detailed topographical maps. They traveled along ridges marked on the maps and identified ponds and lakes they came upon by the size and shape shown on the maps. Details on hills and mountains also helped determine their approximate location. This was long before we had access to GPS equipment.

The handler said they used bright colored flagging tape, a different color for each day. The area was a maze of thick brush, rock, steep hills, and marshlands. Added to the inhospitable terrain, were of course, swarms of mosquitoes and black flies. Moving through the country was slow and laborious. Neither the police nor the SAR members had any form of reliable radio contact in this remote area.

Mel asked me to conduct a search the next morning on my own, while he and a SAR team returned to an area they were still searching. I reluctantly agreed, but on the other hand, was excited to be involved. Mel had pre-arranged that I meet a bush pilot hired by the Mackenzie detachment at a wharf on Carp Lake, southwest of Mackenzie and accessible by road. The pilot would fly Trapper and me to a small lake west of Mackenzie, within the search area. After the drop-off, we would then move south from that lake for about two miles to another lake. After searching the circumference of that lake, we would then double back to the first lake and search around it. We would then wait for the aircraft to return and transport the dog and me back to Mackenzie. Judging from the size of the lakes on the map, it would be a full day's job.

Early the next morning, I double-checked my backpack and gear while I waited at the wharf for my airplane. I had a map of the search area, flagging tape, compass, shotgun, revolver, ammunition for both firearms, food for both dog and me for two days, matches, flares, coat, extra socks, small tarpaulin (for a lean-to), thin rope, bug repellant and a space blanket. The weather was overcast and it looked like it might rain. I waited for about an hour and was starting to become anxious, when I spotted a small aircraft coming in for a landing on the lake. It set down effortlessly and taxied over to the wharf. As it closed in to the wharf, the pilot cut the single engine, stepped out of the cockpit onto a pontoon to meet the wharf.

The pilot appeared to be approximately 40 years old. He was of medium height with a solid, strong stature. His hair was short and he had about three day's growth of a dark beard. His long sleeve woolen shirt was haphazardly tucked into soiled, grease-covered blue jeans, without a belt or suspenders. The long laces of his dirty white running shoes were undone. He spoke gruffly with a thick eastern European accent and introduced himself as "Ivan," without the usual handshake. I do not recall the make of aircraft that he had, but to me it did not appear to be in the best of condition. However, I was not familiar with aircraft and trusted that the Mackenzie members would only hire somebody in good standing. Ivan threw my pack in the back of the airplane's cabin, while I helped Trapper into the back seat.

Ivan announced that he wanted to check the amount of fuel he had on board the plane before take-off. He pulled a two-foot portion of a hockey stick out of the cabin, opened the fuel tank on the wing, and inserted the stick. He withdrew it and looked at it for a moment. He presented it to me and said, "No worry, we got enough gas to get you there!" An alarm bell went off in my head, but I dismissed it. I pulled my map out and tried to confirm with Ivan exactly where we needed to go. "No problem, no problem. I talked to other policeman yesterday. I know where we going. Now get in. We go!"

Ivan untied the plane from the dock and pushed it away. He fired up the engine and we taxied out onto the lake. He gunned the engine. The cabin shook and shuddered as the plane picked up speed on the water. The engine roared with our sudden lift off. Gaining some altitude, Ivan banked the plane over to the west. From my vantage point, I tried to survey the land below and compare it to the map, in a vain attempt to orientate myself. The land was dotted with many small lakes and ponds. After about 15 minutes in the air, Ivan pointed down at a lake. I again tried to compare the land below to my map, but with Ivan's turns and maneuvers, I was still somewhat unsure of our location. I again pointed at the map and indicated to Ivan the lake I wanted. He nodded impatiently and waved his hand at me dismissively. "Yeah, yeah, not problem, that's the one down there," as he stabbed downwards with the index finger of his right hand.

We glided in at tree top level and touched down on the lake. Ivan taxied the plane to the west shoreline of the lake and shut the engine off as the pontoons gently slid up onto the smooth sand. Black flies immediately swarmed us as we disembarked. With my dog and gear safely on shore, I helped Ivan give the plane a mighty push off the bank. He stood on the pontoon and smiling broadly, said, "Hey buddy, I try come to get you tonight! If not, I be here in the morning. OK? No problem!" I was somewhat dumbfounded by that statement. I hoped he would not forget about us.

With that, he clambered back into the plane, started the engine, and taxied out. The aircraft heaved off the lake, circled once, and headed east. With the drone of the plane getting fainter, I took stock of my situation. The bugs engulfed both the dog and me. It was best to keep moving. I pulled out my compass and started on a southerly heading. Generally, the bush in this area was open and the ground flat. It was just after

9:00 AM and the lake to the south was only about two miles away. I figured we could be there within an hour. The air was still and I started to adjust to the "quiet," meaning there were no manmade noises. We were on our own and had to rely on Ivan to come back for us at the end of the day.

Trapper ranged out ahead of me. I needed to keep a close eye on his movements. It was possible that he could "cut" or cross the prospector's track. If so, the dog would indicate and follow the scent. I also had to carefully watch the compass and keep referring to the map. The map showed little change in elevation of the land between the two lakes. I used some bright blue flagging tape every 50 yards or so, just to be sure.

After a half hour, we crossed a ridge and soon after another. I consulted the map and did not see any ridgelines. After a few minutes, the land started to get marshy and the bush thicker. I had been watching the compass closely and there had not been any sudden deviations. I stopped to tie more flagging tape on a tree branch and noticed a small pond to my right. According to the map, there were no bodies of water between the two lakes. I re-checked the compass, wondering if we had gone off course without realizing it. The bugs closed in to torment us. I decided to continue south for a while longer and within a few minutes came to another ridge, which was certainly not on the map.

I cursed to myself, wondering how I could have allowed us to get into such a situation. I doused myself with more bug repellant and studied the map. South of my intended destination, the map showed ridgelines and a pond. Suddenly it clicked in my head. I wondered if Ivan had mistakenly dropped us off at the wrong lake. Changing my course 180 degrees, we started back. Thankful for the flagging tape, we made good time and returned to the lake from where we started our hike. At the same shoreline, I was able to get a good idea of the shape of the lake. Comparing the shape to the map, I determined that Ivan had indeed dropped us off at the wrong lake. Trapper and I were already at the lake we were supposed to head for. This time I cursed aloud and my voice echoed across the lake.

Trapper and I set a northerly course and within an hour arrived at the lake Ivan was supposed to have taken us. We searched the circumference of the lake and started back to the first lake. We searched that lake and by then, it was after 7:00 PM. It was certainly challenging country to traverse. We were bug-bitten and tired. Loons were letting lose with their distinctive cries across the lake. It started to feel lonely and I wondered if my new friend Ivan would return that evening. We still had daylight, but I started to gather firewood and the dog and I ate some of the food I had packed. I wondered if the space blanket and fire would provide enough warmth through the night. At least smoke from a fire would help keep the bugs at bay.

Just before 8:00 PM, as I started to prepare our camp for the night, I heard the slight drone on an aircraft coming from the east. I looked hard into the horizon and saw a speck in the distance. The drone grew louder and I realized that it was Ivan. My resentment towards the man dissipated at his arrival. This meant that I would not have to rough it overnight in the bush. Ivan taxied up to the shoreline, climbed onto a pontoon and with a wave, hollered, "Hi buddy! Bet you happy I come back, huh?" I reconsidered my resentment. I concluded that I did not really like Ivan.

At the shoreline, I packed my gear and lifted Trapper back onto the airplane. As I climbed into the seat, Ivan was scratching his chin. He looked at me pensively and asked, "Hey buddy, how much you weigh?" At first, I thought it was an unusual question. I told him that I was over 220 pounds. He scratched even more and asked, "How about dog and pack?" My stomach dropped as I suddenly realized there might be a problem with take-off. The dog and pack were probably an additional 120 pounds. Ivan explained that he had not considered the extra weight going out until now. He reasoned that the lake might not be long enough to get enough altitude to clear the trees. In a cavalier tone, Ivan stated, "Hey buddy, we try, OK? Hang on!"

We had already taxied to the very south end of the lake, when he turned north and gunned it with everything that the old plane could muster. I was now prone in the very back of the cabin, holding on to Trapper. I could only see the sky as we gathered speed. The plane shook and bounced over the water and the engine strained loudly. Ivan's big shoulders were hunched over the controls and his head bobbled like a child's toy. With a mighty heave, he pulled back and the engine screamed as the plane lifted off the water. Ivan did not turn to me, but yelled over the noise, "Hang on buddy. Here we go!"

I strained my neck to get a better view out the side window. We were climbing, but I did not know if it was enough. To my horror and amazement, the tops of pine trees whizzed passed the wings of the plane. I heard Ivan laugh like a lunatic as he started to slowly bank to the right. He looked back at me and laughed again. We had obviously made it. I glanced over at my dog. He was looking out the window on the other side. I wondered if he had the same feelings about the pilot as I did.

We arrived back at Carp Lake before dark and I was never so happy to touch down and be away from Crazy Ivan forever.

Trapper and I remained on the search for a few more days with Mel and the SAR people, but we did not locate the prospector. We returned to Prince George and about eight days later, the prospector walked into the town of Fort St. James. The town is about 60 miles southwest of Mackenzie through inhospitable terrain. He was in good condition despite loosing a considerable amount of weight. Apparently, he had lost his way and eventually worked out a course that took him to safety. He was fortunate to survive that unforgiving country.

One night in late September 1982, a high-speed pursuit started in the downtown of Prince George. Two plain-clothes members from the General Investigation Section or GIS tried to stop a car with two male occupants. One of my dog handler counterparts always referred to the GIS members as "Guys in Suits." GIS was what other police forces would call their detectives. I joined the pursuit along with a few other detachment units. The chase proceeded east out of the city on Highway 16. Two highway patrol cars, returning to the city, also joined the chase.

After about ten miles of hair rising speeds, the suspect vehicle turned north off the highway onto the Old Giscome Highway. This road was "old" and not much of a "highway." It was a narrow, dark road, winding through thick brush and around rocky embankments. The chase was treacherous for all concerned, with cars sliding around tight curves and the flashing red and blue police lights giving off eerie shadows in the gloomy bush. Radio traffic was hard to decipher over the din of the sirens and garbled radio transmissions of excited members talking over each other.

We screamed through the tiny hamlet of Willow River and careened along for another ten miles until we came to an abrupt stop in a second hamlet named Upper Fraser. I overheard the animated voice of a GIS member yelling over the radio, "OK, they've stopped! Oh damn, their bailing, their bailing! Get the dog man up here, right now!" His voice labored from the excitement and rush of adrenalin. That was my cue and I was stuck at the rear of the pack.

Within a minute, I joined all the other members gathered around waiting for me. The driver's front door and front passenger's door were wide open on the light colored sedan. The engine was sputtering with the headlights on. I quickly harnessed my anxious dog and he circled in front of the abandoned car. His head went down when he located the scent and he moved off so fast that the nylon line burned my hands despite the fact I had gloves on. Both GIS members were with me on this "hot" track. In response to all the noise we had created, lights were coming on inside some of the homes and at the opposite end of the small community, a dog barked incessantly. I was breathing in big gulps of air, not just from the exertion, but also from the pure adrenalin rush. We were moving at a dead-run as we crossed a small bridge over a stream. Trapper abruptly turned right and we crashed through back yards, over fences, down a laneway, through brush, back onto another laneway, over more fences and finally stopped in a back yard.

Trapper circled frantically a few times and with me hanging on for dear life, we dashed up a long flight of wooden stairs, to the back door of a house. He jammed his nose hard on the handle and turned to look at me. The inside of the house was in total darkness. I clicked on my flashlight and saw two men sitting on the kitchen floor, breathing heavily. Their eyes blinked because of the bright light and they held their hands up, trying to protect their eyes. I tapped on the door window and pointed my index finger at them as if to say, "Gotcha!" Simultaneously, the shoulders of both men sagged. They knew it was all over.

I pointed at the door handle and yelled at them to open the door. With great apprehension, they both cautiously approached the door and just as one reached for the knob; Trapper lunged at the door and barked furiously. I praised the dog and ordered them to move faster, since the dog had obviously lost patience. The GIS members arrested both men. The frustrating part came next. Both men apparently had nothing to hide. They had simply become "freaked out" when the two GIS members "eyeballed" them downtown. We did not find any incriminating evidence on them or in their car. They were charged with dangerous driving and failing to stop for police. It had been an unnecessary event, and therefore for me, it was a hollow victory.

It was a busy night shift in late October. Trapper and I were on patrol in the downtown part of the city, when dispatch broadcast a call of an armed robbery. The staff member at a small convenience store, situated at the north end of the city reported that two masked young men, one brandishing a rifle, ran off with a wad of cash from the till. Several cars responded, including me. It had been so busy earlier, that I had been unable to take a much needed bathroom break.

When I arrived at the scene, I saw that the store was nestled in a large bush area on the east side of the highway. An older, dark colored car was parked about 100 yards south of the store.

More members arrived as I quickly harnessed Trapper and circled him around the store. He picked up a track that went about 200 yards south of the store. He suddenly stopped and started to dig at the ground. He uncovered a .22 caliber rifle buried in the sand. I gave Trapper extra praise, since it was such a big relief to find the weapon. The track ended at that point.

I returned to the store and cast the dog again and he hit another track. This time we went about a 100 yards southeast and the dog started digging, recovering a set of car keys. A member with me tried the keys in the parked vehicle and it started. We now believed we had the suspect's car.

The dog located a third track east from the car into the bush. Since tracking is at a jog, it only intensified my urge to use a bathroom. We covered about 300 yards, when the dog's nose went to the ground again, where this time he dug up a bag of cash. The track continued with numerous twists and turns. It was frustrating for both Trapper and me since the suspects were obviously having difficulty making up their minds. The members were more than satisfied with all the evidence that we had gathered. It would not be difficult to identify the suspects.

Other high priority calls were coming in and everybody started to clear the scene. I intended to be the last to leave, since the dark bush was an ideal place to relieve myself. I drove my truck to the edge of the bush and quickly exited, leaving the door open. Trapper stood in the back of the vehicle, watching me run to the bush.

I was sweating from the earlier exertion. I dropped my gun belt and pants to the ground, with intentions of re-arranging my clothes afterwards. In mid-stream, two terrified young men stepped out of the bush, with their hands held high. One screamed at me, "We give up! We give up! Don't shoot!" Despite complete surprise and embarrassment, I could not stop peeing.

The headlights from my truck were in the suspects eyes and they could not see my predicament. Mustering as much authority in my voice as possible considering my situation, I yelled back, "Down on the ground, now! Move! Don't look at me! Keep your faces in the ground, or I'll let the dog loose!" Trapper could see what was happening and he was now at the open truck door, barking and growling at the two suspects.

Finally, with my gun belt and pants up around my knees, I awkwardly ran back to my police vehicle. I knew that the dog would keep a close eye on the two men. If they attempted to escape, Trapper would have them in a moment. I praised the dog and told him to "watch" them, while I got on the police radio. Sergeant Kessler was on patrol and the only member available to answer my call for help. He was a tall, older man that made younger members like me feel uncomfortable to be around him. He was a serious minded man and did everything by the book. He was very knowledgeable about police work and demanded perfection from all the members on his watch. He was always stern and never smiled.

I knew Kessler was a slow, deliberate driver and that I would have plenty of time to get myself sorted out. The two suspects were still face down when Kessler finally arrived. He rambled up to me and glanced at my prisoners. Kessler had been monitoring the radio traffic earlier and was aware of our efforts. He glared at me, with his big, bushy eyebrows pulled down in his trademark frown and asked, "How the hell did you find these two?" I had been too busy to come up with a plausible story and felt intimidated by his fixed stare. I looked the sergeant in the eyes and replied, "I was taking a pee, when they walked out of the bush." His eyebrows shot up and I thought I noticed a slight smile on his lips. He nodded slightly, trying to comprehend my statement, and walked over to the prone men. I helped Kessler handcuff both and escort them to his police car. He did not say anything else and calmly drove off.

Early the next morning, I was at the detachment preparing for a court case later that morning. Kessler's watch all went home at 7:00 AM, but I discovered an envelope in my mail slot. Inside was a copy of a neatly typed memorandum, addressed to the chief superintendent in charge of the detachment. Kessler wrote the memo, giving me high praise for my "dedication to duty", "perseverance," and "strong work ethic" that resulted in the capture of two armed robbery suspects. It was high praise and I meant to thank the sergeant the next time we met. When I did see him, he was his aloof self and did not appear interested in discussing the matter further.

My first experience at a riot was at the provincial jail in Prince George. Early one afternoon, a group of prisoners overpowered a guard and took possession of his keys. Within minutes, the general population of the prison was out of control. The guard managed to escape, but the prisoners started to create havoc, smashing windows, fighting and starting fires throughout the prison. The guards could not restore order and had to retreat to the perimeter of the institution. The guards mounted a brief counterattack and forced some of the inmates into the open exercise yard. That still left most of the inmates in control of about half the prison grounds.

The majority of the Prince George members on duty that day responded, along with three dog teams, including Trapper and me. With the beleaguered guards, we quickly set about making plans to contain the situation. It had calmed somewhat, but was still very volatile. Fires burned and inmates roamed freely in restricted areas. They taunted and yelled at us, looking for a confrontation. Some guards had armed themselves with revolvers and rifles and the place resembled a war zone. The guards told us that the general population was organizing to attack the protective custody (PC) wing of the prison. That area was still intact, but it would be easy for the general population to get at the PCs. That unit consisted of child molesters, sex offenders, and informants. The general population would inflict retribution, with beatings, torture and possibly murders.

The Officer in Charge (OIC) of the detachment attended to take personal command of the situation. The Old Man had a reputation of being firm, fair, and not afraid to make decisions. I respected and liked the man. He was a breath of fresh air over some of the other commissioned officers that I had known over the years.

We three dog handlers watched him talking to the prison supervisors and other senior RCMP staff members. He was in full uniform but within minutes, took his jacket off, and threw it on the hood of a parked police car. He picked up a bullhorn and while rolling up the sleeves of his shirt, walked over to us. He had a waxed, handlebar moustache, with his forage cap cocked to one side of his head like a city bus driver. He had trouble hiding a half-grin on his face as he related his plan to us. "OK, boys, this is what has to be done. With the help of the guards and members with riot gear, we are going to drive a wedge between the general population and the PC unit. We will go through that gate, proceed down that fence line, and force all the inmates into that open yard with the rest of them. Hopefully, we'll have them disorganized long enough to get over to the PCs and get them the hell out of there."

The three of us were excited and anxious for some action and readily agreed to the Old Man's plan. He continued, "I'm going to be at the front of this thing and I want all three of you on my ass the entire time! Got it?" We all nodded and the OIC finished with, "Be careful I don't get bit though. That wouldn't look good." We collectively agreed and said we would do our best. We were surprised that he would put himself into such a dangerous position. The rioters would certainly single him out as the leader and focus their attention on him. We started to prepare the dogs and ourselves. Behind a building, where the prisoners could not see us, we harnessed the dogs, which sensed something was going to happen. They barked, whined and paced.

I had a bad case of dry mouth and broke out in a cold sweat. Before us were over 180 inmates. Including the guards, we were barely a quarter of that number. We desperately needed the element of surprise. Some of the armed guards worried me. I did not like the way they carelessly handled their weapons. Another handler told me he noticed two armed guards excitedly talking to each other and during the conversation both absent-mindedly pointed their rifles at each other. While the guards and our members prepared for the assault, the dogs were feeding off our anxiety and nervousness. The dogs were continually barking and growling. We did not know this until later, but some of the prisoners had broken down and cried when they heard the dogs barking. The dogs were already creating a considerable psychological advantage.

With the Old Man in the front, we flanked him with our dogs. About three dozen police and guards were behind us armed with riot gear, shields, and batons. We advanced and the momentum built up quickly. The OIC was up front, shouting orders to the prisoners with his bullhorn. The dogs barked and lunged in their harnesses, as we fed the lines out and reeled them back in. The inmates quickly fell back as the dogs closed in. Some screamed in terror at the frenzied dogs. One prisoner lost his footing, fell to the ground, and scampered backwards on his hands and feet. Trapper quickly overtook him and bit him on the leg. The man lay in a groveling, crumpled heap and I encouraged the dog forward. It was important to maintain the momentum, letting the following guards take custody of the casualty. All the while, the riot squad behind us was loudly beating on their shields in unison, like medieval soldiers going into battle, creating their own psychological warfare. We also kept an eye on the Old Man. He had not bothered with any of the protective gear offered to him. With his forage cap still jauntily in place, he kept the pace up, yelling orders over the din of the conflict.

A few inmates were captured in the fray and we moved the rest into the exercise yard. They were all in one place for now and somewhat shocked and disoriented. The OIC stopped the procession. Trapper and the other dogs still wanted to go, but we needed to catch our wind. The Old Man turned to me with a wide grin on his sweat-streaked face and exclaimed, "Brad, hold this damn bullhorn! That coffee I had at lunchtime has gone right through me!" I obliged him as he darted round the corner of a building for some privacy. He called back to me, "Holler if things start to go to hell!"

With the general population contained, we quickly moved to the PC unit. The other prisoners saw this and started to boo and jeer us. They were obviously disappointed that we were going to save the PCs from them. We opened the PC cells and quickly escorted the prisoners to waiting vans. The 27 inmates would be housed at the detachment cells for their own protection. All were noticeably relieved and started to thank us. We were not in the mood for their gratitude. Some of the members openly told them that if it were their decision, they would gladly turn them over to the general population. The PCs glumly moved to the waiting vehicles without any more conversation.

With the PCs out of danger, we could give our full attention to the other prisoners. Guards set up strategic points around the field filled with prisoners. Fires still burned around the prison and it looked like a scene from "Dante's Inferno." High echelon people from the correction service arrived from the provincial capital of Victoria, to attempt negotiations with the inmates in an effort to end the situation without further violence. It was early spring and the nights were still cold. The sun was setting and the prison director arranged to bring food in for the prisoners, staff, and members at the scene. Prison staff distributed blankets and essentials to the prisoners. It was all in an effort to calm the situation as much as possible. Negotiators with the correction service attempted to set up a dialogue with the inmates.

We dog handlers stood by through the entire night, along with several detachment members. By mid-morning, all the efforts by the prison staff to end the standoff had disintegrated. Loudmouths and instigators within the convicts had stirred them all into frenzy. Prisoners were openly taunting and threatening guards and police. Tempers flared and the guards heard prisoners saying they would attempt a mass escape at the east gate of the yard. All the dog teams and several members quickly made their way to the east side. The general atmosphere was gloomy and many of the inmates were in a dark, foul mood.

There were two 15-foot high perimeter fences with gates around the field. The situation rapidly and violently escalated. All the prisoners suddenly charged the first gate. Unbelievably, they hit the gate with full force and it started to topple. The dog teams were between armed guards and the last fence, with a throng of maniacal inmates charging for it. The screaming and yelling grew to a loud roar. The wave hit the second gate and I knew we did not stand a chance. Suddenly I heard numerous gunshots coming from behind me. The guards were firing their weapons over us at the advancing throng. I heard the buzz of bullets going over my head and I hit the ground. Bullets ricocheted off the fencing and kicked up puffs of dirt on the ground. One prisoner, who was an instigator, fell wounded from a shot. He lay in the dirt screaming, holding his leg. The momentum of the charge had been broken and the crowd fell back. Guards quickly recovered the wounded prisoner. He was not seriously hurt. Rocks and dirt kicked up from the rifle bullet had hit his leg. He thought he was badly wounded, but only had bruises.

The charging inmates and the rifle shots passed my head had left me shaken. The lack of proper sleep and constant stress had also taken its toll. We re-grouped and the negotiators went back to work. By early afternoon, small groups of convicts peacefully surrendered and by sundown, all but three were in custody. The prison director asked that the dog handlers search the yard, filled with debris, clothing and blankets. Trapper quickly located one man hiding under a blanket and bit him on the arm. The other two, realizing it was futile to hide, quickly surrendered.

My duties as a dog handler included working with the Prince George Emergency Response Team (ERT). Many of the large detachments throughout the province had such teams, specially trained, equipped, and prepared to deal with situations involving armed people. This included barricaded persons, hostage takings, and heavily armed suspects. Select detachment personnel, constituted of these teams, which were available for callouts at all times. It was the responsibility of dog handlers to train with ERT, to familiarize themselves with the weapons and tactics of this unit. It also gave ERT members the opportunity to work closely with dog teams. Dog handlers could complement ERT on some of their tasks.

During the summer of 1983, the Quesnel detachment had several complaints about a man breaking into summer cabins along lakes west of town. Firearms, ammunition, food, clothing, and other essentials were stolen. People in the area noticed a stranger and some had talked to him on several occasions. He had an American accent, always wore military camouflage clothing, and, to most, appeared to be eccentric. He always carried a rifle and shotgun and he would not tell anybody where he was from. A recent bulletin circulated to RCMP detachments and other police forces referred to a man wanted by authorities in the United States. He was mentally unstable, armed, and dangerous. The Americans believed that the subject was somewhere in the interior of British Columbia.

The physical description in the bulletin matched the suspect in the Quesnel area break-ins. The detachment requested dog handler and ERT patrols of the area. Owen, a big, powerfully built ERT member, was happy to ride shotgun with me. We were making a patrol in my unmarked suburban along a remote logging road about 40 miles northeast of Quesnel. Each of us was armed with the ERT issue AR-15 .223 caliber, semi-automatic assault rifles, and 9 mm pistols. We wore camouflage uniforms and bulletproof vests.

As we slowly patrolled, Owen and I planned that if we encountered the suspect, we would back off and call for support. We rounded a curve in the road and ahead of us about 300 yards was the suspect, walking nonchalantly along the road. Upon hearing our approach, he turned, and stuck his thumb out for a ride. Owen let out a low whistle and exclaimed, "Holy shit, that's our man!" I was fixated on the man. The metallic noise of Owen locking and loading his AR-15 sent a chill up my spine. Both rifles were between us, with the barrels pointed at the floorboards.

We slowed a little, but did not want to stop for fear of alarming the subject. We could not see any weapons, but thought that he could have stashed one in the bush or under his clothing. Owen now had his rifle between his legs, with the barrel still pointed downwards. Since I was driving, I could not get to my rifle, but it was close by. We had to change our plan. At about 100 yards, we decided to take the man down. After bringing my vehicle to a stop in front of the hapless hitchhiker and exiting with the dog, I would run around the front of the truck and confront the man. Owen would stay seated, with the door unlatched and as soon as the truck stopped, would fling the door open and cover the suspect with his rifle. If the man made a move for a firearm, Owen was prepared to shoot him pointblank.

We pulled along side him and our plan went down like clockwork. As I flew out of the truck with Trapper, the suspect stood stone still, with mouth agape, as Owen pointed the business end of the rifle in his face and exclaimed, "Police, don't move!" I had Trapper by his collar, ready to release him. The dog barked, snarled, and surged ahead at the astounded man. Owen ordered the man face down on the ground and searched him, as Trapper and I covered Owen. The subject had a rather large, wicked looking knife concealed under his coat.

We handcuffed the compliant prisoner and placed him in our truck. Despite the rude introduction, he was friendly, talkative, and freely admitted to all the offences in the area. He cooperated by taking us to his camp about three miles from where we arrested him. The suspect was happy that we came along. He had become rather lonely and the novelty of being a "bushman" in the wilds of British Columbia had worn thin. His camp was inadequate for the conditions, with only an open lean-to. It was crammed full of stolen goods, including canned food, clothing, several more knives, a .357 caliber rifle, a pump shotgun, and a large array of ammunition. This was our lucky break. The Quesnel investigators quickly arranged to have the man extradited to the United States.

On a night shift, I responded as back up to a uniformed member named Greg, who was attending a noisy party complaint. Just prior to my arrival at the residential address, I overheard Greg radio the dispatcher, informing that he was at the scene. By the time I pulled up, I saw him at the front door of the crowded house. The windows were open and loud music blared out into the street. From the curb, I could see the house filled with boisterous, voluble people. Five or six partygoers were outside, at the corner of the house. All were openly swigging beer and one man let out an ear-splitting whistle upon seeing me. They all laughed and continued their rowdy banter.

I grew somewhat alarmed at seeing Greg suddenly walk into the party-house without someone to watch his back. I could clearly see that the partiers were all adults. It was not the usual teenage gathering. Leaving Trapper in my police vehicle, I sprinted to the door.

The entrance was still open by the time I arrived and saw Greg disappear into a group of men standing in the hallway off the living room. I got a bad feeling as I pushed my way passed some loudmouths. Most seemed quite brassy and one man made a vulgar comment as I went by. I ignored the remark, only wanting to get to the member, now surrounded in the narrow hallway.

I burst through and finally got beside Greg. I had worked with him on numerous occasions in the past. He was an even-tempered investigator with lots of experience, but that night Greg seemed hurried and oblivious of the situation I perceived was developing. These people were not happy to have us in the house. Greg told me over the din that the owner had invited him in, but then ran into the hallway when Greg tried to talk with him.

I became more uneasy as five or six men now had us trapped at the end of the hallway. They seemed to feed off each other as they became increasingly brash and offensive. One even threatened to assault Greg if we tried to shut the party down. The obstinate expressions on their faces showed that they were beyond listening to any of our suggestions to tone the party down. Most of these revelers appeared to be rather formidable, rough individuals and with the mixture of booze and bravado, were turning into an unpredictable bunch.

Now fully realizing the seriousness of the circumstances, Greg quickly radioed the dispatcher with his portable, requesting immediate back up. While he was on the radio, I tried to desperately reason with the increasingly combative men. Fists were starting to clench and they were stepping in closer. They tried to egg us on into fighting with them.

One younger fellow at the back of the group suddenly reached over the shoulder of a friend and took a swipe at my face. He missed as I quickly pulled back, staying tight against the wall. Reacting, I kicked the friend hard in the shins. The recipient of the toe of my hiking boot let out a scream of pain and instinctively moved back a step. This temporarily increased the distance, but the group pressed forward, again closing in on us. My assaulter became even more aggressive by swinging wildly at me, but continued to use his crippled friend as a shield.

Over the portables, Greg and I could hear other members responding to the dispatcher's request for more back up to our location. I made a good mental note of the chap that was intent on hitting me. I planned to arrest him when our back up arrived. It seemed to take forever for the "cavalry" to arrive. The situation was worsening by the moment, especially after I had booted the man in front of me. Greg was talking up a storm, desperately trying to get these men to be reasonable. I could easily discern the increasing anxiousness in his voice.

To our relief, other members finally appeared at the party house. Over a period of several minutes, the situation slowly started to defuse. The owner agreed to shut down the noise and people were encouraged to leave. Now that we were out of the hallway, I was looking for the man that tried to splatter my face across a wall. I could not find him and assumed he had left.

I went to my police vehicle and climbed in the front seat. Trapper was in the back of the vehicle, quietly taking in the events around us. My hands were shaking from the confrontation and I took a deep breath to calm myself.

The dog had a habit of silently sitting at the back of the truck until any unsuspecting individual got too close. At that point, the dog would explode against the windows, barking and snarling loudly. The effect was usually instantaneous by scaring the hell out of the person. Trapper seemed to find enjoyment in that practice.

Even if other members got too close or were getting in the vehicle at my request, he would bark and growl aggressively until they seated themselves. For the passenger of course, it was a very unsettling experience. It was Trapper's way of showing the world that the police truck was only good enough for the two of us. However, he showed leniency for children and usually only greeted them with a loud sniff on the ear.

I took notice of several partiers walking passed the passenger side of the truck. As I watched them noisily walk away, a loud bang on my driver's door made me jump. The man that I was looking for earlier was now standing at the door. He had kicked it to get my attention. With a leering grin, he motioned at me to roll down the window. As I did so, he mockingly said, "Hey you jerk. Why did you kick my friend? I outta pull you out of that truck and kick your ass." Surprisingly, Trapper remained quiet.

I suddenly had a change of plan. I really did not feel like going through the mound of paperwork involved in arresting this moron. Besides, the Watch Commander would probably release him before my shift ended anyways. Perhaps a little street justice was in order. I rolled the window all the way down. I could sense that Trapper had this man in his sights. I told the moron that I could not hear him and invited him to come closer and repeat what he said.

Not clueing in that I had a police dog in the truck and feeling safe with the fact that I had remained seated, the man confidently stepped up and placed both hands on the truck door. As he bent down to repeat his threat, I swiftly reached up, grabbed the front of his jacket and pulled his head and shoulders into the truck. On cue, Trapper leapt at the man in a burst of absolute fury. The growl started at the back of the truck and as he reached the man, it turned into a roaring snarl. The dog's teeth snapped loudly together within a millimeter of the man's right ear.

I had leaned downwards to allow the dog a clear path and even though I knew what was coming, it even frightened me. For the man that wanted to "kick my ass," it was obviously a terrifying occurrence. I was astounded at the amount of strength he suddenly displayed.

He pulled backwards, out of my grip with such force that it knocked the rear view mirror off the truck door. It flew high in the air and crashed on the pavement. With a piercing scream, the moron also flew through the air. He landed flat on his back. He continued to scream as he fought to get back on his feet.

As I quickly climbed out of the truck, Trapper was barking feverishly. I knew the dog was not finished yet, but it was all over. I told Trapper to stay and closed the door. The dog continued to bark from within the truck as I made for the man, who was still trying to get off the pavement.

I reached down, grabbed his jacket, and jerked him up on his feet. His lower jaw was trembling uncontrollably and he mumbled between quick, shallow breaths. His face was white and the wide eyes remained glued to the dog in the truck. He did not appear to hear me when I told him to move on and not bother me anymore.

I did not care about the mirror. I would just report it as damaged while I was in the house and, besides, it was a lot less paper work. I let go of the man and he scampered off into the darkness.

A woman that lived by herself in the north end of Prince George called the detachment late one evening. She frantically reported that steel ball bearings were coming through the windows of her house. I was one of the units that responded.

The house was in a semi-residential area and did not have streetlights. I arrived at the front of the house and saw a deep dark ditch along side the roadway. I could see the woman peering out her front window. Even from the roadway, I could see the terrorized expression on her drawn face.

Another member who arrived just before me had talked briefly with the complainant. Whoever was firing the ball bearings was doing so from the front of the house. I quickly called Trapper out of the vehicle. He was primed and anxious to work. I held him back to get the tracking harness and long line on him.

As the harness snapped in place, the dog charged down the steep, dark ditch. He was only about a lines length from me when I heard a muffled grunt. In the long grass, a male subject suddenly raised up into a sitting position. Trapper had bit the man on the left thigh. The man yelled out, "No more Mister! Call your dog off! I give up!"

I pulled the dog back and ordered the subject to get his hands up where I could see them or I would release the dog again. "No, no, no!" he repeated and willingly held his hands up for me to see. He wore large horn rimmed glasses that looked too big for his pinched up face. I instructed the man to get onto the road and stand in front of the police vehicle and to keep his hands up.

The other member on scene ran up to assist me. He searched the suspect and discovered a large slingshot in his back pocket. In a small backpack, the man was wearing, the member found a large number of ball bearings, similar to what went through the woman's windows.

Trapper had delivered a nasty puncture wound to the miscreant's thigh. The member handcuffed the suspect and placed him in his police car. A computer check of the man's name revealed an extensive criminal record including a conviction for animal cruelty.

The complainant quickly identified the suspect as the neighborhood "weirdo." She had a brief confrontation with him a week previously and he admitted that he was only paying her back for making him look bad.

The member booked the suspect at the detachment cells after he refused treatment for the dog bite. I could not help but think that Trapper had provided a bit of pay back for the animal cruelty case.

A call regarding an armed robbery sent several units, including Trapper and me to a small "Ma and Pop" type convenience store in Prince George. The suspect, armed with a full-length shotgun, relieved the terrified elderly owners of a considerable amount of cash. They last saw the bandit running passed the front window of the store. He had also threatened to murder the couple if they reported the incident.

Upon arriving, I harnessed Trapper and cast him at the front of the store. The dog's nose went down immediately as he picked up a fresh scent going westbound through a bush area behind the scene.

We covered only about 200 yards when Trapper stopped dead. He located a large black sport equipment bag hidden in the grass and brush. The dog pulled it out by the handgrip.

Inside the bag, I discovered a loaded but disassembled shotgun. Also in the bag was a large amount of cash in small bills and a black leather wallet. In the black wallet was a picture driver's license. The physical description on the license matched that of the suspect.

I continued for about another 2-300 yards and we eventually lost it on pavement. All our efforts to relocate the track were negative, but we had recovered a considerable amount of evidence, including the stolen money. The man identified on the driver's license did not live far from where the dog lost the track.

Investigators went to the suspect's residence. When confronted with the evidence that the dog found the man admitted to the offence.

Trapper and I were becoming more experienced and adept with the constant onslaught of police work. On another occasion, work called us out from home on a Sunday evening regarding another armed robbery. It was another convenience store and the lone culprit made off with a considerable amount of cash.

We pulled up in an alleyway near the scene. The investigator met me to give me a quick briefing. Since time was of the essence, I called Trapper out of the truck to harness him as the member spoke to me.

Trapper popped out of the truck and suddenly bee-lined it down the gravel alleyway. I left the member standing and took off after the dog with the harness and line in hand. Trapper went a block south then turned left into an unfenced back yard. I was running at full speed, trying to keep up. We went through the yard and Trapper suddenly scaled a wooden fence of the neighboring yard. All I saw was his tail as he leapt over the fence. As I followed over the fence, I could see the dog making a large circle in the yard. Upon landing in the yard, I looked left and saw a man sitting on the ground, with his back to the fence. In the beam of my flashlight, he was still breathing heavily and his eyes were wide with excitement.

The dog did not see the subject, but was homing in on the scent of the track. I got to the man before the dog and as I did so, the chap quickly reached inside his half-open jacket. Fearing he was reaching for the handgun that he allegedly used in his crime, I had time only to react by kicking his arm.

The force of the kick did not necessarily hurt the man, but suddenly the air filled with money, all in small denominations. One, two, five, and ten dollar bills floated to the ground. The suspect later told me that he knew it was over and was only reaching into his jacket to hand me the money he stole. He did not have a firearm. During the offence, he only told the victim that he had a gun inside his jacket.

A high-speed chase with a stolen car through city streets one cold winter's night ended and the two male occupants escaped on foot. Trapper and I attended and located a scent from the vehicle. Despite the cold, Trapper was adamantly tracking. After about five blocks, we were proceeding down a laneway and came to the "T" intersection of a road.

Trapper crossed the road and headed for the ditch. Road clearing crews had piled the snow from the roads into the ditches and as Trapper was going over the snow pile, two men rose up out of the ditch. It was so sudden that it surprised both us.

Trapper was immediately disadvantaged when one man placed his hands on the dog's shoulders and pushed him down. Fearing that the suspect was then going to kick the dog in the ribcage, I reacted with a sweeping blow across the man's chest.

I was holding an RCMP issue yellow plastic flashlight when I struck the man. These flashlights were notoriously cheap and I was only using it since I had temporarily misplaced my usual, more reliable flashlight. The force of the impact had little effect on the man except to surprise and stun him. The flashlight exploded into numerous pieces.

This gave Trapper time to react and get out of the precarious position. He reached up and bit the sleeve of the suspect's large down-filled winter jacket. The air suddenly filled with white goose down. It appeared that it had started to snow again. Both suspects surrendered peacefully.

It was a quiet Sunday evening shift in Prince George. Trapper and I were driving home for the night. As we crossed the bridge over the Netchako River, I glanced over to my left and noticed the old brewery along the river. It was not in production at this time of night, but the breeze from the west still brought the strong smell of hops wafting over the highway and bridge.

The police radio had been unusually quiet most of the evening, when it suddenly crackled to life with the voice of the Prince George dispatcher. She announced a "10-72" at the brewery and asked a car to respond. In police terms, a "10-72" was an intruder alarm. I grabbed the radio mike and informed the dispatcher that I was close to the scene. I overheard another car tell the dispatcher that he would attend as well. As I maneuvered my truck onto the underpass that would take me directly to the brewery, the dispatcher advised me that the brewery manager was on the scene. He was the person who phoned in the complaint and would meet me at the front office when I arrived.

Within a minute, my vehicle slid to a stop at the front door. An older, rotund man emerged from the building with a large red flashlight in his hand. His eyes were wide and he walked quickly despite a pronounced limp. Huffing and puffing, he met me at the front of my police vehicle. Between breaths he said, "Damn good of you to get here so fast. I was at the office here tonight, trying to catch up on some paper work, when I hears noises in the back! Kinda scared the shit out of me and you know we have break-ins here from time to time." That was old news to me since I had attended a few break-ins at the brewery in the past. The brewery was a target for those in the community that liked free beer, even if it meant stealing it.

My back up had not arrived, but I knew he was close. Trapper recognized the brewery from past visits and barked anxiously in the truck. I went to the truck, called him out and he ran excitedly to the office door. He waited impatiently for me to catch up. I grasped his choke chain as the manager put the key in the big metal door and heaved it open. The lights were on in the front and the overpowering smell of brewing hops hit me like a wall. I could hear the low hum of the big lights on the ceiling as we entered. Two men were standing within 30 feet of us, each holding four cases of beer. Their mouths dropped open in complete astonishment. They looked like deer caught in the headlights of a truck. I shouted, "Police, don't move!" Both men dropped all the beer on the concrete floor. With the breaking of glass, Trapper strained hard and barked furiously. I yelled again, "Stop or I'll let the dog go!" Both men paid no heed as they ran into a darkened room behind them.

I released Trapper. His claws scratched along the smooth flooring as he quickly gained speed in pursuit of the suspects. As I was running, I saw the dog disappear into the darkened room where the suspects had entered. Everything was silent as I entered the room and clicked on my flashlight. The dog was circling menacingly around one man, who stood, stone still, with his eyes closed tight. Trapper jumped up and pawed at the man, enticing him to move, but the man just gritted his teeth and remained statue-like. The dog had likely found the man standing still and since there was no movement, did not bite him. My gait-impaired manager was just behind me, desperately trying to keep up. My back up entered the building and I called him to our location. He entered and pushed the rigid suspect to the floor.

Before I could say anything, Trapper bolted out of the room going deeper into the darkened part of the building in pursuit of the second man. I heard a scream behind large vats of beer, in the eerie half-lit structure. When I got to the second suspect, he was laying face down on the cold floor, with his face buried in his folded arms. Trapper circled the prone body. I noticed that the man was missing one entire sleeve from his jacket. Trapper had the sleeve in his mouth. I praised the dog as he shook the sleeve proudly and pranced around the suspect as if it was a victory dance. The manager arrived in time to see Trapper's display and between sucking in deep breaths, laughed aloud. I handcuffed my prisoner and ordered him not to move.

I wanted to check on my back up and ensure he was not having any difficulties with the first man. I left Trapper sitting, watching the second man as I ran back. The manager mentioned that he would stay with the dog. The back up had his prisoner handcuffed and was busily escorting him out of the building. I quickly returned to Trapper and the manager. Nothing had changed except for the manager standing over the prone prisoner, with the large, heavy flashlight poised high over the head. It was a dramatic pose and I guessed the manager intended to give the prisoner a good whack if he moved. I helped the suspect to his feet and we all walked outside to the police vehicles. The back up member and I spent a few minutes exchanging information for our reports, while both suspects sat quietly and gloomily in the back of the police car. The dog and I had spoiled their evening.

As I turned to walk Trapper back to my vehicle, I saw that the back door was wide open and to my disbelief, the manager was sliding cases of beer into my truck. As the manager started to limp back to the building for more beer, I called out to him to stop. His face was red with exertion, but he had a wide grin. "You and your dog made my day! In fact, it made my entire year! That was incredible and I gotta do something to show my gratitude!" As diplomatically as possible, I explained to my new friend that I could not accept the beer, even though I thought it was a wonderful gesture. He gave me a perplexed look and replied, "Hell, I gotta do something!" I suggested a quick note or a phone call to the officer in charge of the detachment would do me a lot of good. The manager's face brightened with a beaming smile. "You got it. By the holy hell, you got it!" He thanked me profusely and shook my hand. I helped him unload the beer before leaving for the night.

Early the next morning, I walked in the detachment to check for paperwork in preparation for my dayshift. The staff sergeant in charge of administration at the detachment and the right hand man to the officer in charge saw me and called me to his office. He was waving a paper in his hand and said, "Kuich, get over here, I got a letter for you!" As I walked into his office, he plastered the paper onto my chest. Staff continued, "The manager of the brewery was in here at seven o'clock this morning with this. He kept going on and on about how great you and your dog were last night." I glanced at the letter, typed on brewery letterhead. Before I could say anything, Staff whispered, "The Old Man already saw it and passes on a 'job well done'. A copy is already on your personnel file. Now get to work, before your head swells up so much that you can't get out the door." I tucked the letter into a file folder I was carrying and went happily to work.

1992, Shuswap Lake, in the south central part of BC.

Niki, 2 ½ years old, visiting family on time off. We were temporarily stationed in Kamloops at the time.

Chapter 6
Vernon Detachment

Trapper and I continued to work at Prince George and all the satellite detachments until the fall of 1984. Trapper had been working four years, was in excellent health, and enjoyed working. I however noticed some white hair on his chin, which indicated he was starting to age. The Staffing and Personnel section of the RCMP decided to transfer us to Vernon detachment. We arrived in mid-October 1984 and started work immediately. At that time, the detachment had about 60 members serving the small city of about 35,000 people. Vernon is nestled in the northern part of the Okanagan Valley, at the northern tip of Okanagan Lake. The valley is in the south-central part of the province of British Columbia. The community has a reputation for orchards, fine wines, tourism, hot summer weather, and sunny beaches. I enjoyed the challenges of Prince George, but was now looking forward to living and working in Vernon. I was one of two dog handlers at Vernon and would be responsible for providing support to the smaller satellite detachments of Lumby, Armstrong, Enderby, Falkland, Salmon Arm, Sicamous, and Revelstoke. It did not take long to get into a busy work schedule.

On the last day of October 1984, I was on duty in Vernon, when the Revelstoke RCMP detachment called for my assistance. A prisoner had escaped on foot while sheriffs were escorting him to the courthouse. Driving time to Revelstoke from Vernon is about two hours and just before my arrival, members recaptured the escapee. Instead of returning to Vernon, I decided to stay in town that night and work an evening shift. It was Halloween and I thought the members would appreciate extra help. Winter had arrived early in Revelstoke, which is situated along the Trans-Canada Highway in the Rocky Mountains. Snow was already on the ground and the temperature dropped dramatically with the approaching darkness. I made a few telephone calls at the detachment and finished some overdue paperwork. Afterwards, I took Trapper for exercise at the back of the detachment. The embankment of the Canadian Pacific Railway tracks was about 75 yards from the back of the police office.

After a few minutes, we returned to the front of the building and got in my police vehicle. We pulled out of the driveway and as we started down the street, I heard a tremendous explosion, similar to a loud clap of thunder. It was so intense that it felt like the back of my truck had lifted off the ground. I looked back to see a large black cloud rising high in the air behind the detachment.

I quickly returned and ran to the back of the building. The building did not appear damaged except for some metal flashing blown off the cinder block wall. I was astounded to see a hole about six feet in diameter and about eight inches deep in the frozen ground, exactly where I was standing only two minutes earlier.

The detachment's civilian night guard poked his head out the back door. He was wide-eyed with astonishment. At the time of the explosion, he was sitting in a chair, leaning against the back wall of the detachment. The force of the blast knocked him out of the chair. He was guarding the re-captured prisoner and nobody else was at the detachment. Investigators told me later that the local train crews often used dynamite in their everyday work and at times explosive charges went missing. I harnessed Trapper and he quickly located a fresh scent on the railway tracks, westbound from the detachment. After about 200 yards, the scent turned north, down the embankment to the paved parking lot of a strip mall. The track ended and I circled Trapper several times, but could not re-locate it. I was in a state of absolute shock, but felt fortunate with the timing of the event.

Investigators estimated that from the size of the hole, the suspect(s) threw a bundle containing at least four sticks of dynamite at the detachment. The suspect(s) stood on the tracks to hurl the explosives, then ran west. A lengthy investigation did not identify any suspects.

On a cold winter's day in January 1985, members at Lumby detachment called. A homicide occurred in British Columbia's lower mainland and investigators had reason to believe that the male suspect was hiding in Lumby. The members in Lumby asked me to search a location in town. I agreed, but in turn, asked an ERT member to assist me. Kelowna detachment, 40 miles to the south of Vernon, had an ERT and some of its members worked at different detachments in the Okanagan Valley. On that particular day, an ERT member named Bud was on duty in Armstrong. All ERT members work regular duties and are always available to assist. Bud anxiously accepted my request and met me at the Vernon detachment. He had all the necessary equipment and weapons with him. We headed east for the 15-minute drive to Lumby.

At Lumby detachment, the two members on duty informed Bud and I that there were now two locations to search. We decided to search both places simultaneously. The two Lumby members went to one, while Bud and I, with the dog, checked the second location. It was a mobile home on the outskirts of town. We were about a block away from the mobile home, when we saw an SUV carrying six men, pull out of the driveway, and come towards us. Just before we met the vehicle, I activated the emergency equipment on my unmarked suburban and drove in front of the oncoming SUV. I had blocked the road and the SUV stopped. Bud and I exited the police vehicle with our AR-15's at the ready. I had Trapper on leash, beside me.

Bud ordered all the people out of the SUV, one at a time, starting with the driver. As people emerged, Bud made them lay face down on the roadway, with arms extended. We were not about to take any chances with a murder suspect. Trapper was whining with anticipation and clawing at the ice to get closer to the six men. Trapper and I covered Bud as he methodically searched each man on the icy ground. Each had identification and we were satisfied that the suspect was not amongst the six men. Bud determined that the driver of the truck was the owner of the mobile home and he gave permission for us to search it.

Trapper and I searched the yard and under the mobile home. I then decided not to take the dog inside the mobile home. I was confident that Bud and I could adequately search the interior of the small dwelling. We moved systematically from front to back, and stopped in the bathroom. The room only contained a tiny vanity with a sink, toilet, and bathtub. Bud sat on the vanity while we discussed other areas we could search. After a few minutes, we left the mobile home to meet with the detachment members.

After spending two hours checking other locations around town, we begrudgingly drove back to Vernon. At Vernon, we overheard an RCMP highway patrol member on the radio, informing dispatch that he had the murder suspect in custody. The member later related that while he was driving down the highway between Vernon and Lumby, he saw a man fitting the murderer's description, walking along the railway tracks that intersected the road. The suspect told the member that while Bud and I were in the bathroom of the mobile home, he was hiding, doubled up in the vanity. He related the conversation Bud and I had in the bathroom almost verbatim. If I had taken Trapper into the mobile home, he would have located the suspect by scent within seconds. It was poor judgment or complacency on my part that bothered me for years afterward.

In mid-February 1985, Trapper and I responded to a callout in Salmon Arm, which was about a half hour drive from Vernon. A lone, male suspect held up a downtown gas station with a sawed-off shotgun and ran southbound from the scene. The suspect obtained a considerable amount of cash from the robbery. By the time I attended, I knew the track might be too old, but decided to try. There was snow on the ground and it was below freezing. To my pleasant surprise, Trapper did locate scent and followed it southbound down an alleyway and across a park to a church. From the church, it continued south along a street. He lost it near 4th Street and 2nd Avenue, SW.

Salmon Arm members were patrolling the area and I radioed the lead investigator, Corporal Barker, to advise him of the area where Trapper lost the track. We re-grouped at the detachment and I could see Barker was deep in thought. He was an outspoken man and a hard worker. He conferred with the other members and I overheard him say, "You know, I can't help but think of a guy that lives in that small apartment block close to where the dog man lost the track. He matches the description and he wouldn't be above pulling a stunt like this." Another member replied with the name of one local character. Barker exclaimed, "That's the guy I'm thinking of! The description matches and he's capable of doing this. It's a long shot, but let's go for a visit."

We all clamored out to our cars and drove to the apartment block in question. I left Trapper in the vehicle while I went with the members to the apartment door. Barker's suspect was at the residence along with two other males and a female. Barker engaged the suspect in an amiable conversation outside and after a few minutes, the man agreed to allow us into the apartment to conduct a cursory search.

I and another member stayed in the kitchen with two of the male residents. A member was talking to the female in the dining room, while Barker and a third member kept talking to the suspect. Barker continued his friendly banter with the man. None of the residents seemed nervous or upset. Everybody was cooperative and cordial. The member in the kitchen with me opened the cupboard door under the sink and glanced inside. Not seeing anything, he started to close the door. However, from my vantage point across the kitchen, I had a more direct view into the open cupboard. I saw the sawed-off stock of a shotgun, jammed up behind the sink. I yelled a warning to the members as I drew my revolver. My greatest fear was that somebody might have easy access to the rest of the weapon. We ordered all the residents into the kitchen and searched them. The suspect lost all the color in his face. His calm, cool demeanor suddenly disappeared. Barker now had a wide grin on his face. He knew he had the man in a corner and started to press him further. With a gray face, the man admitted to the robbery. We recovered the stolen cash in the apartment along with the clothing the suspect wore during the offence.

I took Trapper to the back alley of the apartment block and he quickly located a box and packaging for the shotgun that was stuffed under a dumpster. The suspect had just purchased the shotgun a day before the robbery. After further conversations, the female led Barker to a shed in the same alley, where he located the rest of the weapon inside.

Part of my duties as a dog handler was making presentations to the public about police dogs. We referred to this as "PR" or public relations. I talked to schools, colleges, service groups and other community organizations. Most commonly, I attended elementary schools, giving a short lecture and a demonstration. For me, these appearances were enjoyable and all my dogs took particular pleasure in hamming it up for the appreciative crowds.

During a presentation to a service group, I had come in early and hid some soft drugs under a chair that an audience member would sit on and in a few other locations in the room. After the group gathered, I gave my short lecture, followed by a demonstration with Trapper. A man, who was obviously a professional in the community, unknowingly sat in the bait chair. The audience was enthusiastically watching the dog work. I purposely kept the dog out of the search area. After a few minutes of unsuccessful searching, the group was becoming a bit perplexed and anxious.

I then brought the dog close to the man in the bait chair. Trapper gave a strong indication and pushed his nose hard between the man's knees, trying to get to the source of the drug scent. The man's mouth dropped open and his face turned white as I announced that the dog found drugs on my unsuspecting participant. The dog did his sit confirmation as I tossed the ball to him for his reward. The man was now standing, professing that he did not use drugs. I quickly explained what I had done earlier and the crowd took a good deal of pleasure in the man's dramatics. He swiftly recovered from the ordeal and laughed at his predicament. Trapper found the rest of the drugs to the amazement of the people and we concluded with questions and answers.

The young students at schools were the most gratifying for me. They were always exuberant and filled with loud anticipation.

One trick that I had trained all my dogs to do was "speak." It took a little time to accomplish this. I simply started by repeating the word "speak," using a lot of animation. Of course, the dog did not know what I meant, but as soon as he whined or barked, I immediately praised him. Soon the dog realized what I wanted when I asked him to "speak." While saying, "speak," I always opened and closed my hand, touching my forefinger on the thumb. After a little practice, the dog barked when he saw me only using the hand signal. With consistent repetition, I refined the hand signal to a discreet tap of a finger along my pant leg or arm. The dog would attentively watch for the signal during the presentations. Before bringing the dog in to meet the kids, I always gave them some information about my dog, including his age. When the dog was in front of the young crowd, I would then ask the dog how old he was. With my subtle signals, the dog barked once with each tap and I stopped at the required number. I do not recall ever having a child notice the trick and I know some teachers were also baffled. On other occasions, before I brought the dog in, I sometimes gave the dog's ball to a student. I instructed the child to keep the ball hidden so the dog had to use his nose to find it. When the dog entered, I simply said, "Find your ball!" He then ran through the squealing throng of kids sniffing out his ball. Teachers and children alike were always thrilled with the effortless exercise.

Regarding the "speak" exercise, I recall a fellow dog handler explain to me how he solved a crime. He and his dog tracked an individual from the scene of a break-in. The track went for a considerable distance through urban environments; however, they lost the scent and could not re-locate it. About a half hour later, patrolling members located a man walking through a park. It was late at night and he was the only person on foot in the area. He had been sweating from physical exertion and he acted suspiciously. However, there was no physical evidence to link him to the break-in, or to the dog handler tracking him. The handler had already returned to his vehicle, but seized on a novel idea and asked the members to hold the man until he arrived.

The man was slightly puzzled when the handler placed the police dog in a sitting position about 15 feet in front of him. The handler had a brief conversation with the man, explaining that the man was a suspect in a break-in and wanted to confirm, one way or the other, if his dog had been tracking him. With that, the handler stood beside the man and turned to his stationary dog. Without the suspect realizing it, the handler extended his arm behind the suspect and asked his dog, "Is this the guy you were tracking, Boy?" As soon as he asked the question, the handler quickly opened and closed the hand of his extended arm, in plain view of the dog. The obedient canine barked profusely in response to the question. With that, the suspect's shoulders drooped and he replied, "Yeah, OK, I did it. Jeez, those dogs are so damn smart!"

Since circumstances always changed, I sometimes did not use the dog when responding to calls. Suspects might peacefully surrender or not attempt to escape from a crime scene. At times, all that was required was the presence of the dog, or the psychological value of having a trained dog on hand that might defuse a situation.

In late June 1985, I had an experience where I did not have the chance to use the dog; however, his presence was of special psychological value only to me. Trapper and I were working in Vernon, when a call came to assist members from the Armstrong and Enderby detachments. These small communities are approximately ten and 14 miles north of Vernon, respectively.

Members from both detachments responded to a rural area near Enderby concerning a drunken man walking around the neighborhood, indiscriminately firing a high-powered rifle. It took me about 20 minutes to drive to the area and join the four members on a gravel roadway, about 300 yards from the suspect's house. The members had been there for about 40 minutes and nothing had occurred since they arrived and the locale was again quiet. It was a cloudy, dark night, but I could still see the outline of the shooter's house, across an open field. No lights were on in the house and the members reckoned the man had passed out. He did not have a telephone and the only way to make contact with him was to approach the house. We figured that the best course of action would be to wait until daybreak. At least then, we would be able to see properly and it would be easier to deal with the character, when he was in the foggy stupor of a bad hangover. The man had a history of being violent and unpredictable, so we did not want to take any chances.

Three of the members decided to drive further along the road and take up new positions, while the remaining member and I stayed where we were. Keeping the headlights off on their patrol cars, they slowly rolled away. Suddenly I saw a bright flash at the suspect's house and instantaneously heard a loud buzzing sound go passed my left ear. A fraction of a second later, I heard the distinctive, loud crack of a high-powered rifle.

The two of us had probably not moved so fast in our entire lives. We dove, headfirst into the shallow ditch behind us. There were a couple inches of water in the ditch and I felt the cold, dank water soak the front of my shirt and pants. The member with me was a French Canadian and he swore an oath, in French and English. For some unknown reason, I started to laugh nervously at my friend's expletives. My portable radio was crackling from the animated voices of the other three members. They continued making repeated attempts to contact us. Trapper was barking excitedly in the truck, parked on the road in front of me. He always responded aggressively to gunfire. I radioed the others and advised them we were fine and to hold their new positions. It was quiet again except for Trapper whining anxiously in the truck.

I keyed the repeater on my portable radio to raise the dispatcher at Vernon. I updated our situation and made an urgent request for the ERT in Kelowna. At that time, Kelowna was a city of approximately 70,000 people, situated in the center of the Okanagan Valley, 35 miles south of Vernon. It would take at least two hours to muster the team members and drive to our location. Some of the members lived and worked at other towns in the valley and I appreciated the time lag.

I had to get to my dog, firstly for his safety, since he was in the direct line of fire and to have him with me in case some other event occurred. I crawled out of the ditch, onto the roadway and crept to the truck. I pulled myself up onto the passenger side, which was furthest from the suspect's house and opened the back door. I had the interior lights disconnected a few months before, to prevent the illumination of the interior when the doors opened at night. On this particular night, I was very pleased with the added safety feature. The dog was at the door and ready. I spoke to him in a soothing voice to keep him calm and quiet, as I gathered my shotgun, tracking harness and flashlight. With Trapper beside me, I darted back to the relative safety of the ditch. I radioed the others to let them know that I was going to circle wide and take up a position on high ground, behind the suspect's house. We all agreed to spread out, contain the area as best as we could and wait quietly for ERT to arrive. It took some time for me to get into my vantage point. I had thick, dark bush, to conceal the dog and me. We settled down for a long wait.

The house remained totally silent and dark. My eyes were accustomed to the dark and I would be able to make out shapes, if there was any movement. My biggest concern was that the suspect could be wandering around and might attempt an ambush. He knew that we were in the area. I tried to minimize all my movements and kept quiet. Some mosquitoes found our location and antagonized both of us. I had the radio turned as low as possible to maintain contact with the others. Dispatch called periodically to check on our status. I was depending on Trapper's acute senses to alert me, in case the shooter was moving around. It was reassuring to have my canine friend at my side.

While waiting, I thought back to a well-mannered, friendly man named Fred, who was the butcher at the store in my hometown. He always had a big smile to go along with his pleasant disposition. Fred was an older member of the small farming community, but that did not slow his enthusiasm, quick wit, and hard-work ethic. Fred was also a veteran of the Great War and had served as a machine gunner in the hellish trenches of France. Not unlike many Canadian soldiers, he liked souvenirs and folks sometimes talked about the German army helmets, that adorned his fireplace. Fred always attended the annual Remembrance Day gatherings at the local legion. To me, he seemed rather stoic during these ceremonies and unusually reserved.

On one particular occasion, Fred told me about some of his experiences on the Western Front. It was unsolicited on my part and I was awestruck that he would share his vivid memories to me. At one point in his oration, he said, "You never hear the one that gets you!" He explained that, in other words, the victim of a gunshot never hears the report of the weapon that kills him. He is already dead by the time the sound gets to him. At the time, I did not understand the theory, but now realized that Fred's analogy was so true.

Another excruciatingly slow hour passed by. My clothes were still wet from the ditch and I shivered uncontrollably. I was thinking of ERT's progress, when the dog turned his head sharply to the left and his ears perked up. He was looking into the thick bush and I started to feel uncomfortable, wondering if the suspect was prowling about. I was looking hard into the shadows but could not see anything. I nearly jumped out of my skin when I heard, "Pssst!" There was a slight movement low to the ground and I saw the faint outline of a darkened face. The prone figure slowly crawled towards me. He smiled and waved at me. I recognized him as one of the ERT members, dressed in camouflage pants and smock. He paused to speak into his radio headset and in muffled tones, informed his other team members that he had made contact with me. He crawled closer to Trapper and me so that we could have a conversation. Four more ERT members were close by and they would join us shortly. At least six others were at strategic points around the suspect's darkened house.

As the other four appeared, they quickly briefed me on their plan. It was simple. All five members were prepared to do a "hard entry" at the back door. In other words, one way or another, the back door would come down and they would enter to arrest the suspect. Their plan included Trapper and me. We would follow them as they entered and be nearby, if required. At least, I would have an active role in the arrest. With precision and stealth, the five men cautiously approached the building. They gathered at the back door, kicked it wide open and rapidly entered. As Trapper and I followed up, I heard a blood-curdling scream pierce the night air and shouts from the ERT members.

The suspect was asleep in bed when ERT entered. It must have been a terrifying experience for the man to wake up to five big, burly men, with blackened faces, wearing camouflage uniforms and all armed to the teeth. They grabbed his arms and threw him face down onto the floor. Trapper was barking and filled with excitement, however it was all over. An ERT member kneeled on the man's back and placed plastic flex cuffs on his wrists. I took some consolation at seeing the prisoner's wide-eyed, petrified face in the ghostly flickering of the ERT flashlights. He must have felt certain that he was going to die. One member grabbed the man's shoulder and pulled him upwards. Looking into his face, he asked him where the rifle was. I do not believe the suspect even comprehended the question. He just stared back, blubbering and crying, with spittle dripping off his pointy chin. The member glanced at me, rolled his eyes, and shook his head. A quick cursory search of the house revealed a recently fired, high-powered hunting rifle, stashed in the attic. The detachment members took custody of the man along with the weapon and left the scene. The ERT members all gathered and swiftly prepared to depart as well.

Afterwards, I took the time to search the area around the house in the event the suspect had dropped or stashed another rifle. Night was relinquishing its hold and daybreak was pending. Everything was peaceful and tranquil as birds happily chirped in the trees, preparing for their morning. In a state of exhaustion, I dropped down onto a large log. I called the dog close to me and we sat quietly for a while, taking in the beautiful start to a new day.

Being a dog handler was never routine in the sense of boring or mindless; however, Trapper was working well and we enjoyed an excellent daily routine of work, training and playtime. During off-duty time in the summer, I would often take the dog for long runs of two or three hours, up and down the abandoned logging roads on Vernon Mountain. The mountain was just east of Vernon and a quick drive from the city. At the higher elevations, it was cooler and a pleasant escape from the warm valley. During the winter months, with snowshoes and a pack, I would take Trapper to the same area and hike for hours. Both of us enjoyed the wilderness and it was an escape from job stresses.

Most of our work was at night, responding to alarms, break-ins in progress, thefts, robberies, disturbances, noisy parties, and acting as back up to the detachment members on complaints. We were locating evidence and suspects on a frequent basis and some cases we solved almost effortlessly. On one of my few day shifts, I assisted the detachment drug squad with a search of a residence. As I was walking the dog from my truck to the house, he stopped and indicated at the back of the suspect's car, parked in the driveway. In the trunk was kilogram of marihuana.

At the scene of a single vehicle accident, the driver had fled on foot. As I arrived with Trapper, I heard a voice call out in the bush area near the accident scene. The driver unexpectedly emerged and surrendered to the investigator. He had been watching the events unfold from his vantage point but when he saw, "those two police dogs, I thought I better come out!" When the investigator heard that comment, he had the man submit to a breathalyzer test, which he failed miserably.

During a night shift, investigators called me to search the back yard of a residence. The male suspect threw a .22 caliber pistol into the yard during a neighborhood dispute that had escalated into an attempted murder. The culprit was enraged at his neighbor and fired the weapon, narrowly missing the intended victim. Five members at the scene were unable to locate the firearm in the overgrown grass. When I attended, I placed Trapper in a down position in the yard while one investigator briefed me. As the member spoke, I saw the dog, still in his down position, stuff his nose into the tall grass. I cut the conversation short and walked to the dog. Trapper reached into the grass and picked the missing handgun up in his mouth. As I got to him, he stood up and met me, proudly wagging his tail.

The Armstrong detachment requested my assistance late one afternoon. A shooting had occurred more than a year previously, just north of the town. Investigators never located the .22 caliber rifle used in the offence. New information had now surfaced. The suspect had tossed the gun into a large hay field, about a half mile from the scene, immediately after the offence. Nobody was injured, but the member still wanted to proceed with charges and needed the evidence.

When the member and I attended the location, it was now a large fallow, farm field. It was a real long shot, but I agreed to go through the motions. As Trapper leapt out of the police truck, he ran directly into the field. He only went about 20 yards and put his head down to the ground to smell what I thought was a stick protruding about ten inches from the soft earth. The dog glanced back at me and did not move away from the object. As I got closer, I realized what I had thought was a stick, was, in fact, the rusted barrel of a .22 caliber rifle. The member with me witnessed the event and just stood with an incredulous look on his face. I pulled the rifle out of the ground. Heavy farm implements had chewed the stock off the rifle; however, despite some rust it was still intact. There was absolutely no human scent left on the weapon and, if there were any other scents on it such as gunpowder or oil, it would have been very minute. The environment would have surely assimilated most of those smells. It was probably just good luck that the dog took the time to smell the object.

Other files were not so easy or safe. During closing time at a downtown bar in Vernon, several patrons were milling around in front, when a sudden shotgun blast, wounded one man. Others saw the shooter standing by the railway tracks across the street before disappearing into the darkness. They described the suspect as short and thin, wearing a long coat that went passed his knees. The railway tracks intersected the street where the shooting occurred. I attended a few minutes later and Trapper picked up a scent going northwest along the tracks, leading out of the downtown area.

Using my portable radio, I informed all the patrol cars of the direction we were traveling. Two members working together in the same patrol car had the forethought to park about six blocks north of my location on another street that intersected the tracks. They parked the car behind shrubbery and within a minute, observed the suspect approaching their position. Both members were big, strong men, quite capable of looking after themselves. They stepped out of the police car and confronted the winded man. He was surprised and reached under his long coat. One member, with lightening speed, gripped the man's neck in a vice-like chokehold. The man immediately lost consciousness and crumpled to the ground, with the shotgun clattering onto the tracks. Trapper and I arrived just as the members were handcuffing their prisoner. Apparently, the shooting was not random. The suspect later claimed that he only intended to scare the man he shot because of a small drug debt.

One evening, a hit and run accident occurred. When the suspects' car drove away, the victim pursued the vehicle. After a short chase, the culprit stopped and fled on foot. The victim exited his vehicle and chased the man. I had a very capable auxiliary constable with me that night. We arrived at the scene and Trapper quickly picked up the scent of both men. With the auxiliary as my back up, we tracked the two men for about six blocks. Eventually, we came across two men fighting in a field. I yelled at the men to stand still. Both immediately complied.

As we got closer, one bolted, but the other man grabbed and held him. I placed Trapper in a down position and intervened to determine who the suspect was. He was a big, well-built man, about 27 years old and I could smell liquor on his breath. I grasped his jacket to turn him around to search him. He started to turn, then suddenly whirled about to hit me. I saw the haymaker coming and ducked, but in doing so, slipped on ice and fell to the ground. Before the auxiliary could react, Trapper hit the suspect full force with his body, biting the man on the right side of his rib cage. He fell to the ground with the dog on him.

The man stopped fighting and I took control of Trapper. With the help of the auxiliary, I handcuffed the culprit and stood him up. We all started to walk back to the scene, when the prisoner, without provocation, turned and tried to kick the dog. Trapper deftly jumped out of harm's way and I kicked the suspect's legs out from under him. He crashed to the ground, flat on his back. My prisoner said he finally had enough and promised to cooperate. He also failed the breathalyzer test.

One summer's evening a murder occurred in Salmon Arm. The suspect was on foot. During my high-speed drive from Vernon, the members advised they now had the suspect in custody, but I continued to the scene. At a house in the northeast part of the city, Trapper searched a yard and found a small caliber handgun hidden in tall grass. The dog then picked up a track in the yard. We followed the scent eastbound along the shoreline of a lake for a few blocks. It then turned south, crossed a street and ended in another yard. The investigators told me they found the suspect standing in that yard, prior to my arrival. This evidence helped tie the suspect to the handgun and the scene.

The provincial sheriffs were escorting a male prisoner to court on a hot summer's day in Vernon. As they descended the stairs into the basement of the building, the prisoner, Joe Smith, lashed out at the sheriff closest to him. The biggest mistake in this case, was that the prisoner had his hands cuffed in front of him, so the cuffs were essentially weapons. The victim of the assault had lacerations to his head and face. Smith struck the other sheriff that tried to stop him and ran down an alleyway. Smith had an extensive criminal record with many past dealings with the police.

Over the next two hours, the detachment was flooded with calls from people reporting sightings of the handcuffed escapee. I attempted to locate the suspect repeatedly, but was becoming frustrated. At the end of the day, we were no closer to apprehending the elusive Smith. Over the next three days, I assisted with several searches for Smith, but each time it seemed that he was one-step ahead of us. At times, Smith would receive assistance from the public. In one instance, a man sawed the chain off, between Smith's handcuffs. Smith still had the handcuffs on his wrists, but now had total freedom of movement.

On the afternoon of the fourth day, a witness saw Smith at a store near a popular beach in Vernon. I was on duty and made my way to the area, along with another patrol car. The witness called back saying that Smith was walking north on the railway tracks that went passed the store. The other patrol car came in from the south and stopped on a road that intersected the railway tracks. The member radioed that he could see Smith walking on the tracks, about 50 yards north of the store. I happened to be coming from the north, along a road that ran parallel to the railway tracks. I pulled onto a side road and stopped in front of the tracks about 200 yards ahead of Smith. He did not recognize my unmarked vehicle. His full attention was on the marked car south of him. I radioed the member to stay where he was and just let Smith keep walking towards me. I remained in the truck with Trapper, who was now on high alert. He could also see the man approaching our position and I started encouraging the dog. The member climbed out of his police car, folded his arms on his chest, and leaned against his car. Smith kept coming closer to my position. I was surprised, since he was a very street-savvy individual. He still had not clued in that we were waiting for him. The dog knew that something was going to happen.

By the late 1800's, police in Germany were using the German Shepherd dog extensively in their work. They had already developed a stringent methodology in the training and use of dogs. The German Shepherd, originally bred to help farmers herd sheep and cattle, had extraordinary qualities of stamina, loyalty, courage and intelligence, well suited for police duties. German dog handlers used the word "hag" as a command for the police dog to attack and stop a suspect.

Of course said quickly, the word has a sharp tone to it. The RCMP officially started to use dogs in police work in 1935 and borrowed many of the tactics and style of training dogs from the Germans. RCMP handlers used the word "hag" as well, but added a Canadian flare to it. The command "hag" evolved in to "hag 'em".

By now, Trapper was ready for action. He whined with anticipation and focused totally on the unsuspecting escapee. Smith had a bewildered expression on his face, as he again looked back at the member leaning on his car. I too, glanced over at the member, to see a wide grin on his face and he was waving at Smith. As the culprit stepped in front of my truck, I rolled the window down and yelled, "Police, stop!" Smith startled and stared at me with a look of total disbelief.

He took a few short steps and then suddenly broke into full run down the tracks. I bailed from the truck, leaned away from the doorway and shouted, "Hag'em!" Trapper exploded from the police truck in quick pursuit. Smith could run, but he was no match for 85 pounds of determined dog. The dog rapidly closed the distance as I ran to catch up. Smith turned to confront the dog in a fighting stance. Trapper did not slow down, but hit the man full force with his body and at the same time bit him on the right shoulder. I could hear the scrunch of the gravel as Smith's body hit the railway tracks. The dog still grasped the shoulder and Smith kept fighting. He was screaming in terror and pain as I finally arrived at the fray. Smith tried to stand up, but I elbowed him hard in the chest. He fell back onto the tracks and finally surrendered. The member attended and took custody of the recaptured Smith.

As Trapper and I were walking back to the police truck, a civilian came running up to me. He was wide-eyed with excitement and exclaimed, "I just wanted to say that I saw the whole thing!" My first impression of the witness was that of a do-gooder wanting to complain about how the dog and I arrested the escapee. Then to my surprise, the man proclaimed, "Yes, I saw the whole thing and it was excellent! Good work!" Before I could reply, he turned and ran back to his car.

A few months after the episode with Smith, I was conducting my weekly examination of Trapper. It is imperative that the handler regularly checks his or her canine partner on a regular basis to ensure the dog does not have an injury or the start of a medical condition. Police dogs lead such a robust, active lifestyle that it is important that they are strong and healthy. I noticed one of Trapper's top canine teeth had a small chip at the end. The dog had not shown any sensitivity or difficulties, but I decided to have the veterinarian check the tooth.

The vet conducted a thorough examination. Trapper was always a good, cooperative patient and did not mind the vet probing and prodding him. At first, the doctor was not too concerned about the chip until he discovered a crack on the inside of the tooth that extended from the chip upwards, far enough to compromise the inside pulp and nerve of the tooth. The prognosis: very soon, infection would set in and the tooth would have to be extracted.

However, the vet had a novel idea. He suggested surgically shortening the tooth and having a root canal done. After that, a prosthetic tooth would cover the stump and take the place of the damaged portion of the tooth. I had numerous questions about the procedure and the viability of the prosthetic. The doctor was enthusiastic and felt the results could be quite favorable and that Trapper could continue his duties unhampered. The only drawback was that the vet did not have the proper facilities for canine dentistry. He quickly suggested a local dentist that had assisted the vet previously on other cases.

I would have to pass this by my superiors at headquarters in Vancouver for approval of the funds, but decided to wait until I heard back from the vet's dentist. Meanwhile, the vet took radiographs of Trapper's teeth. Later the same day, the vet telephoned me to say that he showed the radiographs to the dentist, who was game for the job and was already formulating a plan for the surgery. Knowing that they had carefully considered the case, I made the phone calls to Vancouver. They were somewhat perplexed and had many questions. This was a unique request, but a day later, they agreed to the surgery, saying they would cover all costs to ensure Trapper received the best care.

Within a week and a half, Trapper went in for surgery at the dentist's office. It was a Saturday, a day off for the dentist, but with the help of an assistant, he opened to accommodate the dog. The vet had his equipment set up to sedate and monitor the dog throughout the procedure. Trapper jumped up in the chair and stretched out. I stayed with him to offer reassurance and keep him calm. The vet introduced me to the dentist and assistant for the first time, but I was sure I had met the dentist before, but could not recall under what circumstances.

The dentist was enthusiastic about the surgery and showed me a tool that he had devised. He explained that the canine tooth is, of course, much longer than any human tooth and, therefore, he had to construct his own instrument to remove all the nerves from the deep root of the tooth. To the average nonprofessional like me, it looked rather wicked. The dentist then showed me the prosthetic, which was an impressive alloy of metal and gold. A week before, the vet had taken an impression of Trapper's damaged tooth to assist in the construction of the prosthetic. Trapper was relaxed and cooperative. He was not overly anxious and allowed the assistant to place a bib around his neck. The vet sedated the dog and the operation started.

The dentist shortened the tooth by half, and bore a hole up the middle of the tooth. Using his homemade instrument, he extracted all the nerves and applied the new, shiny prosthetic that covered the entire tooth to the gum line. It was a success and the vet brought Trapper out of his deep sleep. I moved in to comfort the dog as he groggily awoke. He tried to sit up in the chair. The vet monitored the dog for a while to ensure he was recovering properly. Later, I picked Trapper up in my arms and carried him to the police truck. I suddenly remembered where I had met the dentist before. He was the man that congratulated me upon the recapture of Smith. Trapper went back to work two days later.

Besides my police duties, I took time to train and work with the local Search and Rescue team (SAR). These unpaid volunteers maintain high standards of training in a variety of profiles. Since I worked with these professional searchers from time to time, they allowed me to attend training that particularly interested me. This included man tracking, map and compass work, rock climbing and avalanche rescue work.

Man tracking is an art perfected with years of practice. A walking person always leaves traces in the environment walked through. Clues left behind include footprints, crushed or disturbed vegetation, and/or debris. Astute trackers can easily distinguish subtle traces such as a turned leaf, broken twig or overturned rocks. With practice, most people can become proficient man trackers.

Map and compass work was always important for my job, as these were the days before GPS equipment. I spent hours practicing with a compass, taking bearings and identifying landmarks from maps. We estimated distances hiked, by tallying the number of paces walked.

Rock climbing required a number of skills, including tying proper knots in ropes, using carabineers and special harnesses and safety equipment. Ascending and descending steep rock faces was exciting work and had a practical application to my duties.

Most of the province of British Columbia is mountain ranges and Vernon, within the Okanagan Valley, is no exception. There is also a popular ski resort near Vernon. Vernon SAR had a specialist provide training on avalanches, which again was beneficial for me.

Within the RCMP police dog service, certain dog handlers receive instruction in backcountry skiing, working in avalanche conditions where the dogs train to search for buried victims.

The training is rigorous. Dogs and handlers had to take annual courses and pass stringent tests. I did not take such training, but those that did became proficient.

A young woman had a bitter breakup with her husband. She was now living with her parents in the town of Enderby. Late one evening in October 1985, her estranged husband turned up, uninvited at the parent's house. He demanded to talk to his wife, but the father refused the man. An argument started and escalated to the point that the father shot and wounded the man with a 20-gauge shotgun. Dad fired at least three more rounds at the gunshot victim, as he ran across the front yard in an effort to escape.

Although badly wounded, the man got to his pickup truck and drove himself to the tiny Enderby hospital, two blocks from the scene of the shooting. Police arrested the father and recovered the shotgun before I arrived at the scene. I suggested that Trapper and I could search the yard for shotgun shells and wadding from the fired shells. The front yard consisted of overgrown grass, along with an array of junk and garbage.

We set to work and the dog located an orange 20-gauge shotgun shell near the street, in front of the residence. Then the dog located two spent shells by the garbage can in the front yard and plastic wadding on the far side of the street. The location of these exhibits would assist forensic investigators in determining what transpired and where the shooter was in relation to blood evidence left by the victim. The victim did make a full recovery, but I am sure he did not go back to that house again.

A life altering event happened to me in August of 1986. Because of a serious off-duty car accident, I was unable to work for over one year and would require ongoing surgeries and therapy for another two years. As a result, I could not continue with my job as a dog handler, which for me was devastating. In my early stages of recovery, my bosses explained to me that Trapper was still healthy enough to work for another year or so. They reluctantly decided to assign him to another handler.

Normally RCMP police dogs stay with their handlers for their entire working life. At retirement, most dogs have medical problems and if their condition severely affects quality of life, the dog is humanely destroyed. A few handlers keep their dogs as pets, even if they go on to train a new dog. Each situation is different and the decision is usually left up to the respective handler. Trapper went to a well-respected handler stationed in Whitehorse, Yukon. Despite some jealousy on my part, I was relieved to hear that handler and dog bonded well and they were catching their fair share of crooks.

My recuperation progressed much better than anticipated and I set a goal to go back to dog handler duties. Nearly a year after the accident, I had a surprise telephone call from the Training

Kennels. The staff sergeant said that Trapper's new handler had suddenly decided to leave the police dog service and asked, "We have an old friend of yours here. Do you want him back? We can send him home tomorrow!" I was flabbergasted and filled with emotion. I quickly accepted the offer.

The next afternoon, I was at the Kelowna airport and went to the air cargo center. I heard the familiar, distinctive bark of Trapper in the cargo area of the large building. I impatiently completed the paperwork and was directed to the off-loaded cargo, which included a big metal dog crate. Trapper was anxious to get out of the crate and barked continuously. As I got closer, I fumbled with the key for the padlock on the crate. It was hard to see because of the tears that kept welling up in my eyes. The anxious barking intensified until I talked to the dog with a soothing voice. He stopped in mid-bark and for a few seconds, it was very quiet. Suddenly the crate started to bounce and rock on the platform. Trapper had recognized my voice. Now he was more vocal with loud, sharp barks, mixed with pitiful whining. I unlocked the crate and the door flew open to an ecstatic dog. He spun in circles and jumped up at me, barking enthusiastically. It was nice to have my old friend back home. During the half-hour drive home, the dog kept his muzzle on my shoulder, only lifting it to lick my ear periodically. Having the big dog back in my life was an incredible boost to my morale.

About four months after his return, I was preparing for a social engagement one Saturday evening. I took Trapper out to a field near my house for one of his daily runs and he bounded around happily. The rest of the time, he spent in the fenced yard, the house, or his kennel in the back. After his exercise, I put him in the kennel and went to the house. About 20 minutes later, I came out with Trapper's evening meal, before going out. As I approached, I saw his head resting on the stoop of his doghouse door. As I got closer, I noticed that he did not raise his head as he always did. At first, I wondered if he was losing his hearing. It was very unusual. As I opened the kennel run door, a premonition hit me. Trapper was dead. I dropped the food dish and put my hand on his big head. I turned him slightly and looked into his lifeless eyes. I returned to my house in a state of shock.

I contacted my veterinarian, who drove over immediately. He took Trapper to his clinic for further examination. I remember standing at my living room window, choking back sobs, as the vet drove my best friend away. At first, I was convinced that the dog must have ingested a poison. The vet determined that Trapper had an infection in his prostate, which traveled to his heart, killing him instantly. I was devastated. I had lost a truly dear friend indeed.

My health steadily improved and I began to tire of duties that confined me to a desk and an office. I worked at getting back into good condition and made application for re-entry into the police dog service. The Training Kennels contacted me and advised that like other applicants, I would have to pass some physical tests including a timed, four-mile run. I had to complete the run in less than 36 minutes. I worked feverishly at achieving the new standards and then re-contacted the Training Kennels. A staff sergeant came to Vernon for the interview and tests, which I passed. They would advise me of the first available training course.

In September 1990, over four years since the accident, the Training Kennels telephoned me. My old job was now available and a new course started in two weeks time. If I wanted it, it was mine. They had a potential dog that they immediately sent to me in Vernon, to bond with before training commenced. I knew it would be an uphill battle. The course was very demanding and physically, I would have to buckle down.

Everybody at the Training Kennels warmly accepted me back into the fold. However, I knew that they would be watching me closely to ensure that I made the grade. It was ten years since I had last trained and there had been many changes, including new trainers and staff members. The mood of the place had changed. It was more intense and businesslike. The course was still 16 weeks long. Our accommodation would be at a motel in the city of Red Deer and we had access to a kennel van for the 30-minute drive to and from the Kennels each workday.

My group consisted of three other trainees, of which only one was an RCMP member. Of the other two, one was a member of the Fredericton City Police and the second was a deputy sheriff from Montana. The force will often train dog handlers from other police departments and agencies. Our trainer was a sergeant named Kyler. He was very knowledgeable and a professional. He had years of experience as an operational handler. He was a hard worker who expected the very best from his group.

The course was still divided into three levels of training. At the end of the second week, Kyler and I could see that the canine that I had been assigned, would not fit the grade. We reluctantly removed him from the program. I was disappointed. As usual, the dog would go back to his old owner, or in the event the owner did not want the dog back, procedures for adoption to a new home were in place. The Fredericton handler's dog was having difficulties, but Kyler hoped the dog would come around.

I was without a dog and there were no replacements. At the time, the RCMP was having great difficulty acquiring suitable dogs anywhere in North America. The demand for dogs was much greater than what was available. One of the trainers named Joel had the sole task of acquisition. It was a big job, but he was enterprising and attacked the problem with innovative ideas. In one instance, he made contact with a dog broker from the east coast of the United States. Through the broker, the RCMP purchased a few dogs from Western Europe. The results were mixed, but Joel was persistent and kept after the broker for more and better dogs. In the mean time, he learned that former Eastern Bloc nations such as Hungary, Poland, the Czech Republic and Slovakia, had German Shepherds and Belgium Shepherds for sale. The broker agreed to visit some of these countries and purchase dogs on behalf of the RCMP. It would take a week or more to see what the broker found.

The RCMP has predominantly utilized German Shepherds due to the breeds suitability, stamina, and adaptability. However, Belgium Shepherds were used for some time with good results.

Since I did not have a dog, I had the choice of going back to Vernon or waiting a week at the Training Kennels. The only stipulation if I stayed at the Kennels was that the OIC did not want me hanging around. It all had to do with money. He was not prepared to pay my expenses just for me to sit and wait. If I went

189

back to Vernon, I feared that I might be overlooked. I figured that staying would keep me in the game. I took a week's holiday time and remained in the area, staying with friends and family.

The week slipped by without results. I pestered Joel on a regular basis, but he did not hear from the broker. I was becoming very anxious, since the Old Man was not conducive to me hanging around, even if I was not on expenses. I feared that he would send me home. To my surprise, Joel contacted me on the Monday after my week off. The broker called to say that he purchased eight dogs and the first two would be arriving at the Calgary International Airport Tuesday evening. Joel asked if I would pick the two dogs up. I could choose which dog I wanted to train. I enthusiastically agreed to his offer.

I arrived at the airport more than an hour before the scheduled arrival of the dogs. To my dismay, both dogs had flown from Eastern Europe to the US east coast, then immediately directed to Calgary. By my calculations, this subjected the dogs to 26 hours in a kennel crate, stashed in the belly of an airplane. I knew Joel would talk to the broker about this and give him a wakeup call.

Eventually I saw the kennel crates on the floor of the cargo terminal. I did not have any information on the dogs except they were both male German Shepherds, about one and a half years old. Both apparently had training in bite work and aggression. The names of dogs were written on large envelopes, attached to their respective crates. Inside each envelope were documents on the dogs. I also gathered all the paperwork from the airlines for Joel's records.

I took "Lutz" out first. He was cooperative and obviously happy to be out of the cramped crate. "Niki" was next. This semi-long haired dog with a coal-black face and muzzle calmly stepped out and checked his surroundings. He looked directly at me with dark eyes that seemed to show intelligence and a good nature. He wagged his tail slowly. I put leashes on both dogs and quickly took them outside to relieve themselves. I remembered Joel's offer about having my pick. Despite the grueling trip, both dogs appeared calm and confident. This was appealing to me and I found myself gravitating to Niki. I liked his temperament and easy-going demeanor.

I did not want to put both dogs together in the back canopy of the pickup truck from the Kennels. Two male dogs, in close quarters could be disastrous, so I put Niki in the cab with me for the one and a half hour drive north to the Kennels. Niki seemed rather pleased with the soft seat and sat upright, attentively looking out the front window as I drove. I patted the seat between us with my right hand and he understood the offer to lie down. He obliged, slumped down, and stretched out on the seat. He intentionally placed his head on my lap. This cemented my choice. I would take Niki as my dog.

About half way through our trip, I pulled off the highway to check on Lutz. I had made a soft bed of blankets in the back for him to lie down. He raised his head from a slumber, to give me a perturbed look when I opened the canopy. I got back in the cab and Niki resumed his position. It was nearly midnight by the time we arrived at the Kennels. A staff member had prepared two separate kennels for my passengers, along with a small bowl of food and fresh water. Both dogs ate their food and drank some water. I stayed for about an hour to make sure they were comfortable. Whenever I checked, Niki would see me and slowly wag his tail in recognition. I looked over the records that came with the dogs and discovered both came from Budapest, Hungary. I noticed earlier that both dogs were unusually thin and their teeth were more yellow that they should have been for such young dogs. I wondered what kind of diet the dogs had lived on in Budapest.

The next morning, I returned to the Kennels earlier than usual and checked on both dogs. They seemed more energetic than last night and the kennel staff said they were voracious eaters. To prevent the dogs from becoming sick, the staff was cautious about how much they fed them. Niki was a bit more bouncy and quickly recognized me. I took him out for some exercise, but I could see that he was still tired from the long flight.

Kyler and Joel came out to assess the new arrivals. Neither said much, but I could tell that they were not pleased with the physical condition of both dogs. Kyler pointed at Niki and commented, "This dog is not ready for training. He is underweight and looks lethargic." Kyler took me aside and with a concerned expression suggested, "I don't think these dogs should train until at least next week. Just take your dog for short walks and bond with him. See what he's like around people, loud noises, and shiny floors. You know what I mean. Also, see what his prey drive is like. Throw a ball for him. All the regular stuff. Feed him six or eight times a day, but small amounts. The poor buggers need some weight."

I told Kyler that I shared his concerns and both dogs would need time to adjust to their new surroundings. We knew very little about their backgrounds. Another more senior handler than me was also re-training and offered his detachment patrol car that he had brought to the Kennels. I gladly accepted and over the next five days, I drove Niki from place to place in central Alberta. I was impressed with his determination to fetch a ball. He would not stop searching for the ball when I intentionally hid it in high grass or bush. He was tenacious, yet always calm and collected. He took all the tests with ease and confidence. Open staircases and shiny, slippery floors are a big challenge to some dogs, but Niki reacted positively. He had a truly voracious appetite, but never growled or snapped if I took the food dish away from him, while he was eating. This showed that he accepted me as the leader of our new pack. I could best categorize the dog as being an "old soul." His easy-going nature made him a pleasure to handle.

The following Monday, we started our training. I had fallen too far behind to re-join my old group. The training staff finally removed the Fredericton handler's dog from the program, so he was also starting over with another European dog that had arrived at the Kennels. Both of us ended up with two other handlers that had just arrived, but we would retain Kyler as our trainer.

All the handlers, trainers, and staff were curious about the European dogs. They had protection training, but we did not know how much. One day, a handler from another group, without any warning, made an aggressive move at Niki. The dog's passive nature changed in a heartbeat. Niki lunged and narrowly missed biting the surprised man. The dog's reaction was instantaneous and serious. There was no warning, such as barking or growling. Niki stared at the dumbfounded member with fierce, menacing eyes, waiting for another move.

Whomever had trained Niki in aggression, had done an outstanding job, but there was a lot more to police work than biting people. Overall, Niki's reaction to all the training was remarkably good. With a proper diet, the dog was quickly gaining weight, muscle, and endurance. He was eager to please and loved to work.

Winters on the prairies are usually not favorable for training, but that winter was not as severe and we progressed well. At one point, all the groups in training had to move to the RCMP Training Academy or "Depot" for one week of riot control training. I had not been back to Depot since my recruit training, but I looked forward to visiting the "Swinging Arm Ranch" as some members affectionately referred to the training center. A few days before the six hundred mile drive east across Alberta and Saskatchewan, the weather turned incredibly cold, with temperatures well below minus 40 degrees Celsius.

By the time we started our training at the "Ranch," the weather improved greatly and we utilized the new recruits during the evening hours for our riot training. During the day, Kyler ensured that we kept to our normal training schedule and, therefore, I did not have much free time to reminisce about Depot.

Something we were not accustomed to at Regina, was the prodigious number of jackrabbits that roamed the area. One morning, we took our dogs out to a large field for exercise before work. We accidentally scared up a squad of the bouncing, long-eared animals in front of the dogs. The result was pure pandemonium. The rabbits seemed rather unconcerned about being pursued by prey-driven dogs and their handlers trying to call their respective dogs off the chase. I am sure the rabbits had lots of practice in the past, eluding coyotes and farm dogs.

Once the riot work concluded, we returned to the Kennels to resume our training schedule. By early February 1991, Niki and I successfully completed the course. I had my personal pickup truck at the Kennels and therefore could drive Niki back home with me, rather than having him flown home commercially. I felt the dog had enough of airplanes for a while.

Immediately after the course, Niki and I left the Kennels, bound for Vernon. We had a late start to our seven-hour drive but the dog sat proudly in the seat as we made our way over the Rockies on the Trans-Canada Highway. At approximately 1:00 AM, we stopped in a pullout for some rest. It was cold and I let the truck idle, with the driver's window cracked open for fresh air. The dog and I settled in for a sleep.

About an hour later, I woke with a start from a sharp wrap on my window. An RCMP highway patrol member, who I had never met, was making a vehicle check. He noticed that the breeze was carrying the exhaust fumes from my truck onto the cab and was concerned about our safety. He asked for my driver's license and I complied without letting him know who I was. I knew he would return to his patrol car and radio the dispatcher for a check of my license. We had parked in an area served by the dispatch in Vernon.

A few minutes later, he returned with my documents. As I rolled the window down, his portable radio crackled and I recognized the female voice of the dispatcher exclaiming, "Oh, make sure you say 'hi' to Brad and welcome him back. We missed him!" The member shot me a baffled look as he handed over my license. I did not explain or elaborate, just thanked him for his concern, and said good night.

Before I had trained Niki, the staff sergeant in charge of police dog services in British Columbia informed me that there was no permanent dog handler position available for me. I would likely remain in Vernon, until a position came available in BC. My old position in Vernon was filled before I went back into the police dog service and so, effectively, I was an extra dog handler for the province. In RCMP jargon, that meant that I was "Surplus to Establishment" or STE.

A few days after I returned to Vernon, the staff sergeant had me temporarily transferred to Kamloops detachment. One of the two dog handlers posted there, suddenly had to re-train a new dog. Kamloops is diverse community supported by ranching, farming, and the forestry industry. The city is on the Trans-Canada Highway, about 300 miles northeast of Vancouver. It is also about 70 miles northwest of Vernon. Since it was a temporary transfer, I would keep my residence in Vernon, but commute for each working day. Most of my shifts were from 6:00 PM to 4:00 AM. The RCMP provided me with a police vehicle, for work and commuting. There were also off-duty times when I would be on call for Kamloops and area. Besides Kamloops, the remaining handler and I were responsible to support the satellite detachments of Blue River, Clearwater, Barriere, Cache

Creek, Ashcroft, Logan Lake, Chase, Merritt, Lillooet and 100 Mile House.

I was driving home along the Trans-Canada Highway after a long night shift in Kamloops. It was about 4:00 a.m. but still fully dark. It was early spring and ghostly patches of fog hung along the ditches and into the farm fields near the highway. A small car with Province of Alberta license plates was just ahead of me on the quiet road. There was nothing unusual about the vehicle or the way it was being driven, but I routinely radioed the dispatcher with the plate number. I quickly received a reply that it was reported stolen from the city of Calgary, three days previously. Calgary is about 500 miles east of Kamloops. A backup unit was dispatched from Kamloops, but I was already about 12 miles east of the city and the unit would take some time to catch up to me. I patiently followed the vehicle, but since traffic was very light, it was hard to remain inconspicuous. It appeared to have four occupants, but because the windows were covered with dew, it was difficult to see into the car. After a few miles, the stolen car started to move erratically, by slowing down, then suddenly speeding up. My backup was frantically trying to close the gap and I was becoming more anxious with each passing minute.

Finally, I had no choice and decided to stop the vehicle. I was about 20 miles east of the city, when I activated the emergency lights on my unmarked suburban truck. The car abruptly pulled off the highway onto the gravel shoulder and stopped. Niki was on full alert. He sensed my anxiousness through my actions and tone of voice. He was staring hard at the car, whining with anticipation. It was a remote, rural area and the rolling fog made for an eerie scene. The occupants did not try to exit the vehicle. I knew my backup was trying his best, but time seemed to drag by. Suddenly the car lurched forward about 50 yards and stopped again. I pulled my truck in closer and kept my flashing red and blue lights on. I could not wait any longer and decided to approach the stolen car.

I had to make up my mind whether to do the approach with Niki or not. If the dog was with me and the driver or others fled on foot, I had a better chance at re-capturing them. If the occupants all decided to confront me, at least the dog would give me some psychological advantage. On the other hand, the dog could be a detriment. If the vehicle did some other wild maneuver during my approach, there was a chance the dog could be injured. I figured that the best thing under the circumstances was to leave Niki in the police vehicle. I believed that I could get to him quickly enough.

I put the truck headlights on high beam. It would be difficult for the occupants to see me approaching through the bright lights. I drew my pistol (at the time I re-entered the police dog service, all RCMP dog handlers were trained and issued with Sig-Sauer pistols rather than the less effective .38 caliber revolvers) and cautiously walked to the car. As I got to the rear bumper, it suddenly sped forward, with the spinning rear tires throwing gravel onto me. The vehicle abruptly made a "U" turn on the highway and sped passed me. It came so close to me that I was forced to jump into the ditch. The stolen car was now returning to Kamloops. If Niki had been beside me, he likely would have been struck.

I quickly clambered back into my truck and the chase was on. With speeds of over 100 miles an hour, it was difficult to handle the big vehicle and use the police radio at the same time. We soon passed my backup unit that was now desperately trying to turn around. Other units were also frantically responding from Kamloops. They set up a roadblock on the highway, at the outskirts of the city. As the city came into view, I saw the red and blue flashing lights of the roadblock. Of course, the suspects also saw the roadblock. The stolen vehicle suddenly fishtailed in front of me as the driver threw the brakes on. A cloud of smoke from burning brakes and tires billowed up and engulfed my vehicle. The suspect car barely slowed enough to navigate a right turn off the highway, about one block from the police cars. It careened around the corner onto a dead-end road.

Instead of stopping, the car made an immediate left onto the railway tracks that crossed the road and paralleled the highway. I was astonished as sparks flew wildly from the bottom of the car. It banged and scraped along the tracks, all in a desperate effort to evade the police. The pounding on the railway ties finally blew out the two front tires and it came to an abrupt stop. We all converged on the vehicle, with weapons drawn. I ran to the driver's door with Niki beside me. We were ready and I hoped that somebody from the car would do a runner. The engine was still running, but it sputtered and clanked with clouds of steam enveloping the car. The emergency lights of numerous police cars cast uncanny red and blue flashes through the cool, early morning air.

No movement came from inside the car. A member deftly opened the driver's door and pointing his firearm inside, exclaimed, "Don't move!" The response was a shrill scream from the 13-year-old female driver. All four occupants were girls between the ages of 12 and 14 years. They filled the night air with a chorus of screams and hysterical crying. They stole the car in Calgary and drove it to Vancouver to see friends. When I stopped them, they were returning to Calgary. It had been a frustrating and dangerous event for all involved.

To make it even more irritating, after the girls appeared in provincial court later that same morning, the courts turned them over to social services, for their safe return to Calgary. Social services put the children on the Greyhound bus, unescorted, for Calgary. During the trip, all four went missing and the police again had the responsibility to look for them.

Shortly after taking the position at Kamloops detachment, Constable Day, a uniformed member, approached me with a file recently assigned to him. It was a warrant for the arrest of a man under the provisions of the provincial mental health act. Day had personally dealt with the man in the past and was very concerned about making the arrest. The man, Mr. Stone, was irrational, unpredictable, and extremely violent. He was also a martial arts expert.

Stone had essentially confined himself to his residence in a rural area outside of Kamloops. He would not talk to anybody, including his own family. Fearing that Stone may harm himself and others, his immediate family had applied to the police and the courts to have Stone taken into custody and moved to a facility for care. Day had good reason to be concerned about affecting the arrest. Together, Day and I consulted with the Kamloops Emergency Response Team (ERT), to formalize a plan. Family members of Stone also volunteered their assistance. Time was of essence, however. After considering all the possibilities, we had a plan that we hoped to execute without anybody getting hurt.

Stone lived in a split-level house, with the front entrance on the ground level. His adult son had a key to gain entrance to the residence. Part of the plan was to have the son talk to his father in a last ditch effort to get Stone to peacefully leave the house for help. While the son was talking, two ERT members and I, with Niki, would surreptitiously enter at the ground floor. Remaining ERT members along with Day would remain outside to contain the house in the event Stone attempted to escape. If the son was unsuccessful, we would be in a good position to step in. The ERT members were not dressed in their usual "black gear," but in regular uniform. We wanted to maintain the least aggressive posture towards Stone. The ERT members would attempt to arrest Stone, while I stood by with Niki.

I remember the son carried a concerned, anxious expression on his face. He was accepting of our methodology, but I think any son would find such a situation unsettling knowing he was allowing three burly police officers with a police dog, into his father's house. It was difficult to re-assure the young man, especially when we ourselves did not know how events might unfold.

Despite daylight hours, we were able to use other houses and surrounding bush to get to the house without detection. With hesitation, the son put the key in the front door lock and opened it. The door creaked open and the son put his head inside and called out to his father. With no reply, the son opened the door wider and entered. As he did so, we quietly and closely followed the son inside. It was dark inside the house. All the curtains were drawn on the windows and the air was warm and musky. Clothing and boots littered the entrance and the closet doors were open wide. Unopened mail and newspapers lay strewn across the floor and the home was generally unkempt.

A wide staircase at the entrance led to the upstairs. At the foot of the staircase, the son called out to his father once again. This time a male voice upstairs answered and Stone pensively appeared at the top of the staircase. The three of us stepped back into the darkness of the ground floor. Stone did not see us, but concentrated on talking to his son. A light was on upstairs that silhouetted Stone's frame. He was not a tall man, but appeared lean, trim, and fit. Stone pointed his index finger at his son accusingly and demanded that he leave. His actions became more animated and he spoke in quick, sharp sentences. He paced at the top of the stairs and shook his head when his son tried to reason with him. Stone then started to mutter to himself as he paced. The son was becoming more anxious and frustrated as the conversation went on. I could see that he wanted to go upstairs and be closer to his father, but was reluctant to do so. The son turned to us with a look of desperation and despair. He simply walked out without saying anything. This was our cue to move in for the arrest.

Stone had turned and disappeared from the top of the stairs. The two ERT members quietly ascended the stairs, two at a time. I followed with Niki at my side. I was holding the dog by his choke chain. If I had to release Niki, I did not want the leash obstructing him. I wanted a quick, clean release. I was confident of Niki, but in the back of my mind, I remembered that the dog was young, still fresh from training and did not have "street smarts" yet, especially when it came to such a potentially volatile situation. I just hoped that if he were required, that he would do a sufficient job.

I was still bounding up the stairs when both ERT members reached the top. Stone shouted in obvious surprise. One member tried talking quietly and soothingly to Stone, as Niki and I crested the stairs. The kitchen and dining room were all one large room, divided by a counter. Both ERT members were in the kitchen with Stone, about 15 feet to the right of me. Stone became loud, yelling unintelligibly, with wide, glaring eyes. He started to mumble between fits of loud shouts. The members still tried to reason with Stone, when he suddenly lashed out with a flurry of punches and kicks. The members were capable and experienced. At first, most of Stone's kicks and punches were wild, but as the members moved in, Stone's martial arts training started to take a toll. His aim improved and his moves were fearsome. I was reluctant to release Niki, since I was unsure if he was focused on Stone. With a battle in such close quarters, the dog could quickly become a detriment and bite a member.

The unceasing blows, forced both members into defensive positions. Stone broke free and ran to the dining room on my left. As he did so, I looked left and saw a rifle propped against the wall, behind the dining room table. It was hard to see at first glance and I doubted that the ERT members had even noticed it. Although everything happened so quickly, it felt like slow motion. Stone was going for the rifle and I had to stop him. My heart pounded in my throat like a hammer on an anvil. Before entering the house, I had double-checked my pistol as I always did and ensured that it was ready if needed. Niki was barking furiously at Stone, with his front feet off the ground, straining against my hold on him. I had to make a decision. Should I put all my faith in Niki and release him? I was justified to stop Stone with deadly force and was prepared to do so. In that split-second, I made up my mind and released the dog.

Until then, Stone had been concentrating on the ERT members. I do not believe that Stone even realized our presence, until the dog confronted him. In a flash, Niki bit Stone on the forearm and hung on. Stone stopped in his tracks, with a sudden expression of surprise and fear on his face. He focused on the dog, which gave us the chance we so desperately needed. Both members and I bailed onto Stone, forcing him to the floor. He stopped fighting and went totally limp. Niki released the arm and we handcuffed Stone's hands behind his back. Other members from outside entered the house to assist, but it was all over. Constable Day took custody of Stone and escorted him passed his family to a waiting ambulance. The family was visibly relieved and the son stood quietly, with one hand over his face. I checked the rifle. The .22 caliber weapon was loaded and ready to use. Niki and I left the scene.

1987, Vernon BC. Trapper, just shortly after his retirement and return to me. We had been apart for one year, however he still remembered me as if it were yesterday.

1981, Prince George. Trapper posing for a Christmas Picture.

Chapter 7
Return to Prince George

I spent almost one year working in Kamloops. The NCO in charge of police dog services for the province informed me that a permanent position in Prince George was now available. The transfer process is involved and depends on a series of moves and promotions of other dog handlers across the entire country. At that time, there were no other positions and I had no choice but to accept Prince George. Actually, I looked forward to the move back and knew what to expect. Our time in Kamloops had left Niki well-grounded and we would have no problem with the challenges in Prince George. In February 1992, I moved to Prince George and as before, we were one of four dog teams.

A month after returning to Prince George, I responded to a call of a suspicious man that frequented a bush area bordering a residential section, in the west part of the city. There had been a rash of recent break-ins and residents complained that the man might be responsible for the crime spree. Patrol cars were in the vicinity when I arrived at about 10:00 PM. The investigator, named Brock talked to the citizens and he directed me to the bush area where they saw the man about a half hour before.

Niki indicated a track in the forbiddingly dark bush. The undergrowth was thick and I had a nagging feeling in my gut. It was almost as if somebody or something inside me, was telling me to be careful and that things were not right. I had intuitive feelings before and from experience knew to listen to those forewarnings. It eased my mind somewhat that Brock was my back up man. He was a small, but very capable member and I trusted him. Niki pulled hard and despite the dense foliage, we moved fast. The scent was very fresh and the dog surged harder. We went uphill for about 300 yards and then the ground leveled out. I had been so intent on the dog that I had forgotten about my back up. Brock was gone and I suddenly realized that I was alone with the dog. The bush thinned out and we moved faster. We started to go downhill for about 400 yards until we came to a singlewide vehicle trail. The dog turned right and we ran along the trail. By that time, my eyes were well accustomed to the dark and I could see that we were coming to a gate, at the entrance to a gravel pit.

A large tree was at one side of the entrance and upon our approach, a wild-eyed man leapt out from behind the tree. He stood in front of us and screamed. The man's sudden actions dumbfounded and shocked both the dog and me. I yelled back saying that it was the police and ordered him to stand still and show me his hands. I shone my flashlight on his crazed face and he glared back, muttering and cursing. I tried to talk to him, but he suddenly turned and sprinted across the pit. His actions were certainly bizarre and unpredictable. I was unsure if he had committed a crime or was dangerous to others and himself. I could not let him go.

He kept running even after I again ordered him to stop. With Niki beside me, we ran to catch up, but he was getting away. I shouted for him to stop or I would release the dog. He seemed unaware and ignored my demands. I released the dog. Niki quickly closed the distance and bit the man on his left thigh. The pain from such a full mouth bite would stop any person, but to my amazement, the man continued running with the dog attached. Niki seemed astonished as well. The dog released his grip. I re-commanded and encouraged the dog. Niki hit him again, on the same leg. This time the man stopped, but appeared oblivious to the pain of the bite. The dog let go again, but with lightening speed, the suspect reached down and grabbed the dog by his muzzle. By the time I got to Niki, the crazed man had the dog's front feet off the ground. The dog was shaking his head, desperately trying to free himself. I struck the man on the chest with a heavy blow, but it had no effect.

Suddenly, he dropped Niki and whirled around with something in his right hand. I grabbed his right wrist with both my hands and we wrestled to the ground. Niki was biting the subject repeatedly on the arms and legs, with no effect. The pressure from the bites would be extremely painful; however, this person seemed possessed and had no limit to pain. We rolled several times and I ended up on top of the struggling, deranged demon. He was a thin, small framed man, but his strength was incredible and unyielding. For the time being, my only advantage was that I was bigger and heavier than my adversary. He continued to fight ferociously. At this point in the struggle, I could see the unmistakable outline of a small handgun in his right hand. I still had my hands around his right wrist, but he feverishly tried to point the weapon at my face. I was fighting for my life.

Suddenly Niki delivered a fierce bite to the man's right forearm and, somehow, the pain from the bite finally registered on him. The suspect let out a yelp and I felt his strength briefly ebb. I thought of pulling my pistol, but that meant I would have to release my right hand from his wrist. I did not have enough strength to hold his wrist with one hand and besides, during the struggle, my gun belt had twisted and the holster was now in the middle of my back. My portable radio had also come off my belt and was lying in the sand beside me. I could hear the dispatcher and members desperately trying to contact me. I felt my large, three cell metal flashlight under my knee. In an act of desperation, I reached for it and struck the man repeatedly across his head and neck. I hit his right wrist and arm. To my amazement and relief, the gun fell to the ground.

The crazed man lashed out with wild punches that I blocked with my flashlight, however he knocked the light out of my hand, and it flew through the air, landing some distance from me. I grabbed both his wrists as Niki continued to deliver bite after bite. I lost my grip on the man's right wrist and he pulled an object out of his jacket pocket before I could stop him. It was a folded pocketknife and he tried to open it. I once again grabbed both wrists, but he desperately kept attempting to open the knife. I was losing my strength. It felt as if we had been battling for hours, but it was probably no more than a minute. To my horror, he got his hands together and partially opened the knife. I pulled his hands apart again, and the knife snapped closed on his index finger. He seemed oblivious to the sharp blade sawing into his finger with blood running down his hand onto my hand and arm.

We rolled again and he broke my grip and repeatedly stabbed me with the half-open knife, hitting me on the chest, face, and mouth. Somehow, through the fight, he lost the knife on the ground. I was fighting on the rush of adrenalin, but had no strength left. Niki was still with me, but his strength was certainly flagging too, and I feared he might be seriously injured. The demented opponent was still battling with us. I considered one last desperate attempt. I knew that very soon, he would be able to overpower me. I had to be off him before that happened. The question was would I have enough strength and time to take my pistol out and shoot him.

Before I could answer that question, the most incredible thing happened. Four members, including my former back up, appeared out of the darkness. They jumped onto my still struggling foe. With indescribable relief, I rolled out of the fray. Niki remained in the battle, buoyed by the arrival of help. Unsteadily, I got to my feet, reached in and pulled the dog away. After a considerable struggle, the members finally subdued the suspect. Exhausted, I dropped to the ground, holding Niki beside me. I wanted to cry, but held myself in check. Brock stayed with me, while the other members dragged their prisoner away.

I looked up and slowly nodded when Brock asked if I was all right. By the expression of deep concern on his face, it was obvious that Brock did not believe me. In an apologetic tone,

Brock said, "I lost you. One moment, I was right behind you and then you were gone. I tried calling you several times." He was referring to the start of the track. I was probably too intent on the dog or too far away and did not hear him.

I spit out gobs of blood, which alarmed Brock even more. He reached for his portable radio, to call an ambulance for me. I waved a shaking hand at him and protested, "No, no, I'm OK." Brock lowered the radio, put a hand on my slumped shoulder, and with a worried grin, recommended, "You better get checked out. You look like hell!" I pulled myself over to Niki and tried to examine him. He seemed uninjured, but I knew that dogs sometimes did not acknowledge or show pain immediately. I looked over at Brock and asked how they had managed to locate the dog and me. Brock simply pointed towards a sand bank next to the area where the fight took place. Perched upright in the sand, shone the powerful beam of my flashlight like a beacon into the night sky. Brock told me that during the frantic search for me, they suddenly saw the light of my flashlight.

I insisted on searching the scene for the knife and gun, despite Brock's repeated protests. Niki quickly recovered the weapons and Brock drove me to my vehicle. The handgun turned out to be a loaded starter's pistol. The inside of my mouth continued to bleed from cuts inflicted by the knife. At the emergency ward, a doctor used eight stitches to close the wounds. As the adrenalin receded, my entire body started to ache and I shivered uncontrollably.

After my hospital visit, I thoroughly checked Niki. He seemed to be in good condition, but was probably as tired and sore as I felt. I drove to the detachment and told the Watch Commander that I was booking off work for the rest of the night. I must have been a sorry sight, with a puffed-up face, dried blood on my torn, sweat-stained shirt and covered with dirt. He took one look at me, grimaced, shook his head, and told me to go home. In a fatherly tone, he told me not to hesitate to call him if there was something I needed. I thanked him for his concern and drove home.

I had a long shower and dropped into bed. It was well after two in the morning. I was exhausted but could not sleep. I tossed and turned until dawn, before I got up and went out to Niki's kennel. He greeted me at the gate of his run, with a wagging tail. I sat with him for a while and checked him over once more. He leaned his body heavily against mine and I reflected on his performance earlier. If it had not been for his courageous efforts, I was sure that my situation could have been much worse.

As soon as the veterinary clinic opened, I dropped in to have Niki examined. The doctor could not find any injuries except for some bruises. The veterinarian ordered Niki to take a few days off work to rest and recuperate. We returned home and I had another shower. I wanted to wretch when I saw ten tiny bruises on my chest. I still had not fully realized that the suspect had attempted to stab me with the half-closed knife. I took the next five days off with Niki.

Brock contacted the suspect's sister in Ontario. Her brother had a history of mental illness but coped exceedingly well, provided he took his medication. A few months before, he stopped taking his prescription and moved away. Nobody knew how he ended up in Prince George. During his time in jail, he went back on his medication again and was a model prisoner.

On some calls, I did not actually use the dog, but stood by in the event the dog was required. This was often the case involving the arrests of dangerous and armed suspects. In May 1992, I had a telephone call from the NCO in charge of Smithers detachment. It was my day off and I was at home. He requested that I immediately drive to Smithers. The community is about 300 miles west of Prince George along Highway 16. The dog handler stationed at Terrace, a town about 60 miles west of Smithers normally covered that area, however he was not available. During the brief conversation, I learned that another dog handler, stationed at Prince Rupert, along with the ERT from Prince Rupert, would also meet me at Smithers. Prince Rupert is a small coastal city situated about 150 miles west of Smithers. The NCO would not elaborate further. Something big had come up and I was anxious to be involved.

That evening, I arrived at a detachment overflowing with detachment members, ERT members, the other handler, and plain-clothes homicide investigators from the RCMP headquarters in Vancouver. After some quick introductions, we settled in for a briefing from the senior homicide investigator.

The file began on Vancouver Island. Two notorious men, well known to police, drove a man and woman to a remote area outside one of the Island communities. There were issues between all the people involving an outstanding drug debt. The two men forced the woman on her knees and shot her execution style. They then forced the male victim on his knees, but the handgun jammed. After repeated attempts, the weapon still did not work. The two murderers placed the terrified man back into their car and started driving back to town. Along the way, they attempted to shoot him again, but the gun still jammed. The victim promised not to say anything, if they let him go. The suspects agreed and turned the man loose.

Unfortunately, for the suspects, their surviving victim and witness went directly to the police. The suspects quickly learned about the turncoat and fled the island before police could arrest them. One of them owned land on Babine Lake, about 40 miles northeast of Smithers, at the end of Old Babine Lake Road. It was the only road into the lake and police had information both suspects were on that property. Each had lengthy criminal records for violence and drugs offences. They were suspects in other gangland murders and possibly responsible for the disappearance of a Smithers resident a few years before. They were unpredictable, dangerous, and carried weapons. Some also considered them survivalists.

First, police had to determine if the suspects were in fact at the Babine Lake property. The area did not provide adequate cover for an approach and therefore the police would lose the element of surprise. It would be the job of two members from an RCMP surveillance team to get close enough to the property and identify the suspects. The operatives prepared well for the task. They drove to Smithers from Vancouver, with a pickup truck and camper on the back, pulling a boat. These undercover members fit the role perfectly as visiting American anglers. They even had State of Washington license plates on the vehicles.

I had a chance to observe the two operatives before they departed to Babine Lake. They certainly did not look or act like police officers. Both were in their forties. One was a tall, lanky, loose-limbed man, with a long neck. He wore a hat covered with fishing lures and flies. He constantly fidgeted and spoke rapidly, with eyes that darted back and forth. To me, he looked like a nervous wreck. The other operative was the complete opposite. He had an easy-going demeanor with an ample bear-belly exposed at the bottom of a stained T-shirt. He was bald, with overgrown mutton shop sideburns and a mean five o'clock shadow. They departed on their mission with an array of surveillance equipment and everything else they needed to play out their roles as anglers. As they departed, they waved, yelling, "Bye, y'all!"

The entire plan was complex. It depended on the coordinated efforts of at least sixteen ERT members and 2 dog handlers. Two RCMP aircraft were at the Smithers airport: a fixed wing, and a helicopter. Both aircraft were ready for service at a moment's notice. Once the surveillance team was in position, they would contact and confirm the identity of the suspects. The operatives would then report the suspects' movements on a regular basis. We knew the suspects would eventually move. To do so, the only way out was to drive south, along Old Babine Lake Road from their property to Smithers.

Once the operatives reported the suspects were moving, the RCMP aircraft would be in the air and monitoring the movement of their vehicle along the 40-mile road out to Smithers. The ERT and dog handlers would set up an ambush site on the road and wait for the wanted men to drive into it.

The ERT and dog handlers set up camp at a farm along Old Babine Lake Road. The farmer was gracious enough to allow us to stay on the property. He agreed not to reveal to anybody that we were on the farm. We would all stay in the outbuildings on the premises.

The ambush strategy was involved. We picked the ambush site along Old Babine Lake Road, just south of a hairpin turn. The aircraft would keep ERT apprised of the suspects' progress along the road from the lake to the ambush site. The hairpin turn was advantageous since the suspects' vehicle would still be moving slowly and give us the best opportunity to stop it. An ERT member in an unmarked suburban truck would park, hidden off the road, about a mile north of the hairpin. Once the suspects drove passed his position, he would follow them undetected until the ambush site. At the site, an unmarked car would be at the side of the road, hood up, with an ERT member in plain clothes standing beside his "disabled" car.

As the suspects approached the "disabled" car, the plainclothes ERT member would step out in an attempt to solicit the suspects for assistance. We hoped the suspect vehicle would roll to a stop. Then, ERT members and dog handlers could emerge from the ditches after discharging several stun grenades and tear gas on the suspects. We hoped to frighten and disorientate the suspects enough that they would be unable to resist. The ERT member driving the suburban would block the road, preventing the suspects' vehicle from backing out of the ambush.

Over the next three days, we continually rehearsed the plan, making adjustments, and refining our tactics. During the rehearsals, we did not use the explosives or gas. We did not want to draw any attention to ourselves. There was not much traffic on the road except for anglers going back and forth from the lake and a few locals that lived on the road.

Anytime vehicles approached our training positions, we hid the equipment, vehicles, and ourselves. We were big news, with everybody in camouflage uniforms and police dogs. The last thing we needed were news reporters looking for a juicy story and tipping our hand.

Our undercover anglers radioed to the detachment early on the first day of the operation. They had made contact with the suspects. During friendly introductions, the suspects had used their real names. This confirmed the identities of the wanted men. We did not know this until later, but over the next three days, the operatives and suspects all become good acquaintances. The murderers were anglers and familiar with Babine Lake. They offered the friendly "Americans" advice on the types of lures to use and good fishing spots on the lake.

Coordinating everybody's roll in the ambush and keeping good communication was paramount, but the waiting was the worst. The hours and days passed by excruciatingly slow. We slept in the outbuildings and ate packaged meals. The continually overcast weather concerned us. A big part of the plan relied on the use of the plane and helicopter and weather conditions could compromise their effectiveness. On the third day of waiting, it rained, making us miserable. We tried to keep busy, checking, organizing, and cleaning equipment. We went through our plan repeatedly. We even worked out a tactic that did not include the aircraft, in the event they could not fly due to inclement weather. Even the dogs were becoming uneasy. The other handler and I did some of our own training just to keep the dogs focused.

On the morning of the fourth day, the suspects left Babine Lake. As they drove by our members, who were busily fishing, one suspect waved and called out, "Hey guys, good luck with the fishing today. We're going into town." The operatives politely smiled and waved back. As soon as the white pickup truck disappeared around the corner, the members were on the radio, informing us of the movement.

The sun had already poked through the clouds and lifted our spirits, when we heard the operatives report on the radio. The ERT commander simply exclaimed, "It's on! Let's go!" For me, the message was electrifying. The targets had just left the lake. We all went into hyper-drive. We were throwing on uniform and gear that was neatly stacked and ready. We must have looked similar to firefighters before leaving the fire hall. ERT members were checking, locking, and loading their weapons. Checks and double checks were completed on the communications net. Small but equally important details were checked. Simple things, such as ensuring ammunition pouches and gun holsters were fastened shut. Nothing was overlooked.

For me, I ensured that Niki was prepared. He had a quick run before I placed him in his tracking harness. I would be the first member to toss in a stun grenade. In fact, by throwing in the first grenade, I would initiate the ambush. I ensured that I had two grenades and that they were secure in my pockets, but easily accessible. I was dressed in full camo gear, with an armored vest. My long line for the dog's harness was wrapped and ready on my gun belt, in the event we had to track a suspect. I checked and double-checked my pistol and made sure I had easy access to extra clips of ammunition. I even double-checked the laces of my hiking boots. The last thing I needed during the ambush was a boot coming undone. I ensured that my portable radio was on the correct channel and

I double-checked to ensure it was working on the com-net. The compass was in my top left jacket pocket. We were ready for action. Vehicles were starting and we were finally on the move. We estimated it would take 30 minutes before the suspects arrived at the ambush site.

The distance from the farm to the ambush site was about three miles. We quickly drove that distance and hid our vehicles off the road, about 300 yards south of the site. A uniformed member arrived from the detachment. He blocked the road, to ensure no civilian traffic got close to the takedown. Except for the two members driving the suburban and the "disabled" car, the rest of us double-timed the remaining distance.

Niki and I set up a position about 20 yards west of the roadway. We were on a hill, hidden in thick brush, with an open view of the roadway. Two heavily armed ERT members had positions close by me. ERT members and the other handler secreted themselves in the bush across from us. The plainclothes ERT member stood by his "broken down" car. The hood of the car was up and he looked convincingly like an angler, anxious to get back home after a long day of fishing. I caught a glimpse of an ERT sniper, setting up on a ridge, southeast of the road, overlooking the scene.

It suddenly became quiet. Scattered clouds blocked the warm sunshine. It became surreal. A crow cawed incessantly in a tree near the site. Above us to the north, I heard the faint drone of small airplane. The ERT members near me were monitoring the fixed wing pilot's reports. The helicopter was in the air too, but it was in reserve, carrying a team of ambulance attendants. If anybody was injured, medical help could quickly be on scene. Both aircraft were high enough so as not to alarm our targets. We heard that the suspects' white pickup was making slow but deliberate progress along Old Babine Lake Road.

After the rush of the deployment, this new waiting game was torturous. Nobody was using the radio, except for the voice of the pilot making periodic reports. Nothing moved. The crow continued its loud banter. Niki sat quietly but attentively beside me. My insides were churning as I checked the stun grenades in my pocket for the umpteenth time. I would only throw one, but had another in the unlikely event the first one did not work. The stun grenades, if used properly will not harm anybody, other than to cause temporary deafness. The extremely loud bang only stuns, frightens, and disorientates people.

A few more interminable minutes ticked by and I thought I heard a vehicle coming from the north. I strained my ears and pointed north. My two compatriots, nodded to confirm what I heard. The noisy crow either grew tired of cawing or perceived that something was about to happen. It suddenly flew away. My breathing quickened upon hearing the distinctive scrunching of truck tires meeting gravel. The white pickup with the two suspects came out of the hairpin and slowly continued south towards the ambush. With shaking hands, I pulled a stun grenade out of my pocket. Holding it firmly in my hand, I pulled the safety pin and held the lever down in my palm. The grenade would explode a few seconds after I released the lever.

As the vehicle continued, the occupants saw the plainclothes member walk out from his vehicle. The men in the truck had their full attention on him as I stood up and with a mighty heave threw the device at the truck. I tossed it in a high arc. It came down immediately behind the cab of the truck and exploded with a fiercely loud crack. My timing and aim were perfect. The occupants of the truck seemed to rise up in their seats as the pickup slid to a stop.

Immediately, three or four more grenades detonated around the suspects' vehicle. The truck lurched and stopped again. The plainclothes member was already moving out of the line of fire as the suburban barreled in behind the suspects' truck and slammed to a stop. The driver quickly exited and ran to the ditch as he drew his weapon. Two ERT members emerged from the bush on the east side of the road. One member, armed with a 37 mm teargas gun, smashed out the driver's window and fired a gas dispersion round into the cab of the truck. The inside of the truck cab instantaneously filled with the white talcum-like powder. Both occupants looked like snowmen as they coughed, gasped, and wheezed. More ERT members and the other dog handler appeared from the bush and converged on the driver's side of the vehicle.

At the same time, Niki and I, along with the two ERT members ran towards the passenger's side of the truck. The passenger was staring at us with wide eyes, screaming, "No, no, no!" The ERT member to my right bellowed back, "Get your hands up, now!" All the events happened within seconds, but for me, everything was in slow motion and it seemed to take ages getting to the truck. As I arrived, my eyes, nose, and mouth felt the stinging effects of the searing gas. Tears poured down my cheeks and mucus ran from my nose. Ignoring the scorching pain at the back of my throat from breathing in the gas, I opened the door. The passenger was screaming like a banshee, as one burly ERT member grabbed the man's shoulder and flung him out of the truck. His body flew passed Niki as the dog attempted to grab a leg, but missed. The powder-encased man fell heavily to the gravel road and two ERT members quickly handcuffed his hands behind his back. Niki was fiercely barking so close to the suspect that globs of his saliva were actually hitting the man on the face. The driver had met the same fate. The other handler's dog was barking profusely at the prone driver. Both men lay on the ground, trembling in absolute terror. I led Niki away and he stopped barking after I soothed him. The scene became surreal again. The cloud of white gas dissipated and everything was quiet, very quiet. Nobody spoke to one another. Within a minute, uniformed detachment members arrived and took custody of the prisoners. They drove them to the Smithers detachment, where the homicide investigators were anxious to talk to them.

The adrenalin rush that I had just experienced was over and the sudden de-escalation of the intense drama was almost too much to bear. I had mixed emotions. After all that preparation, planning, and waiting, it was all over within a few minutes. I was certainly thankful it was over and that the dog and I were not injured. Actually, I was glad that nobody was seriously injured. It was evident that both suspects had wet their pants. I saw the big wet stains on the front of their pants when the detachment members picked them up off the ground. Under the same circumstances, I figured I probably would have wet myself too. I was tired and just wanted to go home. As the ERT and dog handlers slowly hiked back to the waiting vehicles, we started to chat amongst ourselves. Nobody was exuberant or exchanged "high-fives." It was just a quiet discussion, with a great amount of relief. Several citizens were waiting at the roadblock that was still set up. Some were openly complaining about being forced to wait on their fishing trips, but they all went quiet as we slowly walked passed them.

At the debriefing later that same day, the commissioned officer in charge of the entire investigation stood up before all the participants in the takedown and opened with the statement, "I am happy that none of the members of the public were injured today. I am also pleased that neither of the suspects was seriously injured and that none of the members involved in this operation were injured...in that order." I was surprised by the order of his concerns. Complete silence met his remark and we all sat looking at him. I do not know if he meant to say it that way, but it left me disappointed and disillusioned with the higher echelon, once again.

We did not find any weapons on the suspects or in their vehicle, except for a hunting knife under a seat. Niki and I, along with some ERT members searched their property at the lake, which yielded several loaded firearms. The courts charged both prisoners with first-degree murder. However, while awaiting their trials, the justice system being what it is, released the men. Before their trails could begin, one of the suspects was found shot to death, with eight bullets in his body. It was likely retaliation for the execution murder of the woman. This of course, required the police to investigate yet another homicide.

Niki was always a pleasure to work with and we were doing our fair share of police work. One night in Prince George, several members contained a residential area. A man had violently assaulted his wife and the investigators believed he was hiding within a block of his house, possibly armed with a knife. The suspect had a history of violent behavior. We arrived at the scene and I cast the dog, hoping to locate a track. The alleyway was dark and at first, I did not see the suspect suddenly sprint passed us, but Niki did. The dog broke loose from my grip, and charged after the suspect. The man made it to the street, running head-on into a junior member, standing on the road. The surprised member fell to the ground, but was even more astounded when Niki rounded the corner, vaulted over him, and stopped the suspect with a bite to the leg. I was right behind Niki and will always remember the member's astonished face as the dog leaped over him.

On another occasion, complaints kept coming in throughout the night, about two prowlers in a residential area, breaking into parked cars. We attended each scene and all of our attempts to track the suspects failed. Finally, at about 4:00 AM, we received another report of the men breaking into a car in the same neighborhood. This time Niki picked up a fresh scent and we barreled down a street, crashed through a thicket of bush, crossed a boulevard, ran down a walkway, and turned right onto a residential street. About 30 yards ahead of us, two men were carefully scouting out parked cars, peeking in the windows. They were so intent that they did not see or hear us. As I ran towards them, I reached back and turned down the portable radio on my gun belt, so that any sudden transmissions would not give us away.

We quickly closed the distance and Niki bit the first man on the right thigh as I yelled, "Police, get down, now!" The suspect shrieked in pain and surprise while dropping face down on the ground. I called to the second man not to move. He complied and walked to me with his hands up. I ordered him to lay face down with his partner. Niki barked furiously at both men, who were now lying stiffly on the pavement. The dog and I had moved so fast during the track that I was unsure of the name of the street where we ended the track. Patrolling members had also lost our position. Niki watched the two prone men while I quickly went to a house and asked the half-asleep resident to call the police for help. The members quickly attended to take custody of the two men.

Once in the summer, two suspects left the scene of a break-in on bicycles. Despite the use of bikes, I cast Niki in the area and he indicated the fresh bicycle tracks in the grass. There was probably some human scent floating down onto the grass and the fact the bikes had crushed the vegetation, it was still enough for the dog to follow. The weather conditions were ideal with a cool, calm evening and no other distractions. Niki followed the two men for about six blocks. I advised members over the radio, to patrol a few blocks ahead of our direction of travel. They located two men on bikes, who later admitted to the offence.

In late August 1992, another handler named Jackson and me were assigned to assist the Fort Nelson detachment. Fort Nelson is a northern community about a 12-hour drive north of Prince George. The detachment had a report of a missing hunter, in a remote, untamed region about 70 miles west of the town, along Margison Creek, north of the Tuchadi River. The man was with a group of hunters that had camped in the area for a few days. The night before the hunter went missing, other members of the party felt that he was acting abnormally. His personality suddenly changed, becoming argumentative and sullen. At one point, the man walked away from the camp for no reason and the other hunters retrieved him. Through the night, he walked off again. This time his companions were unable to find him.

The hunters reported the incident to the detachment, the next day, when they arrived at Fort Nelson. The investigator immediately called in the provincial search and rescue volunteers (SAR) and requested dog handlers from Prince George. Jackson and I, with our dogs, flew to Fort Nelson on board a new RCMP fixed wing aircraft. The pilots were very particular about their new plane and did not want our dogs on the seats. Later the same day, several commissioned officers would be passengers and the pilots did not want dog hair on the seats. We were slightly offended, but decided to play nice. To us the dogs were members as well and deserved the same privileges. The pilots stowed all our gear including four days of food for men and dogs, backpacks, clothing, extra hiking boots, shotguns, ammunition, a two-person tent, stove, sleeping bags, knives and compasses.

It was a smooth flight and we landed at the Fort Nelson airport. We met a civilian helicopter pilot, hired by the detachment, to ferry us to the search area. He was a friendly man and helped transfer our gear to his chopper. We asked if the dogs could sit on the seats and he replied that he did not mind at all. Jackson and I turned to each other and laughed. Besides friendly, the pilot was levelheaded and knew the search area intimately.

During the forty-minute flight, we were subjected to a spectacular, panoramic view of some of the most beautiful country in the world. Sparkling white snow crowned the tall, craggy mountains on both sides of us. Rivers and streams wound through thousands of square miles of timber. It was fall in this northern country and colors of some trees were magnificent. The waterways were shades of green, indicating they flowed from cold, glacial formations. As we continued west, the effects of logging operations diminished. It was pristine, unspoiled country.

Over the headsets, the pilot informed us that he could take us directly to the base camp, set up by SAR. The base camp was near the area where the hunter went missing. He also told us about a small fixed wing airstrip, about a five-minute flight from our search area. Fixed wing could bring in more men and supplies for the search and he could easily ferry them to our base camp. The other piece of news that concerned us the most was the fact we would not have radio communication with the outside world. If he was at the site and we needed to contact our people, he offered to take us up high enough in his helicopter so that we could call out on his radiophone.

Otherwise, he would relay written messages to Fort Nelson detachment. Receiving an injury in this country, even a minor wound or sprain could be disastrous. The pilot said he would be out each day, providing the weather allowed flights. He re-affirmed with us that it was fall and the weather could be unpredictable. Added to all that, he mentioned that it was grizzly country and that we would be sharing territory with a big sow and two yearling cubs. We knew it was grizzly country but it was still sobering information. Grizzlies are the second largest predators in North America, next to polar bears.

We arrived at the base camp late in the afternoon where we were met by the SAR people. At first, Jackson and I were dismayed to see only four searchers, but after some discussion, we could tell that they were experienced searchers and outdoorsmen. These well-trained civilian volunteers assist with emergency matters within the province. They are a dedicated, hard-working group. The team leader provided us with many pertinent details of the case and briefed us on their activities, prior to our arrival.

Together, we decided to split up into two groups. Niki and I, with a SAR member, hiked south for about two miles, until we came to a small creek. At the creek, we turned east and followed the creek for about three miles along the base of two mountains. I would be concentrating on Niki, in the event we cut the hunter's scent. The SAR member, armed with a high-powered rifle, watched for bears. We double-backed on our trek and returned to the base camp before nightfall.

It was reminiscent of a search, years before with Trapper, in a remote region, east of Quesnel. We were alone, looking for a missing gold-panner, when I came across the footprints of a grizzly. We cautiously continued until we walked into a small clearing where I saw a large, flat rock, the size of a kitchen table. It had recently been overturned. Next to the rock was an old, rotten tree stump that was shredded. Obviously, the bear had been "grubbing"; eating juicy, tasty grubs. Trapper was nervously looking around, constantly turning, and sniffing the air. I set a compass bearing and quickly walked out of the area, without seeing the bear. Just being near the huge animal was a vulnerable, humbling, and terrifying experience.

At the base camp, Jackson and I quickly set up our tent and campsite. We ate a dinner consisting of canned food and trail mix, washed down with water. We had only one food dish for the dogs, so I decided to feed Niki first and then Jackson could feed his dog. Niki was always a voracious eater. As he was knocking back the food, Jackson's dog stood back, watching Niki. Both dogs got along well, considering the fact both were alpha males. Halfway through his dinner, Niki stopped, backed away from the bowl, and looked at the other dog expectantly. The other dog moved in and finished the food. Jackson and I were amazed at Niki's generosity. Jackson re-filled the bowl and his dog continued, but stopped partway to allow Niki access to the food. Both of us laughed at our good-natured canines as they took turns eating.

We put all our foodstuffs in a backpack and strung it high in a tree with rope, in an attempt to keep predators away. The night air was crisp and bright stars filled the clear sky. Frost was already on the grass as we nestled into our sleeping bags. Both dogs curled up together on an old horse blanket we discovered at the hunter's camp. Just before falling into a slumber, I heard a bull elk bugling in the distance and the mournful howl of a lone wolf.

At daybreak of our first day, we dressed and restarted our campfire to make coffee and eat a breakfast of canned fruit and peanut butter sandwiches. The fire took the chill off and the dogs stayed in their bed, until Jackson fed them their breakfast, which they again shared. During the morning and early afternoon, we split up and conducted more searches. It suddenly clouded over and when we re-grouped at the camp, it started raining. The weather concerned me the most. It was late enough in the year that colder temperatures could bring snow. After a quick lunch, we searched more terrain and returned before dusk. It was a miserable search with the rain and wet vegetation. My boots were soaked and I was cold. We set up a large tarp over our tent and the SAR members tents. It made for a drier area, where we could change out of wet clothes and dry off. It was imperative that we stayed warm and dry. One SAR member fashioned a corner of the tarp to funnel rainwater into containers, so that we would have decent drinking water. We used the water to boil large mugs of tea, which warmed us and lifted our morale.

The SAR leader had sent a message back with the chopper pilot, requesting more people and resources. Meanwhile, we decided to ration our supplies in the event the weather worsened and the pilot could not get back in. We had to make the best of it as we continued our searches. It rained throughout the night and I did not sleep as fitfully as the first. To everybody's relief, the rain clouds broke away letting the warm sunshine pour in the next morning. We worked more search patterns, covering further distances. The only thing I found were old boot prints in some mud. They were the right size for our missing man, but could have belonged to another hunter.

At around noon, I heard the distant thumping of helicopter rotors and from my position in the bush, estimated it landed at our base camp. About 20 minutes later, it left the camp, but returned another 45 minutes later. After a couple hours of searching, I returned to base camp. The helicopter pilot was still there. To my amazement, there were containers of hot, prepared food and a few new SAR members to complement our search party. The chopper pilot had flown directly to our camp, dropped off supplies, then flew to the nearby airstrip to ferry more goods to us. We all appreciated his efforts.

One of the passengers the helicopter brought in was a provincial conservation officer (CO). His concern was the big sow grizzly and her two yearlings within our search area. He suspected that they might be responsible for our missing hunter. The CO knew where the bears frequented and during the flight to our camp, observed all three bears in a clearing about five miles southeast of our camp. Grizzlies often bury their food, to eat later. The CO saw evidence of such a burial in the clearing.

When they maneuvered lower, to have a better look at the burial, the old sow rose up on her back legs while attempting to swat the chopper out of the air. She adamantly protected her kill. We believed that it was worth checking. Two SAR members, armed with rifles, accompanied the CO in the chopper, to re-check the sow's kill. The bears had left the clearing and the helicopter landed. The pilot stayed with the aircraft, keeping the rotors going. The SAR members stood by, with their rifles ready, while the CO checked the buried food. It turned out to be the hindquarters of a moose.

We continued searching for three more full days, without any results. The helicopter made it out each day and with him came messages from the Fort Nelson detachment. They wanted to bring in five fresh handlers and dogs to replace Jackson and me. Half the SAR group was replaced with fresh searchers and they wanted to increase their number with more people. Search efforts were hampered with sudden rainstorms and high winds. The helicopter pilot was truly our hero, since he braved the weather each day. Providing that the weather held, we would be replaced on our sixth day. Fixed aircraft would fly the new handlers to the airstrip and the chopper pilot would fly us from the base camp to the airstrip. In turn, the fixed wing would fly Jackson and me from the airstrip to Fort Nelson.

On the sixth day, the helicopter arrived mid-morning. It was cloudy with blustery winds. The pilot was anxious to fly us to the airstrip. The weather was closing in leaving us a small "window of opportunity" to exit. He still had to transport the new dog teams and their equipment to the base camp. We jumped in with our dogs and gear, for the short flight. From the air, we could see the airstrip in the valley, about five miles away. Rain and wind buffeted the helicopter. Rivulets of water that peeled off the front windows ran along the side windows. A sudden squall hit the aircraft so hard that it felt as if it had stopped in mid-air. I was sure the wind gusts were holding us, suspended in the air. I glanced over at the pilot, but his face did not reveal any concern.

At the airstrip, we met our counterparts, waiting for their flight to the base camp. We did not have time for pleasantries, other than to wish them good luck. It was a wild, bumpy flight to Fort Nelson. At the airport, the same RCMP aircraft was standing by, awaiting our arrival. The pilots anxiously helped us load our gear. The weather to Prince George was worsening as well. As Jackson and I clamored aboard, I noticed both pilots were giving us a disagreeable look. One even curled his nose. Without giving much thought to it, I realized that we had not bathed or shaved for six days. We were sweat stained, filthy, and wood-smoked. I remembered that I had only brushed my teeth once. We joked with each other. Jackson wondered how our dogs could stand us. The pilots quickly closed the door tight, between the cockpit and passenger cabin. We invited our dogs onto the clean seats for the duration of the flight to Prince George.

Sadly, the missing hunter was never located. There was some speculation, from the man's behavior, that he may have suddenly developed a medical condition that affected his reasoning.

Niki and I were involved in an extensive investigation near the community of Chetwynd for about six days. Chetwynd is about a four-hour drive northeast of Prince George. Family members reported a man named Sonny missing. Routine enquiries by detachment members soon evolved into a murder investigation. The dog and I spent considerable time searching for Sonny's remains on his rural property and in different places near Chetwynd.

Investigators soon learned that Sonny was associating with a resident that recently moved to the area. This man, named Barney, also had rural property a few miles from Sonny's home. Investigators also gleaned information that Sonny had a yellow backhoe and it was now on Barney's property. He was not cooperative and police quickly obtained a search warrant for Barney's farm. Barney had a criminal record for violent crimes that went back for years. He had spent many years as an inmate at correctional centers in the province of Ontario. He was also a suspect in at least five gangland murders.

Several members of the serious crime section from Vancouver had been assisting the Chetwynd members. I also had another dog handler from Prince George attend to assist. On the morning of the warrant, several members, including two dog handlers attended Barney's property. Given the suspect's propensity to violence, we decided that once everybody was in position, a member would telephone Barney and have him meet investigators at the entrance to his acreage. Both dog handlers would stand by at the entrance in the event the suspect resisted arrest. Once Barney was in custody, we would all move in for the search.

Barney met us at the driveway and surrendered peacefully. As two members escorted him to a waiting police car, I overheard him say that he needed his prescription for a chronic stomach ailment. Another member retrieved the medicine from Barney's house and sent it with him to the detachment cells. The acreage had an old house and outbuildings with several rusted old cars parked at the front of the property. Barney did not have any animals or livestock. We commenced the search and quickly found Sonny's backhoe in an outbuilding.

We continued an extensive search for any other relevant evidence, including Sonny or any of his belongings. Witnesses in the community had seen Sonny and Barney together on several occasions around the community. Some speculated that Barney had tried to entice Sonny into criminal activities. As the search dragged on, we all became more disillusioned. Niki and I had covered the property several times. The other dog handler only found a gun holster stashed under one of the old cars.

At one point, after seven hours of searching, the sergeant in charge of the homicide team called a meeting. We were close to the end time of the warrant. All we had was Sonny's backhoe. It was not enough to link Barney directly to Sony's disappearance. The sergeant was looking for suggestions. Nobody had any fresh ideas. Barney was close-mouthed and remained cool as ice. There was certainly no chance of a confession.

Auxiliary constables with the RCMP are civilians that complement RCMP detachments across the province. They are all volunteers. The provincial government provides training and uniforms for these people. When on duty, they work only under the direct supervision of regular members. An auxiliary member named Pete, with the Chetwynd detachment, slowly raised his hand.

The sergeant acknowledged Pete, who calmly said that he was a farmer in the Chetwynd area when not involved with the local detachment. Unlike Barney, he had livestock on his farm. The thing that caught Pete's attention was the straw spread over the ground in front of the dilapidated barn. Pete said that farmers use straw as bedding for horses and cattle. To him it did not make sense to have fresh straw spread on the ground. Having been a farm boy, I suddenly realized Pete was onto something. I became irate at myself for not recognizing it earlier.

One member of the homicide team walked over to the straw and moved some of it with his foot. He commented how soft the earth was and could easily dig it with the toe of his boot. Another member found a spade in the barn and started to dig. Soon we were trading off taking turns at the shovel. The hole increased in size and depth. Somebody found another spade and the work progressed. At a depth of about five feet, the plainclothes member digging struck something solid. With a gloved hand, he cleaned the soil off the object he hit with his shovel. With excitement in his voice, he announced, "Hey, guys, it's a rubber boot!" With mounting interest, we gathered around the hole. He picked the boot up and exclaimed, "Holy shit, there's a foot in that boot!" Sonny had been located.

Now that we had Sonny's remains, we could stay on the property until we had gathered all the evidence. Two members went back to the detachment to get Barney's side of the story, but all he did was start to moan and groan, demanding his stomach medicine. It would take another day to unearth Sonny. It reminded me of an archaeological dig. Investigators screened each shovel full of earth, and cataloged every piece of evidence for court purposes.

Investigators established that Barney had shot Sonny and then used Sonny's backhoe to bury the remains. Barney thought nothing of keeping the backhoe for himself. Thanks to an astute young auxiliary constable, we were able to conclude the homicide investigation.

Two weeks before Christmas 1993, Niki, and I attended the Hutka Lake Correctional Camp, situated southwest of Prince George about 20 miles, along Blackwater Road. It was a work camp for over 25 inmates serving sentences in provincial jails in a remote area surrounded by mountains and forest.

During a head count at the facility, the staff determined that one prisoner was missing and a search of the camp failed to locate him. A rural member attended in response to a complaint made at the Prince George detachment. In turn, the rural member requested my attendance.

By the time I arrived at 3:30 PM, the weather was overcast and the temperature just below freezing. Normally at this time of the year there would be a considerable amount of snow in the area, however there was only patches of thin, crusty snow on the ground. I met with the member and camp staff for more details.

It turned out that the missing prisoner named Smith, had recently offered sexual favors to other male inmates. Smith's advances offended some prisoners and one threatened to kill him. Smith was a small, slight man and his ability to defend himself was questionable. The last time the guards saw Smith was around lunchtime.

The facility consisted of several separate barracks that each housed six or eight inmates. The other buildings consisted of machine shops, garages and an administrative building for the staff. The camp did not have fencing or gates to the surrounding area. Prison authorities had deemed these inmates were "low escape risks."

On that day, a junior member named Sid was accompanying Niki and me. It was his day off, but had volunteered to work with us. Sid was a well-liked member and had a strong work ethic. Recently from New Zealand, he enjoyed playing practical jokes on other members, including the NCO's.

I had recently been the victim of Sid's jokes. All members are issued pepper spray, used to immobilize confrontational and uncooperative people. When discharged, the small aerosol cans have a distinctive "pffssst" sound, familiar to all members. During a particular dayshift, I was in the detachment storage room retrieving some equipment. The room does not have windows and is very dark with the lights off. To my surprise, the door suddenly flew open and my heart dropped when I heard "pffssst." The lights went off and as the door slammed shut, I heard Sid's recognizable chortle. I was left coughing, choking, and crying from the spray, fumbling and tripping in the total darkness, trying to get out for fresh air.

Sid was quick to volunteer as my back up on the search and I gladly accepted his offer. I could count on him when it came to the serious business of police work. Sid was anxious to participate. The staff locked the prisoners in their barracks and nobody had been into the bush area surrounding the prison. I cast Niki on the west side of the camp and he immediately located a track. The track was at least three hours old, but the thick bush and ideal weather conditions were in our favor.

239

Niki pulled hard as he settled into the track. Sid and I had to work at keeping up to the dog.

Despite intermittent loss of radio communication, Sid used his portable radio to keep the others apprised of our progress and direction of travel. The area was laced with old logging roads and accessible to prison staff and our members to patrol with four-wheel drive vehicles. The track continued west as night started to descend upon us. The temperature was dropping and the bush absorbed us in its stillness.

We continued west over the rough terrain and thick bush. For about four miles, we were constantly jumping deadfall, crossing frozen streambeds and bogs. We had stopped a few times to catch our wind and report our progress to patrolling members. I had been concentrating on Niki so much that I did not realize that we were gaining altitude and there was more snow on the ground. I saw Smith's footprints more often. Both Sid and I were in uniform and despite the crisp night air; our patrol jackets were wet from the exertion. On one stop, I could see Sid's face bathed in sweat. We had to keep moving to keep the cold away. Niki was anxious to continue the track. Whispering "good boy" to him, his head shot down and he strained hard in his harness, pulling me up another hill.

The track changed direction. Going north for about another mile, we connected with a logging road that we followed for another mile. The track left the road and now headed east. Smith would be familiar with the area, since work parties from the camp labored in this area. We had made a large semi-circle and I believed that Smith intended on getting to Blackwater Road. Sid radioed for members to patrol the road, in the event Smith was walking it.

We tracked Smith for another four miles eastbound until we came to the paved Blackwater Road. Niki wanted to cross the road and we picked the scent up still going east. We only went about 300 yards, when the track turned north, parallel to Blackwater Road. We crashed through thick bush for about another half mile and crossed the road again. The track continued north, parallel to the road.

In spite of our physical exertion, the cold was creeping in on our bodies. My feet were cold and the sweaty shoulders of my patrol jacket started to gather frost. We kept going northbound, parallel to the road. Over the police radio, I overheard another handler coming on duty. I was reluctant to call him for assistance, because I wanted to catch Smith myself. It was just the inherent competitiveness of dog handlers wanting to show who had the best dog. However, it did not make good sense to exclude the other handler in this case.

The handler readily agreed to help, and stopped about a mile ahead of my location on Blackwater Road. Taking his dog, he walked into the bush and cut Smith's track. He tracked Smith for almost another mile where he located the escapee curled up under some foliage. Smith had tried to hide from the handler and dog, however he was not properly clothed for the elements, and suffered from exposure. After treatment at the hospital, the man went back in protective custody at another facility, for his own safety.

Niki and I did not catch the escapee, but with the collaborative efforts of another dog team, we helped make the arrest. I was proud of Niki's perseverance, despite the long distance over rugged terrain in freezing conditions.

On another winter callout, there was a considerable amount of snow on the ground. It was snowing heavily with temperatures of minus ten degrees Celsius. Investigators recovered a stolen car on the eastern outskirts of the city. Footprints in the deep snow indicated that three suspects had walked away from the vehicle. Dispatch called Niki and I out just before midnight. The area was rural with farmyards, fields, and bush.

Niki picked the scent of the three subjects out of the deep snow and the white downfall continued profusely during the pursuit. There was no wind or breeze and the large snowflakes drifted straight down. The tops of fence posts had six to eight inches of snow on them. It was difficult to move continuously through fields and bush covered in two to three feet of the white stuff. At times Niki bounded through the snow, having to keep his head up or else become buried. We followed the tracks for over an hour. The dog and I were near exhaustion. We came to a fence line and as we crossed it, three men stood up in front of us. They were as physically tired as Niki and me. We all just stood looking at each other for some time, as the falling snowflakes accumulated on our bodies. All the suspects peacefully surrendered and I radioed the units patrolling the area, to advise them of my location. With our prisoners leading the way, Niki and I marched them 500 yards to a roadway, where a patrol car took them into custody.

It was a day off and I was fishing and camping with friends west of Prince George, when called back to work. That morning, a man assaulted a teenage girl who had been walking through a small park in the northwest part of the city. The assailant choked the victim with a length of yellow nylon rope. He then tied the semi-conscious girl's hands together and attempted to assault her sexually. A passer-by interrupted the offence and the suspect ran away.

Investigators quickly identified and arrested the suspect. Niki and I attended the crime scene to search it for evidence. The dog located the girl's discarded underwear hidden in high grass. After a few more minutes of searching, Niki raised his head high and gave a slight indication, but then lost the source of the scent. A faint breeze was blowing and I re-directed the dog. Some bushes, about four feet high, had green and yellow foliage. The dog picked up the scent again and I could tell the source was in the bush. I looked but could not see anything. Niki was now balancing on his hind legs and indicating strongly at the bush. I looked closer and saw a piece of yellow nylon rope, about three feet long, on top of the bush. It was the rope used to choke the victim.

I gave Niki high praise and petted him generously. He went right back to work and located a book of matches on the ground. All the recovered evidence would help strengthen the case against the suspect. Rope at the suspect's residence, matched the rope Niki found and the rope the suspect used to bind her hands. Investigators found other books of matches with the same unique brand name at the suspect's house. All of the evidence that Niki located would help to convict the suspect in court.

Chapter 8
Portage la Prairie

In early 1994, I accepted a transfer to Portage la Prairie, Manitoba. It is a farming community of about 13,000 people, located in the south central part of the province. It is about a 90-minute drive west of the city of Winnipeg, along the Trans Canada Highway. The detachment that I worked from consisted of 33 members, which by RCMP standards in Manitoba was a large detachment. For me, it was the smallest that I had worked from during my entire service. I was only one of five RCMP dog handlers for the entire province. My area of responsibility was roughly from the northern tip of Lake Manitoba to the Canada-United States border, west of Portage la Prairie about 50 miles and east to the outskirts of Winnipeg. It was about 18,000 square miles of territory.

Within my area, besides Portage la Prairie (often called Portage), were numerous small detachments of two to twelve members. I also provided support to three small town police departments, Canada Customs at the international border and infrequently at the Winnipeg International Airport for narcotic detection. Added to that, I also conducted periodic drug searches at two provincial jails. There were five RCMP members within my area raising puppies for the RCMP puppy program. All aspired to become dog handlers. I monitored the progress of the puppies and mentored the potential handlers. I worked any shift I wanted, but had to be on call and prepared to work on a moment's notice 24/7. If I was going to be away from my area, I had to ensure one of my counterparts was available to take my calls. If other handlers were away from their areas, I had to cover for them.

The land in southern Manitoba is predominately flat due to massive glacial movements thousands of years ago. When the glaciers receded, they left soil that became some of the best farmland in the country. The entire countryside is a patchwork of thousands of acres of wheat, barley, canola, rye, flax, potatoes, corn, blueberries, strawberries, and sugar beets. Small towns and villages lay nestled throughout and long, flat, straight highways and roadways cross through the country. The southern tip of Lake Manitoba is about 12 miles north of Portage. It is a massive body of water and a summer home to a large variety of waterfowl. During a walk in my neighborhood, one summer's day, I recall a rather large pelican nonchalantly walking down the sidewalk. There was a large pond in the city, and it probably decided to visit.

Manitoba is a beautiful province in the spring, summer, and fall. The only drawback is the overwhelming prevalence of mosquitoes, black flies and many other varieties of insects. In late spring, the wood tick is particularly troublesome. This nefarious tiny insect crawls onto hosts, human and animal, usually without detection, buries its head into the victim, and over a period of days, sucks the host's blood. It will gorge until many times its original size before releasing itself. The tick is a common carrier of Lyme's Disease, which can cause paralysis to the host. The tick lives in high grass and brush and was most common during the months of May and June.

I was constantly combing through Niki's thick fur for these pests. Many times after getting home from long callouts, I sometimes spent an hour grooming the dog. It was common to discover eight to twelve of these pests. After that process, I then stepped into my garage, shed all my clothes and equipment, and checked my own body. After checking the clothes, I immediately washed them. I sometimes found two or three of these nasty critters on me. In the mornings, I always re-checked the dog and sometimes found two or three more already attached to him.

Manitoba winters are fierce. During my first winter, the mean temperature for January was minus 37 degrees Celsius. Added to the cold temperatures were strong north winds and blizzards. I recall winter striking vigorously at the end of October and we still had snow the following April.

Because of my large area of responsibility, a considerable amount of my time was spent driving and my response time could sometimes be hours. In late June, I received a call after midnight. A car had rolled into a ditch and slammed into a power pole. The male driver and lone occupant fled the scene on foot. Witnesses said the driver ran south from the scene, across a farm field.

It was over an hour before I attended the scene on Highway 8, near the community of Selkirk. Prior to my arrival, two RCMP members had walked out into the same farm field for about 200 yards and then walked back.

I quickly harnessed Niki and he picked up a scent going across the same field the members had walked. One of the members went with me as my back up. He commented that the trail Niki was working was exactly where he and the other member had walked. At about 200 yards, Niki stopped and circled once. Again, the member told me that was where the members stopped, turned, and went back to the scene. Niki persisted and did not bring his head up. To me it appeared he was trying to sort something out. Suddenly at the point where the two members had turned, the dog surged ahead and the line went tight again. I praised the dog and he dug in harder going across the fallow field.

Niki had been following all three scents together and when two stopped, he continued with the third track. Tracking or following a human scent is not like "Hollywood." In the movies, the handler shows the dog a piece of clothing or article belonging to the suspect. Perhaps they believe the dog will discriminate from all other tracks and only follow the scent presented to it. From my training and experience, the dog will follow the freshest scent it finds. In this particular case, three scents were together. The first two were obviously fresher, but had ended. Niki had made the correct presumption that this was the scent to follow.

It was a clear night with stars glistening in the night sky. I could easily make out the flat prairie horizon as we moved south across the field. After about a mile, we crossed a fence and continued across a mix of pasture and bush. I could see a farmyard about a mile or more ahead of us and told my back up to radio the other members to patrol ahead and check the farm. If the suspect made it to the farm, I feared he might try to steal a vehicle.

We crashed into a thicket and the dog surged more than ever. From that action, I believed we might be closing in on the driver. Suddenly the line went slack and I heard a man's voice exclaim, "Hey, ow! That hurt!" I smashed through the bush, frantically trying to get to Niki. I praised the dog as I got to him. He stood over the man's prone body, who was face down on the ground. Niki turned to me with a happy, satisfied expression.

Niki had nipped the man on the back of the leg when he found him. The member with me handcuffed the prisoner's hands behind his back. I could smell the distinctive odor of liquor. We both helped the man to stand up, but as he did so, he grimaced in pain and could not straighten up. He was a big, burly man, in his forties and appeared to be physically strong. At first, we believed he might be feigning injury until we started to escort him out to a roadway, about 200 yards ahead. After about 50 yards, he almost doubled over and complained bitterly of back pain. We took the handcuffs off, which seemed to help, but in the last 50 yards or so, we had to support the suspect as he walked. A member took him directly to hospital.

At the local hospital, x-rays revealed the prisoner had crushed vertebrae in his lower back. Doctors immediately transferred him to Winnipeg for emergency surgery. One of the attending physicians later commended us for finding the man when we did. Otherwise, paralysis or worse, shock and death could have been the result.

In the summer of 1994, the RCMP ERT for the province of Saskatchewan requested the assistance of the ERT from Manitoba. The team had a standoff with two murder suspects at their farm near the farming community of Carlyle, in southeast Saskatchewan. It was about a four-hour drive west of Portage la Prairie. A man and his 20-year-old son were suspects in a recent murder and refused to surrender to police. Barricaded in their farmhouse for two days, both men had exchanged gunfire with police. They refused to talk to police. Saskatchewan ERT needed relief and Manitoba ERT obliged. I and another Manitoba dog handler attended with Manitoba ERT.

Investigators met us upon our arrival and briefed us before we took up replacement positions from the Saskatchewan ERT. They gave us a very descriptive history of the two suspects. Both had long histories of violence and criminal activities in the area. The community feared them, and most people considered the brutal pair unpredictable and remorseless. They were suspects in the disappearance of the wife and mother of this dysfunctional household. Rumor had it that the men shot the woman and disposed of the remains by chopping up her corpse and feeding it through a large wood chipper.

On another occasion, the two suspects had a party at the farmhouse. During the gathering, one male guest, with sensibilities clouded by the consumption of large quantities of drugs and alcohol, announced to everyone that he was going to shoot himself. With that, he picked up a rifle that he discovered in the house. In a vain attempt to attract attention and be humorous, he pointed the barrel at his head, reached down, and pulled the trigger. He neglected to check if the gun was loaded. He blew his own head apart. After the brief interruption, the hosts encouraged their guests to continue with the party. It occurred in the kitchen and the revelers had to step over the corpse to get to the refrigerator for more beer.

With those thoughts in our mind, the other dog handler and I carefully deployed around the farmhouse with the ERT members. It was early afternoon and we expected to be on site until 2:00 AM the next morning. This would give the Saskatchewan ERT time to rest and re-group. For the dog handlers, our job was two-fold. Firstly, the handlers and dogs could assist with an ERT assault of the house and secondly, if one or both suspects escaped, we could track or search for the suspect(s).

It was an old two-storey wooden house, with a peaked roof and weather worn white paint on the outside. All the windows in the house were broken, from either gunshots or tear gas rockets fired by ERT members. Several tear gas rockets had missed their marks, embedding in the sides of the house. ERT had intended to fill the house with enough tear gas to force the suspects outside, but the plan proved fruitless. It was evident to me that it had been a very dramatic event and I was surprised that nobody was injured. We did not detect any movement from the house and settled in for a long evening. Niki and I were with an ERT member on the north side of the yard about 200 yards from the house. We concealed ourselves amongst some large farm machinery situated in a row of large trees and tall grass. We had to keep movement to a minimum.

The afternoon dragged on into evening. The sun set on the flat western horizon in a spectacular splash of red, orange, and yellow. We prepared for the enveloping darkness. Hungry mosquitoes appeared and tortured us incessantly. Searchlights bathed the house with stark, bright light that cast ghostly shadows on the eves of the building, which gave it a foreboding, evil appearance.

We had no response to our repeated efforts to make contact with the barricaded men. The ERT commander used a loudspeaker that broke the stillness of the night. At one point, a technician sent a remote control robot to the open front door. Armed with its own camera and searchlight, we hoped it would show us what was happening inside the house. For unknown reasons, it stopped dead at the doorway and the tech frantically tried to retrieve it without success. Nerves were starting to fray and members wanted to assault the house to end the waiting game. The ERT commander urged everyone to be patient.

At 2:00 AM, Saskatchewan ERT and a third dog handler moved in and we stood down for some rest. The ERT commander scheduled us to return at 8:00 AM. It felt good to stand and stretch after a long night of being prone or kneeling. We gladly accepted hot food and coffee while we discussed the feasibility of an assault. Deep down, I was apprehensive about going in the house, but like the others, I was anxious to see this file concluded. We bedded down in tents a few miles away from the scene.

Early the next morning, as we were preparing to go back to the site, the ERT commander informed us that Saskatchewan ERT had made a hard entry at 4:00 AM. They found both the suspects deceased and it appeared they had been so for some time. It was determined that the father had shot his son before turning his own rifle on himself. We were no longer required.

It was difficult not to be distressed at times. Despite remaining objective and concentrating on the job at hand, some of the more bizarre and grisly cases were having an effect on me. I was finding it harder to remain impartial. Investigators from the Lac du Bonnet detachment, northeast of Winnipeg, called me about 3:00 AM, in mid-August 1995. I had already worked another case before the call and had just got to bed. It was a two-hour drive and by the time I reached the detachment, I was exhausted. With the detachment members, I then drove east of the town for almost an hour, into a remote region near the Ontario border. A citizen reported finding a pickup truck with a camper, abandoned in the area.

The vehicle owner lived in Winnipeg, but family members had reported him missing to the Winnipeg Police Service, two days previously.

According to his family, he had become depressed. It was also unlike him to leave without telling somebody. Investigators conducted a cursory search around the truck and camper and recovered several pieces of clothing and the lower jawbone of a human being. In the camper, the members found a suitcase filled with women's undergarments. Dried seminal fluid covered the clothing and because of that, the stench from the suitcase was disgusting.

With the aid of a specially trained RCMP evidence recovery/ search team, Niki and I went to working the bush around the truck. The search team recovered a human skull with flesh and hair still attached along with the upper jawbone. A pathologist would later determine that the jawbones and skull belonged to the missing man. Niki and I continued the search through thick, heavy brush and the dog located a black canvas, homemade bodice, complete with copper rivets. The man's blood covered the bodice. It was similar to other pieces of clothing found in the camper.

We continued for three more hours, but located nothing else. From all indications, it appeared the man had taken his life, perhaps accidentally. We also learned that the missing man was a masochist. Large predatory animals had easily located the corpse, tore it apart and quickly consumed it. Since there was nothing else to do, we headed home.

As I had mentioned before many of my calls required me to be away for hours and sometimes days. Driving time, along with hours of searching for evidence or tracking suspects was time consuming and at times exhausting. One summer's night, dispatch called me out regarding a break-in in Portage la Prairie. I attended the scene within minutes, harnessed Niki, and cast him around the scene. He quickly located a track, went about 100 yards and found three male subjects hiding in a thicket of bush. With suspects in custody and all evidence recovered, I returned home to bed within 20 minutes. It was the complete opposite to what we were used to working.

Niki and I worked at the Headingley Provincial Jail one day in 1994, searching for contraband in the inmate's cells and common areas. Another RCMP handler was working with me. All we found was paraphernalia and trace amounts of narcotics. After a couple hours, we concluded our searches.

Returning from the drug searches, the prison staff invited us to stay for lunch. We knew the prisoners made all the meals at the institution and politely declined. The assistant warden offered a tour of the prison for our information.

During the excursion, we learned the prison was built in 1931. To me it was a rundown, outdated facility. The warden enthusiastically showed us one area after the other. This included the old "condemned cells" that were still used for solitary confinement. During the days of executing murderers in Canada, condemned prisoners waited in those cells. If the appeal courts upheld the conviction, then the prisoner had his date with the hangman.

Actually, the "condemned cell" was a big cell within a room. Guards sat with the prisoner, outside of the cell, 24 hours a day until the appointed time. Guards, a sheriff, and the hangman then entered the cell. After the prisoner's hands and arms were pinioned, they lead him through a large metal door at one corner of the cell. This led directly to the gallows. The hangman placed a canvas bag over the head and then drew the rope tight around the neck. After strapping the legs together, the executioner finally threw the lever that sprung the trap door beneath the condemned. The prisoner fell to his death. The process was apparently quick. From the time the big metal door opened until the trap door sprung, it was usually no more than 30 seconds.

To me, this part of the tour was very sobering. In fact, I found it rather sickening. I stood on the trap door where several prisoners met their fate years ago. I remember staring at the stark green walls of the chamber and having a cold chill run down my back. The warden mentioned that on one occasion, officials hanged two prisoners "back to back." This meant the hangman placed both condemned back to back on the trap door and dropped them together. Our tour guide also related that on a few occasions the hangman misjudged and did not use enough rope. Instead of having their necks snapped, the victims suffered an excruciating death by strangulation. Alternately, during another execution, too much rope resulted in the near-decapitation of the prisoner. There is a graveyard on the grounds of the prison and some of those buried there, died on the gallows.

I soon learned that the jails in my area would no longer be my responsibility. The corrections people had identified a guard to train and handle a black Labrador retriever for narcotic detection. The dog and handler quickly proved to be proficient and I took every opportunity to visit and train with them. They were a dedicated, competent team.

It was nearly midnight, Christmas Day, 1994, when my phone rang at home. Up until that time, the Christmas break had been uneventful. A man had threatened to kill his girlfriend at their house in Portage la Prairie. The young woman escaped, but the suspect barricaded himself in the residence and refused to talk to the police. The man was drunk and had a history of violence.

Within minutes, Niki and I joined the investigators outside the suspect's house. It was a cold, still night and the members were standing with storm coats buttoned up, and fur hats pulled over their ears. One member at the scene, named Larry, was the staff sergeant in charge of the detachment. Larry was a tall, well-built, personable man that was a definite "old school" type. He wanted to end the situation by just going into the house and forcibly arresting the drunken man. I could see that the other members in attendance did not agree to Larry's strategy. In fact, a couple members commented to me that they wanted to wait until the man went to sleep before entering. They tried to convince Larry to no avail. Larry was adamant and he was the boss. The members could still see the suspect walking around, drinking in the house. We did not know if the man had a weapon. I agreed with the members and told Larry there was no hurry. If the suspect kept drinking, he would eventually pass out and then we could arrest him without force. Why risk getting hurt over Christmas.

Larry relented somewhat and backed down, to our relief. I ensured all the members were in position to contain the drunk and we settled down to wait. After an hour or so, we did not see any more movement in the house. We telephoned the residence, but got a busy signal. The culprit had left the phone off the hook from an earlier attempted call by Larry. I suggested waiting a little longer, before making an approach.

Suddenly, without warning, Larry stood up and marched towards the back door. He decided to go in and expected the rest of us to follow him. I grabbed Niki's collar and quickly fell in behind Larry. I motioned to the other surprised members to stay put, except for one member named Doug. I had worked with Doug on several occasions in the past. He was very capable, dependable and had good common sense.

Larry opened the door and strode nonchalantly into the home. The suspect was asleep in the bedroom on the main floor. He was fully clothed, laying face down on the bed with both hands tucked under his body. Incredulously, Larry reached down and started shaking the sleeping man. As Doug and I reached the bed, Larry was still shaking him and calling his name.

In an instant, the culprit flipped around as Doug grabbed at his wrists. Larry was slow to help Doug who suddenly yelled, "Drop it! Drop it! He's got a knife!" I released Niki and in a split second, the dog had the assailant's right shoulder in a full mouth bite. The man shrieked as he dropped the eight-inch long knife from his right hand. Doug and Larry pinned the man and started to handcuff him as Niki let go of the shoulder. I praised the dog and took him away after the handcuffs were on. Doug and another member took the prisoner to hospital for treatment.

The rest of us returned to the detachment where Larry approached me. He knew that he had acted impulsively, endangering himself, Doug, and me. Larry had high praise for Niki and invited me to his house for a "nightcap." By now, it was after 3:00 AM, but I knew that I would have trouble sleeping. I accepted the offer, taking Niki home first. Larry was quite generous with the "nightcap." It ended up being three "nightcaps," all doubles.

It was a cold winter's day and I had just concluded some searches of baggage at the Winnipeg International Airport. It was mid-afternoon but nightfall was already approaching. It was over an hour's drive back to Portage and I was anxious to get home. I took Niki for a quick run before getting back in the truck. I threw his ball for him, but as he charged after it, I heard a slight whine. He returned the ball, wanting me to toss it again. I obliged and I heard him whine again. I checked him, but did not see anything wrong. My heart started to pound and I had a sinking feeling in my stomach. Niki was six and a half years old, which is still young for most dogs, but not for hard working police dogs. I had seen other handlers with dogs younger than Niki develop arthritis and other debilitating diseases.

I tired to be optimistic as I drove Niki to his veterinarian, who happened to be in Winnipeg. It could be something minor or treatable. My world crashed around me, after the doctor took a radiograph of the dog's hips. The worried expression on the vet's face did me in. Niki was developing arthritis in both hips. It was not bad, but bad enough that Niki could no longer work. I felt sick that I had not seen any signs of lameness or pain in the dog before. The vet assured me that dogs sometimes did not show discomfort, especially when they were busy doing something they enjoyed. Niki certainly liked police work.

Following a sleepless night, I contacted the Training Kennels the next morning to update them on Niki's condition. After reviewing my veterinarian's detailed report, the Kennels removed Niki from service. They kindly informed me that they would leave the rest of the details up to me concerning the dog's future. The Kennels advised that I would attend the next training course, in about two months.

I contacted my veterinarian again to give me a prognosis on Niki's condition. The dog would not be in any pain or discomfort for a while. However, even with a more sedentary life, the disease might progress quickly and he would not enjoy a good quality of life. With a heavy heart, I considered putting Niki down, until a local large animal veterinarian contacted me. He told me about a new drug being used successfully, to slow the progress of arthritis in dogs. It was a very expensive treatment, but he made me an offer that renewed my hope.

He suggested that he would take Niki as a pet and mascot at his large animal clinic and provide the treatment, which he could obtain without great expense. I drove to his clinic and talked with him for an hour or so. He was a younger man that lived on his own, dedicating his life to the treatment of sick and injured animals. His facility was impressive and he seemed to be a genuine person. Niki seemed to think so too. I noticed the vet took to the dog as well.

I waited another day to consider the options. Keeping Niki would be very difficult, especially with another police dog around. It would be heartbreaking for Niki and me, when I would have to leave him behind, while the other dog and I attended calls. After careful consideration, I felt Niki would receive good care with the veterinarian and that his remaining days would be pain free.

The next evening, I drove Niki to his new home. I did not care that the vet saw me choking back sobs as I said goodbye to my old friend. Niki looked at me expectantly as I opened the clinic door to leave. I told him to stay and he obediently did so, and then I walked out into the cold, night air, with tears streaming down my face.

I later learned that Niki settled into his new life quite well. He became close friends with the clinic cat. Clients were often amused at Niki carrying the docile feline around the clinic in his mouth. The vet became concerned at one point when Niki kept insisting on herding the cattle that came in for treatment. The doctor was worried that the dog might be injured and put a stop to it. I laughed at this, thinking that Niki was only living up to his breed name - a German Shepherd.

The Kennels gave me priority to retrain. They sent a big, robust, handsome brown and black male German Shepherd named Saber. He was only about a year old and had a considerable amount of energy. Saber had an aloof, independent demeanor. He was hardheaded, but loved to work, probably more to please himself than me.

The dog was a product of the RCMP puppy-rearing program and another handler had taken considerable time to work with Saber. He was a strong tracker and well on the way to a working life. I had about two months before my scheduled course at the

Kennels. Despite other duties assigned to me, I also spent a good amount of my time training and socializing Saber.

This was my third trip to the Training Kennels, but because of the dog's prior training, my instructor accelerated the course. Saber and I completed the training in about seven weeks compared to the regular sixteen weeks. By the end of June, we were back at Portage la Prairie.

1995. Saber, 2 years old, just after completing training at the Training Kennels

Dispatch called me out from home. There had been a lengthy dramatic high-speed pursuit, which ended in a rural bush area about 50 miles northwest of the city of Winnipeg. The registered owner of the vehicle had several warrants for his arrest and was possibly armed with a handgun. The members involved in the chase briefly lost sight of the car, only to find it again, crashed in a ditch, wrapped in a tangle of branches and scrub. The lone occupant of the vehicle was gone.

During the busy summer months, duty called Saber and I out three or four times a week. We had completed our training together a few weeks earlier. Saber was new and still needed some time to get his "street smarts" and prove himself to me.

Saber and I crashed through the dense, tangled bush. The deadfall was heavy, resulting in both the dog and me having to jump over the downed trees as we pursued the suspect. Despite the track being over two hours old, the thick bush held the scent and was now releasing whiffs of it for Saber to follow with his big discerning nose.

We started the track at about 3:00 AM on a clear, warm, starlit, morning and only about ten minutes into the track, my back up man was already falling behind. I did not know this colleague well, other than he was at least 15 years younger than me. He appeared fit and strong. As I vaulted over another tree trunk, I thought to myself, "What the hell kind of young people are we hiring now? He can't even keep up to an old guy like me."

I heard Saber's claws scratching on another tree trunk as he got his footing on the way over. The dog was in a harness and I was hanging onto the end of the 20-foot long line attached to it. Saber was intently locked on to the track. Despite my years as a handler, the adrenalin rush that I always experienced in these situations had become addictive. I loved this part of my job. Using the acute senses of a well-trained dog to find a human being was still exhilarating.

My back up man lagged even farther behind. I tried to wave him off, but because of the distance and darkness, I was unsure if he saw me. From my experience, I knew that he would only be a detriment to Saber and me. Despite the fact the man we were pursuing may be armed, I did not want another person to distract me. The dog and I were better off alone in this pursuit.

During that time in Manitoba, RCMP radio communication in most rural areas was abysmal, especially with portable radios. I discovered the portable that I carried was useless in this area, but my cell phone kept me in touch with the members patrolling the roads and trails in the area.

Saber was a relentlessly tracking and keeping a murderous pace despite the terrain. Suddenly I heard the splashing of water and sucking sounds as the dog's feet sunk in mud and water. We were now in a swamp, but the dog continued onward. Reeds and high grass slapped me in the face as I desperately hung on to the line. I was sure that my back up had finally abandoned us, a prospect that did not bother me in the least. I was breathing heavily and the smock that I wore over my uniform shirt was soaked with sweat. The water was halfway up to my knees and at times, the dog had to lunge through the water. Amazingly enough, Saber was still catching the suspect's scent trapped in the thick vegetation.

I wanted to stop for a moment to catch my breath and adjust my clothing and gun belt. To my relief, we finally came out of the swamp onto dry land. I stopped the dog. Saber looked back at me eagerly as if to say, "Come on, we can't stop now. We gotta get this guy!" We had been tracking almost an hour, through about three miles of bush and swamp. I was trembling from the exertion and my eyes burned from the sweat that ran off my forehead. I grumbled aloud to myself, "Bloody piss-ant, running through this crap!" referring to the suspect. The dog looked at me again. This time he tilted his head as if to ask, "Who are you talking to?"

I took a moment and looked up at the early morning sky. The sky is always much crisper and the stars brighter when not around any artificial light. I quickly found the North Star and determined that we were still advancing in a southerly direction.

I pulled the cell phone from the pocket of my smock. The smock was not part of the RCMP uniform. The year before, I assisted a joint task force made up of members from the Ontario Provincial Police (OPP) and the RCMP. It was a large narcotics operation in the northwest part of Ontario. My assignment was only for a few days, but I became friends with two dog handler counterparts with the OPP.

What amazed me about these handlers was how much equipment and clothing they had at their disposal, compared with RCMP handlers. They must have realized this as well and probably felt a little sorry for me. As I was preparing to return to Manitoba, after the investigation was complete, both handlers presented me with going-away gifts. One of the gifts was the smock. It fit and I added it to my work attire as my "good luck tracking jacket."

I had removed the OPP shoulder flashes and replaced them with RCMP flashes. The smock was battle grey in color and from time to time, when I wore it around headquarters in Winnipeg, I got second looks from some of the senior NCO's (non-commissioned officers). I did not care what these "dress and deportment" types thought of my new uniform. For me, this item of clothing was practical, since it offered protection when running and crashing through thick vegetation.

I thought about taking the time to drain the cold water out of my hiking boots, but decided I would hold off for a while in the event we ended up in another bog. It could just be a waste of precious time to empty them now. Saber was anxious to continue on the track, but I told him to stay. I speed-dialed the RCMP dispatch center in Winnipeg and after two rings a female voice crisply answered, "Telecoms." I replied, "Echo One here. Could you to relay to the patrolling members, we are tracking predominately south. Ask them to keep patrolling at least four or five miles south of the scene." The dispatcher acknowledged my request and asked me to remain on the phone while she relayed my message. In fewer than 30 seconds, she was back on the line. "I let the members know Echo One. Is there anything else at this time?" I thanked her and said I would call later. It was my hope that police cars patrolling ahead could locate the suspect or at least help contain him.

As I put the phone back in the smock, I looked at Saber and whispered, "Good boy." Before I could say more, he turned and put his head back down on the track. The line snapped tight as Saber locked back down on the track. I gave him another "Good boy," as the branches once again slapped across my chest.

Within about a half hour, the sky started to get lighter. I stopped again and took the time to get my boots off, drain them, and ring out my socks. Saber was tired, but he had now settled into a steady cadence, which he could probably maintain for hours.

I had read that biologists, studying the hunting habits of wolves, noted that a pack would track herds of caribou for days at a time. They concluded that the wolves picked out the weak and sick members of a herd from their scent and continued to follow them until the time was right for an attack. I wondered if Saber's willingness and persistence was similar to the habits of his distant cousins.

We were still traversing through thick, tangled bush. This was the toughest track Saber had worked during his short career. In the back of my mind, I began to second-guess Saber. This is not a good thing for a handler to do. Especially since I had some experience. I should have known better. Years before, an old handler commented to me, "Ninety-nine percent of the time, the handler is his own worst enemy. You gotta believe in that dog!" In other words, remain positive and never lose faith in your dog's abilities.

Because of the tough conditions we faced on this track, I started to think that Saber could have abandoned the human track and was following some sort of animal. As I was fretting about his capabilities, we came into a clearing and I looked down and saw a big, beautiful human footprint in the sand. I called out to Saber with relief in my voice, "Atta boy, good dog! Let's get the bad guy!" He responded by pulling harder into his harness. I was elated at the dog's determination and at the same time mad at myself for doubting my obviously capable canine partner.

The sky continued to lighten and the flat eastern horizon was starting to turn a shade of crimson. We came to the top of a ridge and I looked down onto a large, shallow valley. It was light enough now that I could see gravel secondary roads that criss-crossed over the country. It was turning into farmland, rather than just all brush and bogs. I phoned the dispatcher again to let her know that we were still alive and proceeding south. After taking another moment to catch my wind, we continued.

After a half-mile or so, we crossed a road and plunged into another dense thicket. We then came out of the brush onto an open field and continued south. The first thing that came to mind was that we were easy targets on the open ground. If the suspect was armed, he could be waiting up ahead to ambush us. I was getting tired, anxious, and frustrated. The suspect was obviously aware of being tracked by the way he kept going in and out of the brush. This probably was not the first time for him. Suddenly, we were in thick bush again for 300 yards and then we came out onto another road. The dog wanted to go east down the road and we did so for about another 100 yards. The sun poked over the horizon and I heard birds chirping in the tree line along the road. Saber abruptly turned off the road again and went back into the bush southbound.

We popped out of the thicket, crossed yet another field and back into more bush. The dog seemed to be leaning into the harness a little harder now. I was certain that we were closing in on our elusive man. This time the bush seemed even thicker. I was panting and nearly exhausted. At one point, I had to go through on my hands and knees. I could not see Saber, but suddenly the line went slack. I worked my way towards the dog and discovered that he had a black T-shirt in his mouth that he was shaking vigorously. After a brief tug-o-war, Saber reluctantly let me have the shirt. He then immediately turned his attention back to the track.

We continued for another 200 yards and came out onto another gravel road. As we emerged, I saw a shirtless man nonchalantly walking east down the road. This man, that we had chased half the night, was now only about 100 yards ahead of us. In the stillness of the early morning air, I heard a vehicle coming from the west, along the same road. It was some distance away and sounded as if it was moving slowly. The man was still walking away from us and did not turn around. Gathering my final reserves, I dashed up onto the road and sprinted towards the man. Saber was straining hard to get to him. I did not want to release the dog yet. He was tired and if the suspect resisted, I feared Saber would be unable to protect himself. It was best if we got to the man together.

The suspect was probably exhausted as well and perhaps did not hear the dog and me behind him. I did not call out. There was still the possibility of a weapon, even though I did not see one. We were within 50 feet of the suspect, when he suddenly spun around. I quickly released the dog and Saber charged up to him. Saber did not bite the man, who stood stone still. Often a dog will not attack somebody that is not moving. The suspect focused all his attention on the dog, who was warily circling him. The man slowly started to reach behind his back. With one last burst of energy, I plowed into the man, clothes lining him across the upper chest with my left forearm. Now that there was movement, Saber bit the man on his right leg, as we all crashed in a heap onto the road. Winded from the fall to the ground, the man did not resist. With Saber at my side, I got back on my feet.

The vehicle that I heard earlier was much closer. It sped up suddenly. Taking my attention off the suspect, I turned to see that it was a police car. It skidded to a stop in front of us. I could see the member was using his police radio to inform the other units of his discovery. The suspect was now in custody. We did not find any weapons on him and it turned out that he was not the registered owner (RO) of the suspect vehicle. He was an associate of the RO, had a lengthy criminal record, and like the RO, had outstanding warrants for his arrest. He said there was no particular reason he ran from the police, except for the warrants. Still, for me it had been a great success. With the suspect safely tucked away in the back of the police car, I took the time to praise Saber. I got down on my knees on the gravel road beside him. I petted and ruffled the heavy fur around his neck and ran my hands down his back. Saber had certainly earned his "street smarts" on that job and demonstrated that he was a worthy partner.

On a warm, cloudy evening in July 1995, Saber and I were on patrol in Portage when we received a call to assist Ashern detachment with a high-speed pursuit. The community is over 80 miles north of Portage and it took me an hour to drive to the area. During that time, the members lost sight of the vehicle, but after frantic patrols, relocated the car, and stopped it. They arrested the driver, but the passenger ran into the surrounding bush. I was now nearby and Saber quickly located a track going west from the car. After about 400 yards, the dog located a teenager hiding in the bush. The youth was terrified of the dog and did not resist arrest.

As I was preparing for the drive back to Portage, another Ashern member became involved in a second chase. A stolen pickup truck refused to stop, driving at high speeds down a dark, narrow highway near the town. The stolen vehicle was constantly changing directions and driving erratically, trying to dodge the police. I eventually joined the chase and at one point ended up as the lead police vehicle in the pursuit, with my big suburban truck. The Ashern police car had to drop back, because it suddenly developed mechanical problems.

The stolen truck swerved off the highway, bounced through the ditch, with great clods of dirt flying off both bumpers. It headed across an open wheat field at high speeds. I followed at some distance, because the dust from the farm field billowed over my vehicle, it was difficult to see where I was going. I continued through the field, following the tracks and soon drove down a gully into a pasture. It was fully dark but in my headlights, I saw the pickup truck parked at the bottom of the gully. I had lost contact with the other members and my police radio would not transmit. It was another example of a poor, antiquated communications system.

I cautiously pulled up behind the suspect vehicle. Because of a canopy on the back of the truck, I could not see if anybody was sitting in the cab. The headlights were off, but the engine was still running. I stepped out of the truck with my flashlight and drew my pistol. Saber was intent on the truck and I left my door open, in case I needed him. I called out to the truck several times, ordering the driver out with his hands up, but there was no response.

It was quiet except for the police radio in my truck, crackling with unintelligible transmissions. A few mosquitoes whined around my face and I heard frogs croaking in a pond nearby. The night air was still. I told Saber to stay as I slowly and apprehensively approached the vehicle on the driver's side. With each step, my heart beat faster and my breathing increased. My palms were sweaty from holding the flashlight and pistol. The driver's window was up and because of the reflection on the glass, I could not see inside the cab. With the barrel of my pistol, I smashed the window out with one hard strike and pointed it inside the cab. The driver was gone. I quickly reached in, shut the engine off, and took the keys.

I ran back to my police vehicle. Saber still had his harness on from the last track. He was anxious and keen to go. I snapped the long line onto the harness and cast the dog at the driver's side of the truck. He did not locate a track. On the passenger side, he hit a scent and it went in a semi-circle behind my vehicle. A chill ran down my spine as I wondered if the suspect had used the darkness to exit the scene and run in behind me. I felt even more vulnerable. The dog charged ahead and the track went about 300 yards before entering a thick stand of poplar trees.

Saber crashed forward for about another 100 yards, when the line suddenly went slack. I barged up just in time to see a metallic-like flicker. The suspect was sitting on the ground, almost covered by grass and brush. The flicker made me think the man had a weapon in his hand and I instinctively kicked his hands as Saber delivered a bite on the suspect's upper right leg. The man yelled out that he only wanted to give up.

At that time, I heard vehicles drive up and voices yelling my name. To my absolute relief, the Ashern members had finally located me. It turned out that the flicker was a small cigarette lighter, which the suspect claimed he was using to light his face up so that I would see him. He later admitted to several other crimes in the area and led investigators to a large cache of stolen property.

The provincial Department of Natural Resources (DNR) attended a farm about 20 miles east of Portage in early October 1995. They received a report that the owner of the farm had shot a deer without the proper licensing and the farmer was in possession of the deer carcass. The residents were uncooperative and ordered DNR off the property. As they were leaving, one sharp-eyed investigator saw the deer carcass hanging in an outbuilding. Consequently, DNR obtained a warrant and returned to search. The carcass was no longer in the outbuilding, so they called me out to assist them. It was early in the evening and already dark.

Saber located a track westbound from the outbuilding and continued for about 300 yards into a fallow field. The dog abruptly stopped and circled once. Saber put his nose back to the ground but then turned to me with an almost quizzical expression. With my flashlight, I looked at the ground in front of Saber and saw a hoof sticking out. Trained dogs must ignore animal scent, but I can imagine that Saber was thinking that there just were not any other scents at the end of that track. The residents had carried the deer out to the field and attempted to bury it in the loose dirt.

The DNR were happy with the results and the residents admitted to the offence. During the interview, the DNR investigators saw that one suspect had a baggie of marihuana in his front shirt pocket. They seized the drug and asked if more drugs were in the dwelling house. The warrant did not include the house, but DNR asked if the suspects would consent to a voluntary search using the dog. The man's shoulders slumped and he went back inside and soon reappeared with a large bag of the drug. In light of Saber's skill at finding the carcass, the man decided the dog would have no trouble locating the narcotic. The drug seizure only added to the man's problems that night.

On another occasion, a combined Canada Customs and RCMP investigation culminated with search warrants at three farm residences. Investigators wanted to conduct the searches simultaneously. At the time, individuals that lived near the vast, unguarded international border were involved in smuggling large quantities of contraband cigarettes and liquor from the United States into Canada. Information from undercover operations showed that it was an elaborate operation, involving several people.

On the appointed morning, investigators divided into three separate search teams and descended on the farms. I was tasked with floating from farm to farm as required, since they were all within a few miles of each other. At one farm, investigators uncovered a large amount of American whiskey in 26-ounce plastic bottles. A Customs agent showed me how smugglers used syringes to dilute the whiskey with water before sale. They poked a small hole at the bottom of the plastic bottle and drew out a portion of the whiskey. They replaced the whiskey with water and placed a dab of crazy glue over the hole. The agent showed me a tampered and un-tampered bottle. I could easily see the difference in color between the bottles. The smugglers were ripping off their customers.

Agents seized a large quantity of contraband from two of the farms, but nothing at the third. They asked me to conduct a quick search before concluding the warrant. In a small barn, Saber started to indicate "high," meaning he picked up scent coming from above him. The loft was filled to the rafters with loose hay that investigators checked earlier. Using the long handle of a pitchfork, I prodded the hay in several places. I did not locate anything at first, but suddenly the fork hit something solid.

In the hay was a large bale of loose American tobacco. The Customs agents moved some of the hay aside and discovered about 50 bales of tobacco and 20 cases of beer. I had not trained Saber to indicate liquor or cigarettes, but I surmised there was enough human scent on the articles combined with the smell of the contraband, to be foreign to the environment.

An illegal alien had entered Canada in the border town of Emerson, about 50 miles south of Winnipeg. The alien was an American citizen, known to Canadian police. The only member on duty that day in the small farming community, bounced from one reported location to the next without finding the man. At one point, a citizen found the man in a holiday trailer owned by that citizen. The man fled and ran behind the town's Catholic Church. It was almost an hour later when Saber and I arrived. The dog picked up a scent behind the church going west. We went through yards, bush, and fields for about a mile on the outskirts of town.

The track ended at the entrance of the person door to a large car garage on a property. I cautiously opened the door and entered with the dog. The garage contained a number of antique Cadillac cars. The old cars gave off a spooky, uninviting presence. It was cold and quiet in the building. I let the dog take the lead and he went directly to one old car. A head poked up from the back seat and I leveled my pistol on the subject. I ordered him to show me his hands and slowly exit the car. He complied and I took him outside. My portable radio did not work, thanks again to poor communications. I then realized that I forgot my cell phone in the truck.

I escorted my handcuffed prisoner to a house about a block from the garage and knocked on the door. I was in civilian clothes that day and suddenly remembered that I also forgot my identification in the truck. I had my prisoner sit down on the steps and tapped on the door.

A young woman answered with a puzzled look on her face. I understood it must have been unusual for her to see a man sitting on her front stoop in handcuffs and another standing with a big German Shepherd. I told the woman I was an RCMP member and needed assistance. I took out my notebook and wrote down the toll free telephone number for our dispatch in Winnipeg. I asked her to phone the number and instruct them to tell the Emerson member to meet me at the front of her house. She glared at me and did not say anything. With a pleading look, I whined, "Really, I'm a policeman." She grinned and closed the door. Within a few minutes, the member attended and took custody of the illegal alien. After the member left, the woman came out of the house and handed back my notebook. I thanked her for all her help.

The Sandy Bay detachment phoned me on a cold, blustery Sunday afternoon, in December 1995. The members were investigating a break-in of their own police office. I had never been to a break-in at a police office before. Sandy Bay is a small community, about a one-hour drive northwest of Portage.

Members were working at the detachment until about 4:00 AM. Nobody worked Sundays, but an off-duty member came in to complete some paperwork and discovered the ransacked detachment.

By the time I arrived, too much time had elapsed to attempt tracking the suspect(s). The weather grew worse, with increased wind and lower temperatures. Members were busy taking inventory and luckily, all the firearms were in the detachment safe. I could see the footprints of the offenders in the snow and followed them, allowing Saber to search ahead of me. The dog located numerous buried articles including detachment keys, soft body armor, briefcases, paperwork, cameras, camera tripod, a VCR, clothing, uniforms, and boxes of camera film.

In late April 1996, a riot broke out at the Headingley Jail, situated just west of Winnipeg. A call went out for all available members, including me, to attend this major incident. By the time I arrived at 8:00 PM, it was total mayhem. I met another RCMP handler, who had arrived just before me. Fires burned everywhere. People were yelling, screaming, and swearing. Over 275 prisoners had free reign over the facility. Glass, rock, bricks and every form of debris littered the prison grounds.

The general population had already gained access to the protective custody unit and unconfirmed reports were circulating of tortures and beatings. One inmate apparently had fingers severed. Other prisoners intentionally held his hand in an open doorway, and then slammed the large, metal door closed. A head count of the guards revealed that one female guard was missing. Prison staff feared that she might be in the basement of the Intake Building (an administrative center), a building now controlled by prisoners. However, nobody was sure of anything at that point.

More RCMP members were arriving from all detachments in southern Manitoba. This was an RCMP matter, but the

Winnipeg Police Service (WPS) had also responded in force and provided desperately needed assistance. The Manitoba ERT arrived. I had put a call to all RCMP dog handlers, WPS dog handlers and both dog handlers with the Brandon Police Service (BPS) and all were responding.

The other RCMP handler and I ensured that we were available to assist the ERT. Prison staff and RCMP were frantically trying to locate the missing guard and we knew that ERT was formulating a plan for a rescue operation. About an hour later, a guard received a muffled radio transmission on one of their portable radios. It was, as guessed, the female guard and she was in fact in the basement of the Intake Building. She had been able to lock herself in an office. She was wise enough to code her responses so that only the guards knew her location. Prison staff feared that prisoners had accessed the portable radios and were monitoring the guards.

ERT had their plan worked out, which as expected, included two dog handlers. The ERT members surreptitiously walked to the Intake Building in single file, with all their gear and firearms at the ready. The other handler and I brought up the rear with our dogs. We used the walls of other buildings for cover until having to cross a debris littered field. We kept our eyes open, especially the rooftops. Earlier, prisoners had hurled bricks and rocks at RCMP and prison staff from the roofs. The flames and smoke from multiple fires cast moving shadows across the brick walls of the Intake Building. The chilling screams of tortured prisoners from the second floor cut through the volatile night air. My breathing was labored and my heart beat so hard that it felt like somebody was tapping on my eardrums. We had to stay objective and keep moving. We proceeded to the basement steps at the west side of the building. Debris littered the concrete stairs to the basement and we carefully descended and turned down the hallway.

With most of the lights smashed out, the hallway was dark, but we picked our way through the wreckage. The inside of the building had holes in the walls, broken windows, and overturned furniture. Smashed glass and all sorts of rubbish littered the floors. Prisoners had turned on the fire hoses and garbage floated in about three inches of cold water on the concrete floors. Acrid smoke filled the air from the fires.

The partially closed door to the office hung on its loose hinges. Inmates had likely forcibly opened it earlier. I hoped that we were not too late. On the floor above us, I could hear a large group of prisoners, yelling, swearing, and screaming. I prayed they did not have plans to come back downstairs. We quietly entered the office. The dimly lit room was in the same condition as the hallway. Two overturned desks lay on the floor in the center of the room. ERT members flipped one desk up to reveal the huddling guard. She gazed up at the two ERT members as they deftly lifted her onto her feet. I could tell that she was not sure who we were. She had no knowledge we were coming. She shook and her lower jaw trembled uncontrollably. The two members said nothing, but half-carrying her, swiftly escorted her out of the building with the rest of us following. Within a few minutes, she was safely behind friendly lines.

She was a brave soul and very fortunate. Trapped when the riot started, she had the forethought to hide herself with the portable radio. Prisoners did enter the office while she was under the desk. One inmate actually saw her, but did not tell the others. He simply encouraged everybody to leave the office.

The prisoner obviously knew what would happen if the others discovered her. It was certainly her lucky day.

All through the night, efforts to contain the inmates and regain control were slow. A bare electrical wire, coiled around a large amount of metal debris had accidentally electrocuted a WPS dog handler and his canine. They were fortunate to escape the episode without being badly injured. I knew the WPS member well and he had an outstanding canine partner. Talking to the handler later, he was very upset that his dog was hurt. The high-pitched yelps of his companion were almost too much for him to bear. He was sure that his dog only touched a piece of metal the hot wire was touching. Besides the inmates, there was obviously a multitude of other dangers.

By late afternoon of the second day, inmates started to surrender peacefully and the prison staff slowly regained control of the facility. All prisoners were accounted for, but there were casualties. Inmate retribution had been meted out, convict style. Ambulances rushed beaten and tortured inmates to hospital. Five or six lost fingers in the doorways and a guard later found a finger wrapped in a towel that belonged to one unfortunate victim. A few others had some of their teeth pulled out. A viciously assaulted inmate had a broom handle pushed up his rectum. A favored method of torture was to tie a victim into a chair and then push the man and chair down flights of concrete stairs. Personally, I had seen enough. I was sick and tired of prison riots.

Chapter 9
Wrap Up

By 1997, old car accident injuries were starting to compromise my ability to do the job. I enjoyed the dog handler duties, but my jaded attitude towards the justice system was increasing. With a heavy heart, I took early retirement after 22 years service with the RCMP, of which 14 years were as a dog handler. Reluctantly, I sent Saber to the Training Kennels for assignment to another handler.

Reflecting back, I figured that I was fortunate considering the number of dangerous situations that I had been involved in over the years. The murders of two dog handlers that I had worked with were emotionally draining. The fatal stabbing of two police dogs, whose handlers I worked with were sad, heartbreaking events.

Several members that I worked with were involved in shootings and, in some cases, had killed people. One member was shot in the legs with a sawed-off shotgun, while checking a vehicle during routine traffic duties. Another survived a bullet in the abdomen from a high-powered rifle, while responding to a domestic dispute. Both made remarkable recoveries, despite the physical and emotional trauma. Three members, who were not dog handlers, but well respected men who I closely worked with, committed suicide. Two of them had shot themselves in their police vehicles while on duty.

There have been many other cases that I worked on, some humorous to an extent, some sad, some terrifying and disturbing. From all these experiences, I believe that everything boils down to a deficiency or lack of empathy. Without empathy, we are nothing. All the murder scenes I attended remain vivid for me. I recall one scene with the nude corpse of a 16-year-old female; her arms and legs tied with ropes and trussed up amongst trees near an elementary schoolyard. She was a sex trade worker, but she had obviously put her faith and trust in someone that definitely had other nefarious plans. Nobody deserved to lose their life the way that young girl did. I did not locate any evidence at that scene, but the murderer was eventually located, and convicted.

At another scene, the execution style murder of two hitchhikers was very disturbing. The female victim made a vain attempt to protect her face, just as the murderer fired the weapon. The bullet went through a finger before smashing into her face, killing her. Her male partner met the same fate, but did not die immediately. Evidence at the scene showed that he thrashed and crawled around after being shot, possibly trying desperately to escape or to help the female victim. Four other handlers and I walked over 200 miles of ditches, pullouts, service roads, and campsites for five days, searching for evidence on that case. A lengthy investigation later identified the culprit who went to jail for life.

Trapper found a shell casing at another murder scene and along with other evidence; it contradicted the suspect's statement of events. Two innocent, defenseless people lost their lives over an argument with a drunk and a gun. The man went to jail for only seven years, convicted of manslaughter, since the courts deemed he was too drunk to realize what he was doing.

On the upside, I had the opportunity and privilege to work with some of the finest four-legged police officers in the world. My dogs were all good police officers and I must admit I had met many others that were good too. I have listened to many war stories from other handlers and their exploits with their dogs. It was always fascinating to hear how the dogs had such a finely tuned intuition that sometimes baffled the handlers.

I recall one handler relating events on a stakeout. Dog and handler were with several plainclothes members, watching a suspect's criminal activities. The suspect suddenly realized that he was under surveillance and tried to run from the scene. The dog and handler were about 200 yards from the action. Two or three plain-clothes members were in hot pursuit, running down an alleyway. The dog and handler did not see the events unfold, but heard all the commotion. The dog perceived something had happened and suddenly bolted from the handler. The suspect was getting away, when the police dog came around the corner, passed all the members without taking notice of them, and barreled onto the suspect. The handler said he had been reluctant to release the dog, since he feared for the safety of the members. The members were amazed the dog showed no interest in them, but was intent only on the suspect.

Once during a training track in a residential area, Niki ignored the advances of a young mongrel pup that bounced out of a yard as we went passed. The pup was inquisitive and only wanted to play. Without bringing his head up, Niki leaned into the pup with his shoulder, pushing him away. It was if Niki said to the pup, "Sorry, I can't play, I'm busy working!"

I had a large backyard and on a day off, was tossing a Frisbee for Niki. The little family dog was trying to get in on the action, but because of her small size, Niki always beat her to the toy. On one return trip with the Frisbee, Niki finally took notice of the little dog. He bent down enough so the little dog could grasp the Frisbee and together, they returned it to me.

From my experiences, nurturing, training and working with a canine companion over a long period makes the handler appreciate the nature of a dog. I, however, believe that the dog will always know much more about its handler than the handler will know about the dog. While many people are sure how to perceive a dog's action, the dog easily interprets a person's mannerisms. Through the tone of voice, certain physical movements, and/or facial expressions, the dog will instantly know the mood of the handler. It will know if the handler is happy, sad, angry, excited, or distressed. Having been around humans for thousands of years, the dog has adapted well to us. Maybe better than we have to them.

I cannot think of a better way for a person to learn about honesty, compassion, loyalty, trust, integrity, respect, and love than to build a positive relationship with a dog. What better friend could a person have? Time again throughout my service, I have had to depend on my partner. On each of those occasions, he was there for me without question.

At a gathering of handlers and dogs many years ago, I recall one old handler making the profound statement, "Some of the smartest people here today are on four feet." Another handler once remarked, "Don't ever touch my dog or my wife – in that order too!" It was an honor for me to have worked with such brave, dedicated, four-legged police officers.

At the Training Kennels, I recall a trainer state, "Dog spelled backwards is "God!"" At the time we laughed, but thinking back to the all the scrapes and situations with these well trained dogs, I must say that there is some truth in that statement. Any time that I see a German Shepherd dog, I have to take the time to look at it, whether it is a working dog or not. I enjoy watching guide dogs maneuvering their blind charges through congested traffic and streets, or a detector dog at an airport. It is still in my heart. I will always be a dog handler.